GREEK TRAGEDY
IN NEW TRANSLATIONS

GENERAL EDITORS
Peter Burian and Alan Shapiro

FOUNDING GENERAL EDITOR
William Arrowsmith

FORMER GENERAL EDITOR
Herbert Golder

THE COMPLETE EURIPIDES, VOLUME III

T0288772

The Complete Euripides, Volume III

Hippolytos and Other Plays

Edited by
PETER BURIAN
and
ALAN SHAPIRO

OXFORD
UNIVERSITY PRESS

2010

OXFORD
UNIVERSITY PRESS

Oxford University Press, Inc., publishes works that further
Oxford University's objective of excellence
in research, scholarship, and education.

Oxford   New York
Auckland   Cape Town   Dar es Salaam   Hong Kong   Karachi
Kuala Lumpur   Madrid   Melbourne   Mexico City   Nairobi
New Delhi   Shanghai   Taipei   Toronto

With offices in
Argentina   Austria   Brazil   Chile   Czech Republic   France   Greece
Guatemala   Hungary   Italy   Japan   Poland   Portugal   Singapore
South Korea   Switzerland   Thailand   Turkey   Ukraine   Vietnam

Published by Oxford University Press, Inc.
198 Madison Avenue, New York, NY 10016

www.oup.com

Oxford is a registered trademark of Oxford University Press.

Library of Congress Cataloging-in-Publication Data
Euripides.
[Selections. English. 2009]
Hippolytos and other plays / [Euripides]; edited by Peter Burian and Alan Shapiro.
    p.   cm. — (The Greek tragedy in new translations) (The complete Euripides ; v. 3)
ISBN 978-0-19-538878-7; 978-0-19-538877-0 (pbk.)
I. Euripides — Translations into English.   I. Burian, Peter, 1943–
II. Shapiro, Alan, 1952–   III. Title.
PA3975.A2   2009a
882'.01 — dc22   2009031762

EDITORS' FOREWORD

"The Greek Tragedy in New Translations is based on the conviction that poets like Aeschylus, Sophocles, and Euripides can only be properly rendered by translators who are themselves poets. Scholars may, it is true, produce useful and perceptive versions. But our most urgent present need is for a *re-creation* of these plays—as though they had been written, freshly and greatly, by masters fully at home in the English of our own times."

With these words, the late William Arrowsmith announced the purpose of this series, and we intend to honor that purpose. As was true of most of the volumes that began to appear in the 1970s—first under Arrowsmith's editorship, later in association with Herbert Golder—those for which we bear editorial responsibility are products of close collaborations between poets and scholars. We believe (as Arrowsmith did) that the skills of both are required for the difficult and delicate task of transplanting these magnificent specimens of another culture into the soil of our own place and time, to do justice both to their deep differences from our patterns of thought and expression and to their palpable closeness to our most intimate concerns. Above all, we are eager to offer contemporary readers dramatic poems that convey as vividly and directly as possible the splendor of language, the complexity of image and idea, and the intensity of emotion and originals. This entails, among much else, the recognition that the tragedies were meant for performance—as scripts for actors—to be sung and danced as well as spoken. It demands writing of inventiveness, clarity, musicality, and dramatic power. By such standards, we ask that these translations be judged.

This series is also distinguished by its recognition of the need of nonspecialist readers for a critical introduction informed by the best recent scholarship, but written clearly and without condescension. Each play is followed by notes designed not only to elucidate obscure references but also to mediate the conventions of the Athenian stage as well as those features of the Greek text that might otherwise go unnoticed. The notes are supplemented by a glossary of mythical and geographical terms that should make it possible to read the play without turning elsewhere for basic information. Stage directions are sufficiently ample to aid readers in imagining the action as they read. Our fondest hope, of course, is that these versions will be staged not only in the minds of their readers but also in the theaters to which, after so many centuries, they still belong.

A NOTE ON THE SERIES FORMAT

A series such as this requires a consistent format. Different translators, with individual voices and approaches to the material at hand, cannot be expected to develop a single coherent style for each of the three tragedians, much less make clear to modern readers that, despite the differences among the tragedians themselves, the plays share many conventions and a generic, or period, style. But they can at least share a common format and provide similar forms of guidance to the reader.

1. *Spelling of Greek Names*

Orthography is one area of difference among the translations that requires a brief explanation. Historically, it has been common practice to use Latinized forms of Greek names when bringing them into English. Thus, for example, Oedipus (not Oidipous) and Clytemnestra (not Klutaimestra) are customary in English. Recently, however, many translators have moved toward more precise transliteration, which has the advantage of presenting the names as both Greek and new, instead of Roman and neoclassical importations into English. In the case of so familiar a name as Oedipus, however, transliteration risks the appearance of pedantry or affectation. And in any case, perfect consistency cannot be expected in such matters. Readers will feel the same discomfort with "Athenai" as the chief city of Greece as they would with "Platon" as the author of *The Republic*.

The earlier volumes in this series adopted as a rule a "mixed" orthography in accordance with the considerations outlined above. The most familiar names retain their Latinate forms, while the rest are transliterated; *-os* rather than Latin *-us* is adopted for the termination of masculine names, and Greek diphthongs (as in Iphi-gen*eia* for Latin Iphigenia) are retained. Some of the later volumes continue this practice, but where translators have preferred to use a more consistent practice of transliteration of Latinization, we have honored their wishes.

2. *Stage Directions*
The ancient manuscripts of the Greek plays do not supply stage directions (though the ancient commentators often provide information relevant to staging, delivery, "blocking," etc.). Hence stage directions must be inferred from words and situations and our knowledge of Greek theatrical conventions. At best this is a ticklish and uncertain procedure. But it is surely preferable that good stage directions should be provided by the translator than that readers should be left to their own devices in visualizing action, gesture, and spectacle. Ancient tragedy was austere and "distanced" by means of masks, which means that the reader must not expect the detailed intimacy ("He shrugs and turns wearily away," "She speaks with deliberate slowness, as though to emphasize the point," etc.) that characterizes stage directions in modern naturalistic drama.

3. *Numbering of Lines*
For the convenience of the reader who may wish to check the translation against the original, or vice versa, the lines have been numbered according to both the Greek and English texts. The lines of the translation have been numbered in multiples of ten, and these numbers have been set in the right-hand margin. The (inclusive) Greek numeration will be found bracketed at the top of the page. The Notes that follow the text have been keyed to both numerations, the line numbers of the translation in **bold**, followed by the Greek lines in regular type, and the same convention is used for all references to specific passages (of the translated plays only) in both the Notes and the Introduction.

Readers will doubtless note that in many plays the English lines outnumber the Greek, but they should not therefore conclude that the translator has been unduly prolix. In most cases the reason is simply that the translator has adopted the free-flowing norms of modern Anglo-American prosody, with its brief-breath-and-emphasis-determined lines, and its habit of indicating cadence and caesuras by line length and setting rather than by conventional punctuation. Even where translators have preferred to cast dialogue in more regular five-beat or six-beat lines, the greater compactness of Greek diction is likely to result in a substantial disparity in Greek and English numerations.

ABOUT THE TRANSLATIONS

The translations in this series were written over a period of roughly forty years. No attempt has been made to update references to the scholarly literature in the Introductions and Notes, but each volume offers a brief For Further Reading list that will provide some initial orientation to contemporary critical thinking about the tragedies it contains.

ABOUT THIS VOLUME

At first sight, the plays collected here look like a disparate group. What draws them together is that they are among the relatively few surviving Athenian tragedies to deal with specifically Athenian legend. The greatest of Athenian heroes, Theseus, plays a central role in two of the plays, and his children and successors, Demophon and Akamas, figure in a third. The young hero of the fourth, Ion, is destined to become the legendary founder of Athens' far-flung Ionian "empire." In short, Athens is on stage in all these dramas.

Two are overtly "political plays" that bring to the stage great moments in the city's history also commemorated in Athenian public oratory. These dramas don't conform to usual ideas about tragedy, but for that very reason they expand our sense of what a Greek tragedy can be and do. *Children of Herakles* is generally classified as "minor Euripides," but it is a fast-moving and surprising drama. Both the translation here and the introduction to it make a strong case for its importance. A sign of renewed interest in this play is its recent revival in a multicultural performance directed by Peter Sellars, staged in a number of countries and designed to highlight the plight of contemporary political refugees.[1] Even more ambitious

1. An interesting set of articles connected with this production can be accessed at http://www.amrep .org/articles/1_2/welcome.html, a site maintained by the American Repertory Theater.

claims can be made for *Suppliant Women* as a demanding work of art whose complex form embodies a complex vision. Read it not as a political harangue or an exercise in the rhetoric of pathos, but as a drama of the ideals and limitations of communal solidarity it emerges as one of Euripides' great dramas.

The other two plays dramatize the passage of exceptional young men from adolescence to adulthood. Hippolytos' failure to complete the rite of passage is enacted in a tragedy of destructive passions and botched communications that is certainly one of Euripides' masterpieces. Ion's passage is successful, though not without dangers and doubts. He uncovers his true identity in a brilliant blend of tragedy and comedy that still has the power to delight and disturb. These dramas are not overtly political, but *Ion* in particular raises important issues of Athenian ethnic identity and self-definition. Indeed, identity and self-definition are at the heart of both these plays on the personal level as well. Both young heroes have their identity tested when under attack by women with complex and powerful feelings. In both cases, their fathers claim the young men fully as their own only at the end of the dramas.

Hippolytos can be securely dated to 428 B.C., but we are told that Euripides rewrote it after an earlier version was badly received. In the first *Hippolytos*, Phaidra made a deliberate attempt to seduce Hippolytos, her stepson, and this unseemly portrayal of female desire apparently shocked the audience. In the second version, Phaidra fights desperately to hide and control her passion, preferring death to dishonor for herself and her children, only to have her secret revealed against her will. This treatment of Phaidra's desire not only made her character and motivation more acceptable, but it must also have changed the ethical and emotional balance among the main characters enormously. Phaidra's resolution to resist at all costs fails when her old Nurse, thinking to act for the best, betrays her, first wheedling and supplicating to force her mistress to reveal the source of her "illness," then carrying the news directly to Hippolytos against Phaidra's explicit orders. This mistaken attempt to help precipitates the crisis of the drama, but it is just one element: a pattern of speech gone terribly awry.

Hippolytos, whose devotion to Artemis leads him to reject Aphrodite and all her works, reacts to the Nurse's announcement with an intemperate and scathing denunciation of Phaidra and all womankind. Phaidra, sure that her passion can no longer be hidden, plots to salvage her reputation by suicide, leaving a written accusation of rape to "speak" for itself with no possible hope of refutation. Her husband, Theseus, returning from abroad to find his wife dead and the accusation attached to her corpse, curses Hippolytos even before hearing his son's inept attempt at self-defense, made all the more ineffectual because Hippolytos will not violate an oath of silence by betraying Phaidra's secret. Theseus, whose curse precipitates his son's death, discovers the truth too late. In such ways, the drama plays out as a series of powerful but misdirected speech acts: oaths, curses, scathing denunciations, repressions, misguided silences, irrational outbursts, persuasions that are too effective or not effective enough, and one tragically successful lie.

The human drama of *Hippolytos* is framed by the presence of two inimical goddesses. Aphrodite delivers the prologue speech, in which she explains that she will punish Hippolytos, the young man who scorns her, even at the cost of sacrificing Phaidra, her devotee. Artemis appears in the epilogue, to bid farewell to her beloved Hippolytos, explaining that one god does not intervene in the vengeance of another, but that she will have her vengeance in turn on one of Aphrodite's favorites. It is often pointed out that the action of the play, based as it is on the predispositions, hopes, fears, and desires of its agents, could proceed as it does without the gods, but that does not mean that the gods' presence is merely a formality or meaningless. Gods assert, predict, promise, and damn with a certainty unknown to mortals, who (as the play demonstrates to such devastating effect) must make do with uncertain meanings, hopeless wishes, and ineffectual regrets. After Artemis has instructed and rebuked him, Theseus can only wish that he had never cursed his son; those words (ironically, a prayer to Poseidon whose efficacy is evidence of Theseus' divine parentage) cannot be called back. The only effective human speech left comes from the dying Hippolytos, when he forgives his father. In a world subject to the whims of gods like these, humans must in the end depend on one another.

Children of Herakles and *Suppliant Women*, both of uncertain date, but likely to have been produced between 430 and 420 B.C., take up legendary acts of Athenian nobility involving the acceptance of suppliants threatened by impious enemies. In *Children of*

Herakles, by every measure the earlier of the two, Herakles' children are being pursued after his death by the Theban tyrant Eurystheus, eager to destroy the offspring of his old enemy. They arrive at Marathon, in Attic territory, under the guidance of Iolaos, Herakles' now elderly companion, and Alkmene, Herakles' mother. The Athenians, represented by the old men of Marathon who make up the Chorus, and by Demophon, one of the two sons of Theseus who rule Athens, face down Eurystheus' herald, refusing to succumb to fear and reasserting the sanctity of suppliants who have taken refuge at their altars. The Athenians having thus shown their nobility, the children of Herakles prove theirs when Demophon, having taken the omens before the impending battle with the army of Eurystheus, announces that the goddess Persephone demands the sacrifice of a virgin. The city is now torn between their obligation to the suppliants and the goddess' horrible demand; the sacrifice of an Athenian maiden would mean civil war. The impasse is resolved swiftly when one of Herakles' daughters (nameless in the play, but known in later sources as Makaria) freely offers her own life. The safety of the suppliants having been thus assured, she goes to her death, never to be spoken of again.

The battle that ensues continues the triumph of the forces of law and decency. What is most noteworthy about this phase of the drama is that it spins into something like comedy, and then fantasy. When a servant brings news of the battle to come, old Iolaos, in the preceding scene a figure of helpless grief, now announces that he will join the fight against Eurystheus. He meets with the Chorus' disapproval, Alkmene's dismay at being left alone to guard the children, and above all by the servant's scorn and overtly comic ridicule as he hobbles off to war. But this comic departure is simply prelude to Iolaos' miraculous rejuvenation and triumph over his enemy. Against all odds, fantasy becomes the play's reality. Euripides has staged the battle so that Iolaos and Hyllus, an older son of Herakles who has arrived to join the fray with a large contingent of allies, win a triumph for Herakles' clan. Herakles himself, through the miraculous rejuvenation of his old friend, proves his own divinity to those (including his mother) who doubted. Righteousness has triumphed.

Or has it? At this point, the most startling reversal in a play marked by reversals puts an end to the fantasy of an easy triumph of the right ("All things converge at last," 945 / 919, as the Chorus Leader concludes just before the convergence falls apart). In a final, lightning-swift scene, Eurystheus is brought onstage in shackles, Alkmene demands that he be executed on the spot, and the Chorus replies that Athenian law does not permit the killing of a prisoner but she gradually weakens and acquiesces in her proposal to put him to death herself. Eurystheus, whom we have known until this moment only as a tyrant and implacable foe of Herakles and his offspring, reveals himself in his death as a sacred hero, whose numinous bones will have the power to protect Athens from the descendants of the very suppliants the city has just rescued. We have been savoring the requital of vicious lawlessness; now we find ourselves witnessing another act of lawless revenge. Athens stood strong for justice; now (through the Chorus) she condones a profitable injustice. The ending redirects our moral bearings away from a fantasy that, for all its appeal to Athenian patriotism, is too facile and leaves us in the discomfort of hard thought.

In *Suppliant Women*, the gods play a different role, but the limitation of speech and reason, especially in the face of powerful human emotions, is crucial here, too. Indeed, the play swings between the claims of reason and emotion, an oscillation that gives it much of its power. The play is set before the temple at Eleusis, where Theseus' mother, Aithra, is conducting a rite of propitiation for the crops. The Chorus, representing the mothers of the captains who died in the attack of the Seven against Thebes, interrupts and threatens to pollute her rite with its mourning garb and lamentation. This powerful supplication by itself makes a striking emotional case for the mothers' plea. Moreover, they are asking not for protection but rather for Athens' aid in obtaining the burial of their dead sons, which the Thebans have prohibited but is for the Greeks a kind of primal entitlement (as shown by the hard-won burial of Hektor that closes the *Iliad* or the struggle of Antigone for the burial of her brother in the tragedy that bears her name). But when Theseus arrives on the scene he engages not the mothers, but the leader of the Argive attack on Thebes, King Adrastos, whose folly in undertaking the war Theseus demonstrates with the systematic rigor of a Socratic elenchus. It remains for Aithra to convince her son to change his mind, by inserting the mother's need into a larger picture that takes account of the demands of Panhellenic law for burial, as well as her son's and Athens' reputation for heroic action to right wrongs and protect the weak.

With the claims of reason and emotion thus aligned, the play continues on what one might call an optimistic course, with Theseus winning the people's endorsement for his acceptance of the suppliants' suit and debating a Theban herald (largely on the merits and demerits of democracy—of which this legendary king is presented as founder!), to whom he makes clear that Thebes will fight to bury the Argive dead, but only if negotiations fail. A messenger speech makes clear that Theseus has lived up to the moderation of his words, attempting to win the burial before waging successful battle, stopping when his mission was accomplished rather than proceeding to take the enemy city, as his position of strength would have allowed. At this point, however, the tone of the drama changes radically, and with it the meaning of the action. Rather than rejoicing at the victory and its achievement of burial for the fallen, lament for the dead begins in earnest, and painful emotions begin to prevail over the measure and reason with which Theseus and the Athenians spoke and acted. Adrastos leads in the bodies of the fallen in antiphonal wailing with the mothers. Theseus tries to restore balance by inviting the Argive king to give a public funeral oration, such as the war dead of Athens had received in Euripides' day. Theseus and Adrastos prevent the mothers from touching or even seeing their children's corpses, for fear of the access of grief it would produce. But all to no avail—Evadne, a widow of one of the Seven, suddenly appears and in a fantasy of heroic glory mixed with ecstatic, eroticized grief for her slain husband, she throws herself on his pyre. Her father, who has come searching for his daughter, is left to grieve his own loss. A subsidiary chorus of boys brings in the urns that hold their fathers' bones and sing of vengeance yet to come for the slaughter of these noble warriors. (The subsequent sack of Thebes by the Epigonoi, as the sons would be known, was part of legendary history.)

In short, the distinction Theseus made at the beginning of the play between the folly of the Argive cause and the justice of the claim for burial of the fallen has completely disappeared. In a final attempt to bring the action of the play to a positive conclusion, Theseus asks for and receives Adrastos' promise of lasting Argive gratitude for the Athenians' assistance, but a completely unexpected

appearance *ex machina* of Athena, Athens' patron goddess, corrects
him. Reliance on memory and a promise is not enough. Adrastos
must swear to a perpetual alliance with Athens, to which a concrete
memorial (a tripod that once belonged to Herakles, to be engraved
with the Argive oath of alliance) will bear perpetual testimony.
What the drama itself has shown us justifies Athena's pessimism
(or realism, if you prefer) about mere promises, so easily trumped by
anger or ambition, and memory, so easily distorted by grief. When
Athena goes on to predict the war of the Epigonoi, she is not (as is
often said) endorsing renewed violence as she is expressing its
human inevitability. *Suppliant Women* does not deny or denigrate
the greatness of Theseus' humane moderation, but it does suggest
that by themselves, such qualities are never sufficient.

Ion features a young innocent, in some ways like Hippolytos but
tied explicitly to Athenian history and politics. This is a foundling
story with a ground plan not unlike that of *Oedipus the King*: a lost
child long thought to be dead is finally recognized as the royal heir.
Here, however, the ending is at least ostensibly a happy one, and
indeed the shape of the story is more comic (as in the later Greek
and Roman comedies of the recognition of a lost child or sibling
and their dramatic descendants from the Renaissance to the present). Like *Hippolytos* (and also like *Suppliant Women*, as Stephen
Scully suggests in his introduction to that play), *Ion* begins with one
god and ends with another. But the god who is at the center of the
play, Apollo, is missing. Hermes and Athena are not adversaries,
however; both act, in effect, as Apollo's surrogates. Hermes unfolds
Apollo's overall plan in his prologue speech (though, as we shall see,
even a god's plan can go awry in telling ways because of the power of
human emotion). Athena comes to clear up Ion's remaining doubts
in place of Apollo (who, as she says, "thought it best not to reveal
himself to you, lest he be blamed / . . . for all that's happened"
1526–27 / 1557–58).

Ion, the child Apollo fathered with the pure-blooded Athenian
princess Kreousa, has been raised as an orphan at Delphi, Apollo's
great prophetic shrine, and his simple tasks as temple servant of the
god of light fill him with joy. Kreousa, childless since her marriage
to the foreigner Xouthos, has come with Xouthos to the shrine,
where he will ask the god for a child for them both. Before Xouthos
arrives on the scene, Kreousa has time to converse with Ion, and the

two discover the convergence of her story of a child lost and his story of being a foundling. The rest of the story could unfold rapidly and easily from this point, but of course it doesn't. Apollo has decided to give Ion to Xouthos alone, as a child he imagined he fathered on a Delphian girl long ago, when he attended the mysteries of Diony-sos, who inhabits Delphi in the winter months. Kreousa, far from rejoicing at Xouthos' good fortune, is increasingly enraged that Apollo could have given her husband a child and denied her the one he fathered and apparently abandoned. She has been aban-doned, her child lost, and the throne of Athens given to a bastard child who has none of the autochthonous blood of the true Athen-ian. Abetted by her vicious old Tutor, one of the least attractive characters in Euripides' works, Kreousa approves an elaborate plot to kill Ion at a celebratory feast arranged by Xouthos. A dove that tastes wine poisoned by the Tutor and dies saves Ion—Apollo has not forgotten him!—and now he turns on the woman who plotted his death, cornering her at an altar where she took refuge and threatening to kill her.

At this point, the Pythia, Apollo's prophetic priestess, appears with Ion's birth tokens, and Ion accepts that the woman he might have killed is his mother. But is Apollo really his father? Ion, who earlier told Kreousa not to challenge the god in his own sanctuary, starts to do just that, and only Athena's sudden appearance to set things straight ensures that the story ends as it should, though now Xouthos must remain in ignorance about Apollo's lie. Ion has indeed grown up. His rite of passage has readied him to enter the world outside the protected sanctuary of the god, armed with know-ledge about what men and women—and gods—are capable of, for good and ill. Leaving Delphi for Athens with knowledge of what his future holds, he is ready at last to leave behind the guileless happi-ness of childhood and its dreams of serenity and purity.

The translations in this volume were originally published be-tween 1973 and 1996. ROBERT BAGG, Professor Emeritus of English at the University of Massachusetts, Amherst, is the author of five volumes of poetry, most recently Niké and Other Poems (2006). He has published translations of Euripides' The Bakkhai (1976) and The Oedipus Plays of Sophocles: Oedipus the King, Oedipus at Kolonos, Antigone (2004). Sophocles' Outcasts: Aias, Philoktetes, Elektra, and Women of Trakhis, coauthored with James Scully and Mary Bagg, is

forthcoming. W. S. Di Piero, a poet, translator, and essayist, is
Professor of English at Stanford University. He is the author of
five volumes of poetry, most recently *Chinese Apples: New and
Selected Poems* (2007), and of four volumes of essays, including
the new collection *City Dog* (2009). As a translator from Italian,
he has published the *Pensieri* of Giacomo Leopardi and selected
poems of Sandro Penna (1982) and Leonardo Sinisgalli (1983).
Henry Taylor is Professor Emeritus of Literature at American
University in Washington, D.C., where he taught from 1971 until
2003. His third collection of poems, *The Flying Change*, received
the Pulitzer Prize in Poetry in 1986; his sixth and most recent,
Crooked Run, appeared in 2006. Taylor's translations from Bulgar-
ian, French, Hebrew, Italian, and Russian have appeared in many
periodicals and anthologies, as well as in two collections by the
Bulgarian poet Vladimir Levchev and a translation of Sophocles'
Electra (1998). Rosanna Warren is University Professor at Boston
University, where she also holds appointments as Emma Ann
MacLachlan Metcalf Professor of the Humanities and Professor of
English and Modern Foreign Languages and Literatures. She is the
author of five volumes of poetry, most recently *Departure* (2003),
and has also published a book of literary criticism, *Fables of the Self:
Studies in Lyric Poetry* (2008). She edited *The Art of Translation:
Voices from the Field* (1989). Her translation seminar at Boston
University is much admired.

The late Robert A. Brooks was a classical scholar and the
author of *Ennius and Roman Tragedy* (1981). His varied career
included much else, however, including appointments as Assistant
Secretary of the Army and Under Secretary of the Smithsonian
Institution. He was also an actor and theatrical producer and a
poet; a volume of his poems *Roman Epistle* appeared posthumously
in 1984, with a foreword by Richard Wilbur. Peter Burian, a
General Editor of this series, is Professor of Classical and Comparative Literatures at Duke University and has published both translations and critical studies. Stephen Scully, Associate Professor of
Classical Studies at Boston University, is the author of *Homer and
the Sacred City* (1990). *Hesiod's "Theogony": Near Eastern Antece-
dents, and Influence on Classical and European Literature* is forthcoming. His translation of Plato's *Phaedrus* appeared in 2003.

CONTENTS

CONTENTS

HIPPOLYTOS

Translated by

ROBERT BAGG

INTRODUCTION

I

Like so many of Euripides' plays, *Hippolytos* contains the hard knowledge that life without religion is as impossible as life with it. The obstinate mysteries of the religious life seem to me the play's most commanding and intricate theme, and the one most likely to be misunderstood. Readers familiar with the Hippolytos story, either in its mythical form or in dramatizations by Seneca, Racine, Robinson Jeffers, Robert Lowell, and Jules Dassin, will recall that in these the sexual imperative crowds out nearly everything else. Because of its religious and moral fascination, Euripides' play is very different from his followers' versions. Curiously, Euripides had earlier in his career written a play about Hippolytos that resembled his imitators. In this version, now lost, Phaidra was desperate enough to offer herself to Hippolytos face to face onstage.

This early version seems to have outraged its Athenian audience. Perhaps what offended was its picture of a woman reduced all the way to shamelessness by a divinity, a woman denied the dignity of fighting against Aphrodite's seizure (as Helen resists when the goddess orders her to Paris' bed in Book III of the *Iliad*). Possession by a Greek divinity ought not reduce its victim to a *dybbuk*. And if Phaidra is merely depraved she is a less effective illuminator of the purity of Hippolytos. The lost play could not contrast a failed yearning for purity with a victorious one. Hippolytos could not say as a kind of joint epitaph for himself and Phaidra the bitter lines (1587–89 / 1034–35): "There was honor in her death / but none in her, and because my honor / is stronger than hers, it is useless." Most distressing of all to the Athenians may have been the conception of a tragic heroine completely determined in her lust.

In 428 B.C. Euripides returned to the festival of Dionysos with his chastened version, the play we possess, which so pleased the judges they awarded first prize to his trilogy of that year. This time he had taken care not to distress his audience. Phaidra is no longer driven to erotic abandon by Aphrodite. She resists the goddess with what strength she has. It seems clear she would not have falsely accused Hippolytos and killed herself if not driven to it by the Nurse's inept interventions. A clash between something ugly and demeaning (a woman who lusts for her stepson) and something arrogant and inhuman (a man who rejects sex) might be a dispiriting spectacle if presented with ordinary realism. Such a result Euripides avoided not merely by psychological acumen, moral profundity, sympathy, and dramatic tact, but by writing poetry for his characters that is lyrical and subtle but never strident, even at moments of inflamed fury. Instead of offending the members of his audience, Euripides has stretched their sensibilities in several ways. He persuades them to sympathize with Phaidra more than their prejudices would normally allow—all women, especially erotic ones, were suspect in Greek popular morality. He makes Hippolytos' zealous moderation and chastity seem more attractive than such qualities would normally be to a city admiring of balanced complexity and openness to the whole of life. And he stretches his audience's understanding of the gods by placing before it evidence that divine beings behave with an insensitivity crushing to those mortals who must let them into their lives.

Religious power enters the play from two fountainheads, Aphrodite and Artemis, who appear high over the stage. Aphrodite opens the play by informing us of the misery to come; Artemis appears near the end to offer Hippolytos cold comfort for it. We are certain to notice curious features in these divine interventions.

Euripides' portrayal of Aphrodite is as cruel and vindictive as anyone's in antiquity. Because Hippolytos lives joyfully without sex, Aphrodite will see him destroyed. The goddess instills in his stepmother, Phaidra, a passionate desire for him; Aphrodite ingeniously thwarts and transforms that passion until its ultimate consequence is the violent action Theseus takes against his son. Whereas Aphrodite's usual mode of revenge is to make the person she hates fall in love and thus be reduced in hopeless slavery to the goddess, Euripides shows her (as Hippolytos says before he dies) in the act of destroying not just the one enemy but *three* people, two of them innocent of any insult to her. Aphrodite's power clearly is more savage here than is implied in her accepted incarnation as unquenchable but life-fulfilling passion.[1]

---

1. Twice in the play she is praised as a source of life—once by the Nurse (685–86 / 449–50), who is concocting a sophistic argument to justify Phaidra's prospective adultery, and once by the Chorus in a highly ironic context. As Phaidra listens to the Nurse fatally betray her to Hippolytos, the Chorus sings (855–57 / 563–64) of Aphrodite as a hovering bee, who, to enhance Euripides' metaphor, spreads her "savage pollen" on all our lives.

When Artemis arrives to soothe Hippolytos during his last minutes of life, her explanation as to why she didn't save her blameless protégé is coolly legalistic, unconvincing, and detached—even, we imagine, to Hippolytos, whose voice acquires what may be an unaccustomed irony toward her.[2] *I wouldn't have let you die,* the goddess says, *were it not for this rule we gods observe, not to interfere with each other. We don't take pleasure in the deaths of pious people, we're only really pleased when the impious die. We destroy them—children, house, and all.*[3] At this point the message is inescapable: the gods are cheerfully indifferent to the contradiction in their code that allows the supposedly cherished innocent and pious to perish through no fault of their own. Indeed, Artemis promises to continue her vendetta with Aphrodite by killing one of her favorites when the occasion rises (**2123–32** / 1416–22).

The brutal will of such divine beings must have been as obvious to an ancient audience as to our modern one, but with this difference in response. We are free to register contempt for these divinities as they speak and act as characters. Neither Euripides nor his audience quite could; the goddesses were forces outside the theater, both venerable and great. While we as well might find ourselves aware of the gods' enormous significance, qualify our contempt, and so enjoy the play within the imaginative context of the Athenians, to do so takes effort. Understanding Aphrodite shouldn't cause us much trouble—we are accustomed to looking at the experience of passion as both beautiful and painful, a reality that makes life complex and troublesome but one that most of us would not wish to be without. Imagining our way to the divine reality over which Artemis presides is more difficult. Rather than think of Hippolytos as a man in his prime who dedicates his life to a renunciation that he believes will fulfill him, we are more inclined to see him as one who suppresses or fears desire, defends himself from real feeling and sexual love, and does so with arrogance and conviction. In short, we may well consider him an emotional cripple.

This view assumes that the power Hippolytos tries to exclude from his life, sexual love, has a natural, unquestioned right to invade and influence any human being. Suppose our modern world worshipped a divinity comparable to Aphrodite. Every time we indulged in private pleasure (or even communal orgy) we could believe our conduct

2. Hippolytos' possibly ironic lines are "To you, too, lucky maiden, a serene goodbye / You take leave lightly of our long companionship" (**2158–59** / 1440–41). He may not be implicitly revealing his bitterness at her ease of departure but actually marveling at the great unbridgeable distance between mortal and immortal life. The lines do echo curiously his own cutting goodbye to Aphrodite in the first scene (**181–82** / 113). But the irony may be Euripides' own and not his hero's.
3. See **2010–15** / 1328–33, **2023–27** / 1338–41.

inherently religious. But what if we were inclined to a more ascetic nature? We might turn toward a divinity who'd rule out any such veneration for a goddess of sex. Artemis, for the Greeks, was the most obvious figure such a person would turn to. Are there true rewards in following her?

Some of us today might be able to sense what it was like to be possessed by Dionysos or Eros or Ares, but how would we know if we were experiencing the purifying power of Artemis? Euripides has Hippolytos describe this experience with the Greek substantive *sophrosyne* (or the equivalent verbal noun, *sophronein*). I have translated it several ways depending on the context: wisdom, chastity, moderation, character. Frequently the word takes the adjectival form *sophron*. In general, to be *sophron* is to be so strong of character, so free of guilt and clear of mind that you are not even tempted to do the wrong or weak or greedy action. Etymologically *sophron* means "having a mind that is sound and safe." We of the post-Freudian world might have difficulty believing that any person could in truth be as *sophron* as Hippolytos says often and vehemently he is—much of his insistence tends to sound like insecure boasting. But before judging Hippolytos fairly we must overcome the cynicism with which we discount any person's desire to become genuinely *sophron*. One way to assess our respect for the experience of *sophrosyne* would be to acknowledge how much we are missing in not being *sophron*, how much we yearn for it, how much of our life is hurt or diminished or poisoned since we are not *sophron*, and how beautiful life would be if we were. The commonest form taken by our awareness that we lack *sophrosyne* is nostalgia—most of us feel we did have something like it in childhood or youth.

There are many ways to cease being *sophron*, but the one at issue in this play is through sex. Throughout the play, most notably in Artemis' speech to Theseus (1932–2003 / 1283–324), it is made clear that one may not be both *sophron* and susceptible to Aphrodite. Yielding to this most imperious passion would, in Hippolytos' eyes, entail the sacrifice of all the joys and clarity and security of the *sophron* man. When the old servant asks him why he risks offending Aphrodite, Hippolytos answers (157–58 / 102), "Because I prize my purity, I / keep clear of her ..."

Our modern mythology comes close to sharing Hippolytos' belief. It is upon our introduction to sex that we lose our innocence—the sense of safety that we had as children, the sense of knowing where and who we are. Once we accept passion we announce our vulnerability to other forms of temptation and danger. The Nurse speaks of this vulnerability when she says (370–79 / 253–57; 381–82 / 259–60):

> I know we mortals must prepare
> our loves for each other

blandly, keep them dilute,
never so strong that the wine
of sympathy for another
finds the deepest marrow of our being.
Better if the heart's affections
can quicken or relax at will....
My love forces me to feel
all the pain she suffers....

Our vulnerability to intense passion can be brought home to us when we experience any of several kinds of emotion. What is unique to sexual passion is its tendency to make us also feel unclean. To have a passion means to Phaidra that she is stained. She shares Hippolytos' view of *sophrosyne*, though not his commitment. To her Nurse, who has just asked whether Phaidra has been sickened by involvement in some murder, she says (**473–74** / 317): "My hands are clean— / the crime is in my heart." Implicit in this view of passion as vice is the inevitiablity that once sexual desire takes hold, a person becomes capable of self-inflicted violence—as with Phaidra's suicidal fasting—or of violence to others, as when her lust meets exposure and defeat.

Hippolytos avoids sex, among other reasons, so that he might never lose control and harm others. The most confident modern assertion of chastity's indispensable connection to higher moral virtue and to divine insight and euphoria is Henry Thoreau's:

The generative energy, which, when we are loose, dissipates and makes us unclean, when we are continent invigorates us and inspires us. Chastity is the flowering of man; and what are called Genius, Heroism, Holiness, and the like, are but various fruits which succeed it. Man flows at once to God when the channel of purity is open.[4]

Sustaining Hippolytos' devotion to Artemis and *sophrosyne* is a confidence something akin to Thoreau's. If we accept the nobility of Thoreau's valuation of chastity, then we may be ready to appreciate its tragic inadequacy and defeat.

Euripides' plot puts Hippolytos' belief in *sophrosyne* to the test. His very chastity ensures the misery of Phaidra; it leads to her suicide and, with the desolated violence of his father, Hippolytos' own death. The intricate train of causality depends on several failures to understand and some blind responses, but it is enough to say here that *sophrosyne* is simply unable to save Hippolytos; it cannot cope successfully with the passions of his father, his stepmother, or even the Nurse.

4. Henry David Thoreau, *Walden* (New York, 1948), 184.

Phaidra herself articulates the judgment that to be *sophron* and a devotee of Artemis is to possess a real and blessed virtue. She wishes in her sickness for a safe mind, desires not to desire, and yearns to possess what Hippolytos possesses. Her longing for Hippolytos is raised beyond outright lust because it is also a longing for purity—an end to lust, for what is *sophron*. Hippolytos' serenity of life is what she most wants and cannot have. Her longing is constantly before us, from early in the action with her delirious thirst for running brooks, for horses, hunting, forest roaming, the meadow—all the symbolic activities of Artemis—to later in the play, with her calm, acute analysis of her failure to quiet her own lust. Her substitute for the safe haven of the truly *sophron* is the illusory protection of her chaste reputation.

She is herself proof that passion destroys the moral sense; Theseus in his way also is proof. He is portrayed often in Greek myth as a prominent and wide-ranging lecher, a fact of which we are reminded during the first Chorus and by Hippolytos' own conception during one of his violent amours. This fact makes bitter and moving the illegitimate Hippolytos' attempt to win the love and admiration of his father by making himself into someone so pure that his purity lies beyond a worldly man's comprehension. If we cannot understand why Theseus did not believe Hippolytos, namely because his own character led him to comprehend the supposed crime more easily than the actual innocence, we would not believe Hippolytos either and the play would fail for us.

Having said this, and acknowledging the authentic virtue in Hippolytos' pursuit of a unified spiritual life rather than a promiscuous one, we still must agree that there is something wrong with the man. Our minimum objection to him notes his failure to sympathize with the suffering Phaidra, his cold rejection of her, his arrogant, nonsensical diatribe against women; in short, how narrow and pitiless *sophrosyne* can be. Our maximum objection says simply that he is willfully blind to some real urge in himself, and in suppressing it, even for the sake of a just life, he attempts the humanly impossible; he would do better to face up to it. Such an interpretation of the play, which would certainly appeal to a Freudian, could only be sharply supported by one line in the play, and that is spoken by Aphrodite when she sneers that Artemis is the goddess he "honors."[5]

5. Aphrodite shows the jealous symptoms of a rejected woman when she contemplates Hippolytos' intimacy with Artemis—there is a pun in the Greek phrase which I translate "The goddess / he honors is the virgin Artemis" (24–25 / 15–16). "Honors" has a definite sexual implication. Phaidra is so humiliated by his degrading denunciation of women (none of it true of her) that she responds by accusing him of wanting to sleep with her. Theseus assumes that his son's pose of chaste asceticism cloaks the most licentious activities, but we are clearly meant to assume that he is wrong.

At one moment Euripides comes close to telling us why Hippolytos has gone to these extremes of purity (**1667–78** / 1078–83):

> HIPPOLYTOS If only I could manage
> to see myself from out there
> perhaps I'd be permitted tears
> for all this unbearable squalor.

> THESEUS The truth is, my son, your self-regard
> took more of your devotion
> than your own parents ever did.
> A good man would have honored us.

> HIPPOLYTOS I came bitterly from your womb,
> O my cruelly wounded mother.
> Let no one I love ever
> enter this world a bastard.

In this painful effort at the absolute crisis of his life, to look at himself as others would in order to feel emotion, we recognize what has been true from the start: Hippolytos has clung very hard to his self-image at the expense of others. Theseus acknowledges this in his reply; self-regard was Hippolytos' true devotion. And yet in Hippolytos' next speech we glimpse his motive: his desire to be a worthy son of his father was made frantic by the knowledge of his illegitimacy. He wants to be a worthy son. At the end of the play when Theseus accepts Hippolytos' innocence and purity he does so by accepting him as a son with a higher kind of legitimacy.

When we try to answer this question, whether Hippolytos was truly suppressing desire, and so living dangerously to himself and others, we may never find a satisfactory answer. The question touches a mystery of existence. What we can say is that Euripides' play shows a paradigmatic instance of how the world of flawed and passionate human beings irretrievably inflamed by their own appetites, can betray and destroy the *sophron* man as if that very chastity and decency were a vice. The noble mind lives in a graceful body infecting all who see it with promises of pleasure, of the very kind that that mind has renounced.

II

Alert readers of the play have often remarked how redundant the literal intervention of Aphrodite is—everything could happen without her. Though the goddess claims in her prologue to have willed the events we are about to watch, these events are perfectly intelligible as products of interacting human wills. Is there any way to connect the nature of Aphrodite and the other divinities with the seemingly autonomous plot? I believe there is.

As we experience the artful plot we are frequently aware of its essential component—the characters' inability to penetrate and understand each other's inner lives. The Nurse sympathizes with Phaidra's desperate sexual need, but is uncomprehending, numb when it counts, to Phaidra's resistance to her lust and to her pathetic hope that shame and purity might save her. Hippolytos cannot understand Phaidra's desire and recognizes her longing for purity only after she is dead; similarly, being ignorant of what passion can do to the psyche, he does not see why his father is so uncontrollably deranged by Phaidra's suicide and her accusation of Hippolytos' rape. Nor will Theseus perceive that there is authenticity and beauty in his son's claims of *sophrosyne*. Such failures are familiar. The texture of life is rich with our puzzled reactions when confronted by the inner lives of others. So is literature, since most great writers have been obsessed and stimulated by this state of affairs. Shelley proclaimed and Shakespeare enacted the truth that imaginative empathy is the only relief for this bafflement and hence the basis for morality. Robert Frost was fond of saying that literature (like gossip) is our "guessing at" one another. The only solution, said Henry James, is to be very, very intelligent—and yet we know of many intelligent people whose emotions get the better of them.

Euripides focuses on such failures in his tragic plot to dramatize our inability to perceive one another's inner lives. When the characters cannot make themselves understood, or when they miss the real nature of another's action, Euripides' poetry can be excruciatingly fine-tuned to these emotional landmines. But then, what is the dramatic significance of Aphrodite, who is presented simultaneously with these failures of perception as the tragedy's true cause? Euripides seems to have a wonderful awareness that if divinities such as Aphrodite, Artemis, and Dionysos naturally form a part of his culture's (and *mutatis mutandis*, our culture's) imaginative mythology, they (and we) will tend to perceive and to act out their destinies within the myths of one or more these divinities. Such a process, though it has its rewards and powers, will both oversimplify our comprehension of reality and delude us into transposing the behavior of others into the terms of our own myths—with disastrous results. This over-simplification and transposition—Hippolytos does it to women, Theseus to his son—occurs nearly unconsciously, unless one is shocked awake as one should be by a play such as this.

Euripides confronts us with our narrow habits by making the gods, even while he sings their power and grandeur, appear as the emblems and creators of our failure to perceive; emblems, even, of the stupidity of human life. If in the manner of modern playwrights he did not have the gods as facilitators, we would be denied this play's clairvoyance as to the reality of its characters' inner lives. Their lives would be as murky to us as to the characters themselves. But we have only to listen to Aphrodite's hauteur and inspect her empire, and do the same for Artemis, to grasp the tension and weight the characters live with.

The most impressively moving moment in the play bears out this view. As he dies, Hippolytos relieves his father's anguish at the impending guilt of his son's death, by telling Theseus that he frees him of the responsibility for his death. Theseus responds by telling his son he is pious and noble. Each man has given the other what he craved in his troubled heart. They see and love each other now with final clarity. Despite causing all the suffering they have, the divinities have left these two human minds unclouded, free of the gods, at last in the presence of each other's truth.

III

In making this translation my aim has been to re-create above all the dramatic momentum of the action, the impact of each speech and scene. Whenever a literal or lexical translation could not accomplish this I have departed from it, usually in minor or not very perceptible ways, but sometimes more boldly. My other concerns were for the logical interplay of the conversations and for the lyrical power of some speeches and the bitterness of others. I have tried to approach colloquial American speech as closely as the decorum of a passage permitted. The result is a translation of the play as I understand it. A given speech in my version could not be analyzed minutely in order to yield all of the possible interpretations that might be supported by the Greek. Many implications and tones necessary to convey the complexity, size, and richness of Euripides' play simply were left out. I regret losing these untranslated meanings a good deal, but not enough to have made me try to reproduce them with the necessary minute and probably unattainable exactitude; even if successful the result would likely have been a solution to a puzzle rather than a play.

I have relied on the text as edited by W. S. Barrett (Oxford: Clarendon Press, 1964) and been guided in many details of interpretation by his generally authoritative and remarkably thorough commentary.

I do differ with Barrett on one important issue. In his commentary he assumes that the correct view of religion is expressed by the Chorus, the Nurse, and the Servant who lectures Hippolytos at the beginning of the play—namely, that the best way to deal with divinity is always to play it safe and to give the gods what they apparently want. The more intense and demanding engagements that Hippolytos and Phaidra make with the religious and moral life Barrett suggests are foolhardy and mistaken. This view may be appropriate to the comfortable sensibilities of the Church of England and most Oxbridge dons of the previous midcentury, but is hardly the true Greek one. The formulation of this issue by W. K. C. Guthrie seems to me more convincing. Since the passage is interesting and since it throws direct light on the *Hippolytos* I quote it here at length:

> There seem to be two ways of regarding the relationship between man and god which at first sight are diametrically opposed, yet are both strongly represented in the Greek tradition. We become aware of the problem if we try to answer the question: Did the Greeks think it possible or desirable for man to emulate the gods? We possibly think first of the many warnings against the folly of setting oneself up to vie with heaven, of "thinking high thoughts" and forgetting that, as Herodotos said, "the divine is jealous," a maxim which the whole of his history and many of his myths seem designed to illustrate.... This, however, is not the only attitude which has to be taken into account. What are we to say to the conception of man's religious duty which we find in Plato, namely that his aim should be "the completest possible assimilation to god," and the downright statement of his pupil Aristotle that man's chief end is "to put off mortality as far as possible"? ... Which idea, then, are we to take as the more truly representative of the Greek religious mind: that there was a great gulf between mortal and immortal, between man and god, and that for man to attempt to bridge it was hubris and could only end in disaster, or that there was a kinship between human and divine, and that it was the duty of man to live a life which would emphasize this kinship and make it as close as possible?[6]

Perhaps Hippolytos would have viewed this formulation with some rue. He emphasized his kinship with Artemis only to be cut down by Aphrodite for presumption.

In a few instances I have translated lines that Barrett believed spurious and omitted some that he thought might be genuine. These departures are cited in the Notes, in which preparing them I have borrowed freely from Barrett's commentary. My intention was to identify less familiar mythological figures and stories, locate geographical allusions, emphasize the importance of several key terms in Euripides' moral vocabulary, and explain obscurities whenever I knew the probable answer.

The help I have received from friends in translating and revising has been generous and indispensable. The late John Moore of Arnherst read through the entire play with me in Greek; every draft benefited from his

6. W. K. C. Guthrie, *The Greeks and Their Gods* (Boston, 1955), 113–14.

criticism and suggestions. If some of the exhilaration of this experience survives in the translation I am grateful to share it. George Dimock of Smith, the late Thomas Gould of Yale, and James Hynd I thank for their comments and inventive advice. Catharine Carver of Oxford University Press made many helpful suggestions. The first editor of this series, William Arrowsmith, awoke me from many complacent assumptions about the play with his piercing criticism of the manuscript and inter-pretation of the play's meaning. I am conscious that my own mode of translation differs from that of each of the men who helped me, in some cases fundamentally. Therefore it is even more important than usual to absolve them from any responsibility for the infelicities and "mistrans-lations" which remain; these are the result of my practice and principles, not theirs.

I am grateful for the chance to revise both the play's text and its accompanying prose from its original version first published in 1972. Though I have kept to my own and Arrowsmith's injunction "to liquefy the foundations," I have chastened some youthful overreaches and in many places brought the text closer to Euripides' Greek.

I am also grateful to Sharon Fogarty, of the Mabou Mines theater company and Barnard College, who directed a production at Barnard in October 2008 that used an earlier version of the revised text. Her brilliant direction and the talented cast's spirited performance increased my confidence in the new version and encouraged me to make additional improvements.

ROBERT BAGG

HIPPOLYTOS

Translated by

ROBERT BAGG

CHARACTERS

APHRODITE goddess of love

ARTEMIS goddess of purity, the hunt, and childbirth

THESEUS king of Athens

HIPPOLYTOS his son by the Amazon queen Hippolyte

PHAIDRA Theseus' wife, stepmother to Hippolytos

NURSE to Phaidra

SERVANT to Hippolytos

MESSENGER

CHORUS of Troizenian women

LEADER of the chorus

HUNTSMEN subsidiary chorus

SERVANTS (silent)

Line numbers in the right-hand margin of the text refer to the English translation only, and the Notes beginning at page 85 are keyed to these lines. The bracketed line numbers in the running heads refer to the Greek text.

Before the palace of Theseus in Troizen. On stage are two statues, of Artemis and Aphrodite, whose placement figures their antagonism during the play. Paths lead from the palace foreground into the countryside and/or to the nearby seacoast. The living goddess APHRODITE *appears.*

APHRODITE The power I possess is sexual passion—
    which you mortals, in honoring me,
    celebrate in your diverse ways.
    I'm no less the darling of heaven.
    I am the goddess Aphrodite.
    My subjects live in the Mediterranean sunlight
    from the Black Sea to the Atlantic beaches.
    Those in awe of my power I reward;
    but I bring crashing down the stubborn ones,
    so high-minded they despise my pleasures;   10
    for we gods are no different than mortals—
    we return the respect that you give us.

    If you will listen to this story
    the truth of my words is quickly proven.
    In this province of Troizen lives
    Hippolytos, the bastard child
    of Theseus and his Amazon mistress.
    The old king of this province,
    Pittheus the Pure, made him his protégé.
    Now this young man, alone   20
    among his fellows, says freely
    I'm a despicable goddess.
    Marriage is anathema to him,
    he goes to bed with no girl. The goddess
    he honors is the virgin Artemis,
    Apollo's sister, the daughter of Zeus.
    Our young friend thinks her kind of divinity
    the most exhilarating.
    In the pale green forest they are inseparable;
    he drives his killer hounds   30
    until they've slaughtered all the game.
    Such a friendship between human and god

is a remarkable event—
I would not deny him this happiness.
I have no reason to. It's purely his
offences against me that I resent
and will punish—today. My revenge
was long in the planning; now it will
happen with no further help from me.

Once, as Hippolytos passed through Athens   40
on his way to see and enact
the sacred mysteries at Eleusis,
his father's wife, the matchless Phaidra,
saw him and soon was inflamed
in the soft depth of her being
by all the passionate longing
I could exert. That was my plot.
So enamored was Phaidra,
even before coming to Troizen,
she built a stone temple, in my honor,   50
not far from the shrine of Pallas Athena.
From that slope she could look across water
to Troizen, where her new love now lived.
Later, when Theseus fled Athens, after he'd
murdered a hated rival's sons—
defiling himself so badly
his own city dared not keep him—
he elected to spend
his exile year in this country.
So it is here in Troizen that Phaidra,   60
groaning dismally, her mind turbulent
under the lash of continual lust,
fades into a wretched silence.
She has no intimate who can see or cure
what lies at the heart of this sickness.
But her love must not linger in this impasse—
it dissolves as my plans take shape.
The facts I will force on Theseus,
the explosion will be public.
That youth who crosses me must die.   70

His father will kill him. The murder weapon?
Deadly curses granted to Theseus
by Poseidon the sea lord; three times will
the god do anything Theseus asks.
Though her celebrated purity will
survive, Phaidra will not. That she dies,
I regret—but not so keenly I'd
relinquish this great chance to strike
my enemies: punishing them, pleasing me.

Hippolytos must be coming—   80
I see him, just now free
from the exertions of the hunt
So I must disappear.
At his back swagger his friends
chanting a hymn pleasing to Artemis.
He doesn't know that the gates of Hades
are wide to receive him,
or that this sunlight,
with which he sees, through which he swings,
today he will leave forever.   90

Exit.

Enter HIPPOLYTOS *with huntsmen and servants; they*
carry weapons and lead hunting dogs.

HIPPOLYTOS Hunters! Sing out
to Artemis in heaven:
child of god
who protects us!

CHORUS OF Queen, you have our allegiance.
HUNTSMEN We delight in your innocence,
and we adore you, Artemis,
child of Leto and Zeus!
We are moved by your radiance
more than by any of the goddesses   100
who glide through the golden house
of Zeus—most powerful father of all!

19

Yours is a maiden's beauty,
more pure, more grand
than any Olympian's.

HIPPOLYTOS I brought you this green crown,
goddess, fresh from the scene
where I spliced its flowers together,
a meadow as virginal as you are—
where no shepherd would think it wise   110
to graze his herd—a perfect field
no iron blade has yet cut down.
Only the bees looking for flowers in spring
go freely through its cool grass.
Its water flows from the goddess
Restraint, who not only
leads in the rivers herself
but keeps the place a special preserve
for those whom modesty enters at birth,
the instinctively good—   120
these may pick what they will,
but the vulgar are barred from the meadow.
Now, blest lady, take this, embellish
your gold hair—it comes from a faithful hand.

Places a coronal on the statue of Artemis.

No man alive approaches my good luck—
to ride with you, to share confidences:
your voice is distinct in my ears,
though your face I have never seen.
May my luck hold throughout life,
as strong at the finish as now   130
rounding the turning-post.

SERVANT Sir—the word "master" I save
for the utterly masterful gods—
would you take some advice from me
if it seems well considered?

20

HIPPOLYTOS Of course I will. I'd be thoughtless not to.

SERVANT I wonder if you've thought of this—
this fact of human nature?

HIPPOLYTOS Which one? Explain yourself.

SERVANT Don't we always hate arrogance?   140

HIPPOLYTOS I would think *so*. An arrogant man offends us.

SERVANT And don't they give pleasure,
those genial souls who are easy to live with
and have kind words for us all?

HIPPOLYTOS They charm us, yet it seems no strain to them.

SERVANT Would that hold for the Olympian gods?

HIPPOLYTOS I think it would—if gods and humans
share the same inner logic.

SERVANT If you believe arrogance offends,
it's strange you never speak   150
to one proud and awesome goddess.

HIPPOLYTOS Which goddess? Make certain that your mouth
doesn't plunge you into serious trouble.

SERVANT I mean the one who stands
silently there at your gates,
the goddess of passion, Kypris.

HIPPOLYTOS Because I prize my purity, I
keep clear of her, though I pay her
a decent and distant respect.

SERVANT Still, do you sense her holy force,   160
how fiercely she charges everyone alive?

HIPPOLYTOS We all have personal favorites,
            whether we choose a god or a friend.

SERVANT The gods be with you. May you find
         all the wisdom your life will need.

HIPPOLYTOS A goddess whose power reaches its zenith
            when the bed's warm and the night's dark
            leaves me cold.

SERVANT   My son,
            each god makes a claim on us
            that we must pay only in the god's coin—   170
            that's inescapable fact.

HIPPOLYTOS It's time we went indoors, lads,
            to have dinner—we've all earned it—
            a hearty feast, to which a man
            may come home and relax
            after a run with his hounds.
            Grooms, these colts want to be rubbed down
            and pampered—when my hunger is cured
            I'll hitch the chariot to these beauties
            and give them their workout myself.   *To* SERVANT   180
            As for that goddess of yours, Aphrodite,
            I'll just wish her a very polite goodbye.

                    Exit HIPPOLYTOS *and huntsmen; the* SERVANT, *now
                        alone, looks toward the statue of Aphrodite.*

SERVANT But for me, I must not indulge
         in the callow thinking of these young men.
         I am a slave—yours, goddess—and may
         my speech show it, as I address
         your icon:
                        Be merciful if this lad,
         in the inflamed vehemence of his youth,
         mistaking his own interest, speaks
         insane blasphemy to you.   190

Don't hear him—and prove
gods in their wisdom possess
more tolerance than we men do.   *Exit.*

Enter CHORUS *of townswomen.*

CHORUS   I know a ledge where water springs
from the rocks, where the River tunneling down
from his birthplace splashes and sparkles.
There women gather, and dip their quick-
filling pitchers.
Our friend full of news was there,
soaking her colorful clothes in that rush,   200
then spreading them drenched on the rock's
steaming back which the sun keeps hot.

This was her news: that our mistress
was ailing, growing weak in her bed,
confined indoors.
The news was of thick gauzy veils
darkening her chestnut hair.
For three days she's fasted,
shutting her mouth to bread.
She wishes—tight-lipped, suffering—that her life   210
will drive up that beach where Hades
himself presides.
Mistress, is your mind suddenly possessed
because Pan floods it with madness?
Is this Hekate's fury at work?
Should we accuse those holy Korybantes
or the Great Mother of beasts
glowering in her mountains?
Did you forget to provide
a smooth honeyed sacrifice, and that lapse   220
offends the huntress—
Artemis!—who sickens you,
spiriting your vigor away?
Oh that goddess takes the lagoon
in her skimming stride,

23

and when she's sea-borne
she touches down on the dry sandbars
or ranges the shallow salt-water eddies.

Or is the trouble your husband, that man
of splendid birth, the king of Athens—   230
does he keep a girl who gives
him pleasure and loves him
a long way from your bed?
Maybe some ship is anchored out there
in our cordial harbor
(is it from Krete?), whose captain
reports to you, our queen, a tale
so brutal to your soul
you seek repose as the only solution
for such suffering.   240

Could it be this:
our womanly natures
are so poorly composed!
We must live with the misery
of childbirth, all the foolish despondency
leading to it. Once I felt
such chaos in my womb
I cried out to Artemis in heaven,
who loves the hunt and whose care relieves
those giving birth. She came to me then   250
and eased me. She's the one goddess
in heaven I will always admire.

LEADER There in the doorway is the wrinkled nurse,
          bringing our queen outside;
          now we may learn what we crave—
          why our queen's body is wasted,
          and healthy color
          has drained from her skin.

              Enter PHAIDRA *with* NURSE *supporting her; servants*
              follow carrying a pallet on which PHAIDRA *lies down.*

NURSE The gloom of living wears me down,
and ugly sickness piled on that. 260
Now I must cope. And with what next?
Phaidra, here's pleasant sunlight for you
and fresh blue sky to clear your head,
now that I've towed your sickbed
away from the stuffy house. (Here comes
that peevish scrunch of your brow.)
"Take me outside" were your orders all morning.
All right, we're here. Now I expect
you'll grow desperate again for your room.
Today you couldn't be more touchy and cross, 270
nothing pleasant relaxes you.
When I think you're content
with how you've settled yourself
you're frantic to change things again.
I'd much rather be sick than be the nurse.
It's so simple to lie in pain
but nursing is hard on the spirits,
nerve-wracking!
And an ache to your arms as well.
All life is bitter and no end of sweat. 280
If there be something sweeter than this life
I can't see it, the dark mists hide it.
Maybe we've grown to love too much
whatever it is that dazzles us here,
only because we haven't felt on our skins
the strange drench of a new life—we're earthbound.
As for the good things in the World Below—
they aren't talking, though poets do,
and their tales pull us on like the children we are.

PHAIDRA Could you shift my weight a little 290
and prop my head straighter?
Something has melted in my limbs.
Pull me up by my wrists, please,
my delicate wrists.
                    The combs holding my hair

25

are too heavy. Take them out, please.
Turn my hair loose down my shoulders.

NURSE *unbinds her hair.*

NURSE Hold still, child, and cheer up.
It's wrong to keep churning like this.
Your sickness would be easier
to bear if you stayed quiet   300
and minded your dignity.
You learn to suffer if you want to live.

PHAIDRA Ah!
What I most want
is to drink from a cold mossy spring
and to stretch out under a poplar
with the meadow beneath flowing like soft hair.

NURSE Phaidra, what are you saying?
You're talking wildly! In public! Stop
pouring out words that make no sense.   310

PHAIDRA Take me into the mountains—
I will go to the pine forest,
follow our killer hounds
stalking the mottled deer,
closing in—gods, let it happen!
I want to cry on the dogs
and flash a keen Thessalian spear
past my flying yellow braids—
I want my hands grazing the steel
and hefting the spear shaft.   320

NURSE Can you tell me why these pictures
obsess your mind? Child, why do you
leap to this tomboy's enthusiasm—
hunting dogs!—from a silly thirst
for mountain spring water? Do you see
that hillside drenched with springs, sloping
away from our walls? You can drink there.

26

PHAIDRA Lady Artemis, now on your salty lagoon,
        and now in your exercise track
        bombarded with hoofbeats,   330
        I would be there with you,
        riding hard and breaking
        colts from the plains of Venice!

NURSE   More mad words! Child, why are you so strange?
        First you go in this daydream
        chasing game through the hills, now you
        can't stop, your desire keeps galloping.
        Suddenly you love horses racing on packed sand
        where the surf never reaches.
        All this will need some expert   340
        god-watching, to discover which god
        has swerved your mind,
        and has you trembling with madness.

PHAIDRA I must have said terrible things.
        I'm so humiliated! I feel as though
        I'm being shoved hard
        somewhere I must not go.
        Where? My mind's going, I feel unclean,
        twisted into this madness
        by the brawn of a god who hates me.   350
        Help me, nurse, I am wretched.
        Pull the bedclothes over me.
        What I have spoken aloud
        is eating me alive.
        Cover me up! I'm starting to cry
        because my shame is welling up inside—
        can't you see it in my eyes?
        To keep sane, to act sensibly,
        is pure agony for me,
        but this madness is much worse.   360
        It would solve everything
        to let my mind go blank
        and die out of all this.

                NURSE *draws bedclothes over Phaidra's face.*

27

NURSE Yes, I can hide your face.
          And when will Death consent
          to give me—these old bones—
          the same protection?
          But living too long, as I have,
          can be instructive:
          I know we mortals must prepare   370
          our loves for each other
          blandly, keep them dilute,
          never so strong that the wine
          of sympathy for another
          finds the deepest marrow of our being.
          Better if the heart's affections
          can quicken or relax at will, so
          indifference may slacken them
          and free us, or when passion is safe
          the strings may tighten and thrill us.   380
          My love forces me to feel
          all the pain she suffers. I can't bear it. I have my
          own miseries.
          I've heard it said
          living by austere rules
          has broken more good men
          than it's given permanent well-being.
          There's something sick
          in loving her so much.
          I do not like excessive   390
          anything one bit. I like
          moderation much better.
          The calm approach.
          A wise man would tell me I'm right.

LEADER Old woman,
          you take good care of our queen.
          Phaidra's misery is plain to us,
          but none of us knows what sickness it is.
          Can you tell us?

NURSE   I don't know.
          And she's not going to explain.   400

LEADER Not even what first made her suffer?

NURSE Not even that. Her silence is total.

LEADER How ravaged and listless she looks!

NURSE How else should she look?
       She's starved for three days!

LEADER Is this insanity or is she willing death?

NURSE Who knows? But she will surely
       die if she fasts much longer.

LEADER How amazing Theseus lets this happen.   410

NURSE She's calm in his presence and chokes back pain.

LEADER But can't the man look at her eyes
       and fathom she's in trouble?

NURSE Not now. He happens to be traveling.

LEADER There's none but you, then, to make her
       tell us the truth about this illness
       and why she's so delirious.

NURSE I've pressed her very hard. It doesn't work.
       Even so, I don't quit. I'll probe again—
       watch me, everyone here, please be my witnesses   420
       that my concern for our sick queen
       doesn't vanish in a crisis.

                    NURSE *lifts cover from* PHAIDRA's *face.*

       Child, may we erase our previous words
       and start fresh?

29

                                    Try to be more receptive—
stop frowning! You're so tense!
Relax all this. I will stop
my rude badgering of you.
I was wrong-headed, I'll change.
See how gentle my questions are.
Even if your illness is one   430
we don't talk about freely,
remember we're all women here.
Perhaps our tact can find a remedy.
But if you've courage to discuss
your disease with men, speak firmly,
our doctors will take it in hand.
Please answer me. If what I say is wrong
correct me. But if I happen to be right,
come home to my advice.
                                    At least look at me!
You see, ladies, all this turmoil is pointless: 440
we have not moved her. From
the moment her sickness took hold
she's been immune to words.
I promise you this, Queen—
so you'd better decide whether
you'll act like a human being
or thrash around like the wild sea—
I promise you your death will be
treachery to your own children,
since they will inherit nothing   450
of their father's money
or a place in his palace.
It's by the bareback Amazon queen
I swear this, the one who has borne
your children their future master—
a bastard in fact, even though
in mind and everything else
he's an aristocrat. You know who
I mean—Hippolytos!

PHAIDRA Aiiiya.   460

30

NURSE   So that hits the quick.

PHAIDRA Nurse, you will kill me! O gods!
If ever thought of that man
springs to your tongue, crush it!

NURSE Good, you're growing rational again.
But even so, you're still not fighting
to save your children or even your life.

PHAIDRA I love my children. There's a different storm
driving me at the rocks.

NURSE Phaidra, it can't be murder—   470
you've had no hand in some crime
paralyzing you with guilt?

PHAIDRA My hands are clean—
the crime is in my heart.

NURSE Has some enemy hurt you?
Are you caught in some psychic spell?

PHAIDRA No, someone very close,
blood close, destroys me.
Neither he nor I wills it.

NURSE Is it Theseus who is cruel to you?   480

PHAIDRA No. I'm the one who must spare him.

NURSE What's this evil thing that wants you to die?

PHAIDRA Let me go wrong! It isn't you I injure.

NURSE But you wrong me! I am trying to save you.
If I fail, the fault will be yours.

NURSE *kneels and grips* PHAIDRA's *hand.*

PHAIDRA   What are you doing to my hand? Are you
          trying to force my secret from me?

NURSE   I want your knees as well.

                                    She seizes PHAIDRA's *knees.*

          I will not let you go!

PHAIDRA   Madwoman! What you would find out   490
          will be ugly—horrible for yourself.

NURSE   Would that be worse than to see you die?

PHAIDRA   Your questions will kill me—
          and yet I want you to realize
          staying quiet fills me with honor.

NURSE   Why would you hide what honors you?
          Isn't it honest, my wish to know?

PHAIDRA   I must hide it. Shame may be purified,
          it may be made completely noble.

NURSE   Less mysteriously noble   500
          if you'd frankly explain.

PHAIDRA   For god's sake stop, go away,
          let my hand go!

NURSE   I will not let go. Not till you give me
          what I am begging you to give.

PHAIDRA   I will give it. There is something holy
          in your hand's pressure. I'll trust it.

NURSE   I will be quiet while you speak.

32

PHAIDRA I'm thinking of you, Pasiphaë. Mother!
         How savagely you loved!   510

  NURSE She gave herself in lust to a bull.
         Why bring this scandal up, child?

PHAIDRA And my sister Ariadne,
         wretched bride of Dionysos.

  NURSE Child, has the madness come back?
         Why dwell on your family's shame?

PHAIDRA I am the third victim and it
         is hell to be so brutally used.

  NURSE I'm stunned! What are your words getting at?

PHAIDRA At a compulsion that tortures   520
         all the women of my clan.

  NURSE Speak bluntly—it's still too
         elusive. You must say more.

PHAIDRA Ohhh, I wish you would say it
         for me. Don't make me say it!

  NURSE I'm not clairvoyant. I can't
         make sense of vague hints.

PHAIDRA Do you know what really happens
         to human beings when they love?

  NURSE Love brings you sweetness and pain,   530
         almost beyond our power to feel.

PHAIDRA I am now experiencing just the pain.

  NURSE So it is love, child.
         Who is the man?

33

PHAIDRA How shall I call him...speak his name...
the Amazon's...

NURSE Son? Are you telling me it's Hippolytos?

PHAIDRA It came from your mouth, not from mine.

NURSE What next will you make me say?
This finishes me. I can't stand it.   540
Now I know that even the chaste
are capable of the rankest lechery—
oh, they don't wish it, but there it is.
Life is not worth slogging to the end.
It's disgusting. I see nothing
but hate in the sunlight.
I hate what life is in this day.
I'm letting go of my flesh,
I'm letting it rot so I can
vanish from this stinking life.   550
Goodbye. This breath is my last.
I no longer believe Aphrodite
is a mere goddess, she's
more powerful, more ruthless!
Phaidra is past all hope, so am I,
so is everyone living in this house.

                                        NURSE *exits*.

CHORUS We've seen it all now, and heard
our choked and weeping queen
reveal her calamity to us,
better forever beyond our hearing.   560
And better dead than living with such knowledge,
though our knowing brims us with love for her,
for all the agonies swarming upon mankind.
But your own speech laid you open,
doomed child Phaidra! Nothing can change now,
the hours will lapse, each swollen by pain,
all love gliding to the finish fate holds
for you, luckless girl from distant Krete.

PHAIDRA *slowly rises from her bed, to address the* CHORUS.

PHAIDRA May I tell you, because you're close to me,
          Troizenian friends,   570
          how often, when insomnia made endless
          the raw hours before daylight,
          I have worked out in my mind
          why people's lives come crashing down.
          I don't think our failure and suffering
          can be blamed on our blundering minds.
          There's more to it. Most people see
          clearly what's right for them.
          We understand virtue and are even
          attracted by it, but   580
          we can't make it, we freeze—
          because we're lazy or because we're distracted,
          or because we discover a world
          of pleasures more intense than duty.
          And life, especially a woman's, seethes with pleasures—
          exhilarating hours of gossip,
          and daydreaming, that sweet waste of time.
          Even shame gives us pleasure.
          But there are two shames: the kind
          that makes us do what pleases our own soul,   590
          and then there's the kind that tempts us
          to do what the world wants—
          that kind annihilates dynasties.
          If we could always tell
          which of the two shames pleasured us
          we wouldn't have one word for both.
          Once I'd had this insight,
          nothing, not even a magic healing drug,
          could return my mind to a happier mood.
          Let me tell you now what happened to me.   600
          My thoughts grew out of my life.
          I fell in love; the pain, the denial, got fierce.
          I wondered what I could do to survive.
          My first attempt was absolute silence—
          camouflage for my sick spirit.

How could I trust my tongue—which can
set others right, but cannot even sense
the damage it does to itself?
Next I hoped to cool down my passion,
believing in my modesty, its cold power.   610
I was twice wrong. Neither tactic
overcame the lust Kypris made me feel.
Death—I wonder if you understand this—
death was the only solution
I knew would work.
I want people to notice my splendid moments,
but should my life become shameful
I could not stand witnesses!
I knew that my passion, indulged or not,
would make me repulsive to others, especially since   620
I am a woman—our very sex is a disgrace.
There is one woman who should die horribly—
the one who first polluted her marriage,
provoking strange men till they slept with her.
That first slut was an aristocrat,
and what's fashionable in the palace
no matter how truly filthy
soon thrives in every modest street.
I hate those women who speak with chaste discretion
while reckless lechery warms their secret lives.   630
How can such frauds, Kypris, goddess of the green depths,
look quietly into the eyes of their husbands?
What keeps them from shaking in honest terror
at the darkness, their accomplice?
What keeps them poised in the embrace
of the wooden skeletons of their homes
which might any second break their disgusted silence?
Let me say out the thing that is bringing me down,
killing me. I will not let anyone
see the squalor into which I am plunging   640
my husband and the children I bore.
I want them to live openly and speak their minds
in the city famous for that, Athens,
enhanced in their own fame

because I was their mother.
In my thinking a man becomes a slave,
even if he's well born and free,
when he's obsessed by a parent's disgrace.
Only one thing frees a person
to thrive in life's competition,   650
if he's lucky enough to have it:
a decent character braced by self-respect.
Those who are rotten among us, time will expose
just as casually as a young girl
looks in a mirror at her perfect youth;
that's how without warning time's sudden shock
shows up the living sinner.
May I never see my face in such a mirror.

LEADER Such a steady rational mind
is everywhere admired, for its abundant loveliness.   660

NURSE *enters*.

NURSE My lady, the way I behaved just now
was thoughtless—blame the shock with which
your awful dilemma struck home with me.
I was so frightened I was stupid.
We're always wiser about the emotions
when we've had time to reflect.
What you experience is nothing exceptional—
we can be sensible about it.
A violent goddess has invaded you.
She made you love someone. It's no miracle,   670
it's normal. Hundreds receive from fate
exactly this treatment. So, tell me,
are you planning to let love kill you?
What about all the others who love now,
and who will love in the future? Must they die?
For Aphrodite comes on like an enormous
breaker, nobody can stand up to her.
Once you give in, though, she's kind and attentive.
But let her find a man making arrogant claims,

she takes that man and cuts him down to size.   680
And believe me he suffers.
Aphrodite is at home in the high air,
the turbulent ocean is full of her.
Everything alive thrives in her presence.
We are her children, because she starts the desire
flowering that is the seed of us all.
Ask any man of the arts, who is deep
in the things poets have always known,
how passionate Zeus wanted
Semele to sleep with him, or ask   690
what happened to poor Kephalos—
Dawn, who has enough light for the whole world,
flew him bodily where the gods live,
there to delight in his love. So Dawn
and Zeus don't suffer in exile
because they were reckless; they live
in heaven, and are thought good company,
to say the least, by the rest of the gods.
These great ones, you might say, are "resigned"
to their amorous enslavement.   700
And yet you insist you'd hate such defeat.
Maybe your father should have driven
a unique bargain when he conceived you,
or found a different race of ruling gods
who'll free you from our human condition.
How many intelligent men, do you think,
feel their marriages sicken, see their wives
slip away to make love—then don't see it?
How many fathers lend Kypris a hand, putting
a warm young thing in their sons' wild way?   710
For when we face unsavory facts
negligence is wisdom.
To spend your life in a mad craving
for perfection is simply not worth it.
Look at the roof of your own house.
Is there a single timber not slightly askew?
But as a roof it is a great success.
Sexual passion is a big rough sea,

not something you, especially
your frail majesty, can swim through.   720
The best that you, like any person, can
hope for in life is a little more good
luck than bad. It's high time, Phaidra,
to drop your crazy talk of suicide.
No more conceit! For it's ungodly conceit
to think you can win, when you fight
the powers who control your whole being.
Your passion is what the god
has chosen you to become. Accept it.
And though you suffer, be gallant about it.   730
There are certain incantations,
spells with magic potential,
available—cures, I feel sure,
for ailments like yours.
Our men would have little facility
in these black arts, if we women
didn't open their eyes.

LEADER Phaidra, she speaks straight to the heart
        of your present distress. But I respect
        your words more. My praise for your resistance   740
        will sound harsh, I suspect, much less
        pleasant than what Nurse has in mind.

PHAIDRA It's just seductive words like hers
         that make our teeming cities fall apart,
         ruining homes and families.
         It's crazy for us to tell each other
         whatever charms the ear,
         when what we need are words
         that will keep honor in our lives!

NURSE Why this sanctimony? Useless   750
       moralizing isn't what you need.
       You need that man!
                        We have no time to waste.
       So we must be completely frank.

39

If your life were not in deep trouble,
if you were able to control yourself,
I wouldn't have pushed you this far—
certainly not just to satisfy
your lustful fantasies.
The stakes now are too high—
this thing could kill you.   760
Don't despise my efforts to help.

PHAIDRA Woman, I hate what you're saying, it's hideous.
Better to shut your mouth than degrade
us both with any more lewd talk.

NURSE Degrade us? Better for you right now
than any noble stoicisms—now only the act
itself, which saves your life, will do.
Let the good name go which you love
so much and which is killing you.

PHAIDRA Stop it! The gods hear you!
                              No further, because   770
your voice is so full of persuasive ruin!
Love makes me so churned-up and receptive—
if I listen to you, what I want to
hide from will overwhelm me.

NURSE So be it. If this is what you fear
you should have stayed out of love.
Now that you're in it, hear me out,
that is the best thing left.
Something just now crosses my mind.
Somewhere in the palace I keep a medicine   780
potent enough to change love in its course.
It won't disgrace you or derange your mind,
it will free you from this dreadful disease—
if you will only keep your nerve.
We'll need a token from Hippolytos
—either a thatch of his hair or a few
threads from his clothes, from which

40

we'll weave a spell that will bind two
yearnings now fighting each other
into one peace of gratified desire.   790

PHAIDRA This drug, do I drink it,
or will you rub it into my skin?

NURSE I'm not sure. It works
when you give in to it, not when
you know it. Let it save you.

PHAIDRA Your cleverness terrifies me—
I think it will ruin me.

NURSE You're upset, panicked by anything.
But what exactly do you fear?

PHAIDRA I'm afraid you'll give me away to Hippolytos.   800

NURSE There's really nothing to fear, child.
What I do will rid you of agony.

She approaches the statue of Aphrodite and whispers her
prayer.

Aphrodite,
sea goddess, share this adventure with me,
though I have my own tactics, and these,
once I set them in motion, once I share
them inside with a certain young friend,
will carry our affair to its climax.

Exit.

CHORUS Eros, Desire! Our eyes perplex and cloud over
when your essence dissolves within them,
your assault waves of crushing delight   810
pour into hearts marked by you for destruction.
May the cruel hand of your power
never touch me, may I escape

41

ever bearing too much of you, who
stampede to distraction our quiet pulse-beats.
Neither the shooting stars nor the slashing lightning
surpass in terror those shafts of Aphrodite
aimed and thrown by your own hand:
they set our lives on fire.

They are futile,   820
those massive blood-lettings the Greeks make
on the banks of river Alpheus
or in Apollo's house at Delphi,
cattle sacrificed in the wrong shrine;
they are futile
because man's major tyrant,
Eros the god, is never worshiped
by any such honorable slaughter,
though he demands honor, since his keys
open to ultimate delight   830
the dark sensual chambers of Aphrodite—
little wonder he is violent among us,
imagining bitter adventures
for those of our hearts he commandeers.

Think of that free-running filly,
Iole of Oikhalia—
the burden of sex never settled on her body,
no man took her to bed, or married her.
She surged like a translucent naiad
or a reveling Maenad through life.   840
But Aphrodite's hands took hold of her hard,
tearing her clear of her father's house
into the gore and fire
of a marriage charged with slaughter,
marriage with Herakles.
Her bridal song was bloody murder.

Confirm me in this, observant walls
of Thebes, and you, voice of the river Dirke:
speak of the time that Kypris, with lithe

invisible skill, persuaded Semele to lie   850
with Zeus—a pregnancy
which his lightning, whose cutting edge
is flame, cut short in murderous childbirth.
Thus Dionysos was for the first time born.
Hovering at all times everywhere, like a bee,
is the goddess of love, sifting
upon our flowering fields her savage pollen.

PHAIDRA (*listening at the doors*) Silence! Ahh, I will not survive this.

LEADER What is it, Phaidra?
        What has gone wrong inside your house?   860

PHAIDRA You must be still. I can't make out the words.

LEADER We're quiet. From what little we've heard
        this thing does not sound good.

PHAIDRA It's horrible, and it's happening to me!

LEADER What? Why are you screaming?
        Can you make sense of her talk?
        Explain all this shouting, Phaidra.
        You look stunned. What's in those words
        that hits you like a storm wind?

PHAIDRA It tells me I am going to die.   870
         Move here to the door. Listen
         to the chaos coming at us.

LEADER You're right there, Phaidra.
        You tell us the bad news.

PHAIDRA Just this. The child of the horse-loving
         Amazon queen, Hippolytos, is in a huge
         fury, and the one he attacks is my nurse!

43

LEADER   Yes, I hear muffled recrimination—
         not clearly, though; the door blocks most of it.
         But I can hear anger rising in his voice.   880

PHAIDRA His words are plain enough:
         "Salacious bawd!"
         "Slut treacherous to her husband's love!"

LEADER   Dear Queen, it's you who are betrayed.
         Our misery is for you.
         What could we possibly say to help?
         Everything you suppressed
         is now out in the light.
         You have been broken beyond hope
         by your own treacherous, intimate friend.   890

PHAIDRA She told Hippolytos!
         She told him why I was sick!
         Because she loved me.
         She tried to make me well
         with her clumsy frankness,
         but that medicine has death in it.

LEADER   What are you going to do? How are you
         going to fight these impossible things?
         Can anyone cope with your suffering?

PHAIDRA I know one way to fight it.   900
         I will die as soon as I can.
         My mind is so sick and corrupted now
         only death can restore me to health.

PHAIDRA retreats just inside central door, but remains in earshot.

              Enter HIPPOLYTOS *with* NURSE *from side entrance.*

HIPPOLYTOS Mother Earth and Great Sun, whose light
            unfolds the freshness of the clear blue depths—
            could any words be more repulsive?

NURSE Please calm down, child. Don't shout.
       They'll hear us.

HIPPOLYTOS After I've listened to outrage
       you expect silence and restraint?   910

NURSE Please! I am begging you!—
       by your handsome right arm!   *She grips his arm.*

HIPPOLYTOS Don't touch me!
       Stop clawing at my clothes!

NURSE I beg you by your knees   *Now she clutches his knees.*
       not to crush me.

HIPPOLYTOS Why so frantic? Haven't you've been telling
       me what you've just said is blameless?

NURSE This subject isn't for the whole world to hear!

HIPPOLYTOS Come now, charming stories are much more   920
       impressive when an audience hears them.

NURSE You swore you'd never give me away, Hippolytos.

HIPPOLYTOS My *tongue* made you a promise. Not my mind.

NURSE What will you do? Disgrace a loving friend?

HIPPOLYTOS That was nauseating.
       No criminal could be my friend.

NURSE Then have some human kindness! We're all
       capable of making dreadful mistakes.

HIPPOLYTOS Zeus, you made a cosmic mistake
       when you put women in our lives.   930

45

Men chase their glitter, but it's fools' gold.
If your purpose was to ensure
perpetuation of the human race
you could have bypassed women.
A better idea would have been
to let prospective fathers
come to your temples and pay you
in bronze, iron, or solid gold
for seeds which flourish into men,
each father paying for his sons   940
in proportion to his wealth and status.
Our homes would then be free of females.
Now here's why women are an evil
against which men must take
strenuous measures: the father
who begets and raises a daughter,
must find a man who wants her,
then pay him a huge dowry to keep
her from being a lifelong burden.
As for the man who takes home   950
one of these ruinous creatures,
he's thrilled to drape her
like a statue, swathe her
in silks, furiously pouring
money into her lust for style
while his family fortune drains away.
The most tranquil marriage
must be one to a sweet nothing—
though it's still madness to numb your house
with a drowsy useless simpleton. But   960
the brighter they are the more I detest them.
May I never have to live with a woman
bursting with exuberant vitality—
for it's the clever girls Aphrodite
prefers for her adulteresses,
whereas your listless matron
has not enough wit to stir suspicion.
I'd never let a wife have personal servants
unless they were mute dogs,

surly enough to show teeth   970
at the first whisper of lewd gossip.
But as things stand insidious wives
perfect their intrigues behind the scenes,
then send their women abroad on erotic errands,

Turns to address NURSE.

precisely the way you came and offered me
my father's unthinkable conjugal pleasure.
That episode, and all your recent filth,
I'll wash off my skin in a cold swift stream,
swirling its purity through my ears.
How can I do anything evil   980
when even the sound
of evil appalls me?
Listen, woman: only my
religion saves your neck.
If I hadn't been silenced
by sacred oaths you made me swear,
I would take all this straight to my father.
Now, my best course of action
is to leave home until my father returns.
Oh, I won't say a word to him,   990
but when he comes home I'll
walk by his side everywhere,
watching the look on your face,
and on your mistress' face,
when your eyes touch his eyes.
Damn you! I hate women. I'll never stop
loathing them. Some say I'm insatiably
hostile—but women are insatiably lewd.
Either convert them to chaste decency—or
allow me to stomp on them till I'm dead.   1000

HIPPOLYTOS *exits toward the countryside. Enter* PHAIDRA.

PHAIDRA All women, all of us,
         are violated by destiny.

47

The hurt never leaves us.
Too much has gone wrong
and now there are no saving words,
no brilliant maneuvers,
to shake that noose sliding
toward my throat. I deserve it.
In all your expanse, earth and sky,
there's no hiding from what's happened to me.   1010
My hideousness is now naked to all.
Is there a god anywhere
who will stand by me,
or a man who would lend his strength
to see me through chagrin and scorn?
No one will come.
And I think my life is going—
it scares me—over the edge.
No woman is more defenseless than me.

LEADER There's nothing left, mistress, we're through.   1020
Your servant's machinations
have collapsed into a nightmare.

                              PHAIDRA *turns to* NURSE.

PHAIDRA Woman, you are contemptible! Vicious, brainless!
You are the ruin of the very people
you should have loved. May Zeus,
my forefather, tear you by the roots
out of life. Let him drive into your
body surges of his incinerating fire!
I warned you—I guessed your impulse
to tempt Hippolytos—I begged you to be quiet   1030
about those things which now disgrace me.
You couldn't keep your mouth shut.
Because of you, after I die
my name will stink of depravity.
There it is. But now I
must force myself to imagine
how events will work out.
Let me discover in them one new thought.

48

There's such an edge to Hippolytos' outrage
he will repeat to his father your criminal words;   1040
I will be guilty. Theseus then
will make the countryside erupt
with scandal that will savage my good name.
May you be damned, and anyone else
eager to help a friend
by shocking methods, even though
that friend forbids such help.

NURSE My lady, you have every right
      to hate the harm I have done you.
      But the hurt you feel is so severe   1050
      it cripples your judgment—you'd see that
      if you give me a chance to answer you.
      Please listen!
                      You were a baby in my arms,
      your happiness was my life.
      In my struggle to save your life
      I lost the cure and found what nobody wanted.
      If my luck with Hippolytos had been better,
      right now, you'd be delighting in my wisdom.
      Our minds are reckoned only as astute
      as chance will let them be.

PHAIDRA   What!   1060
        After your actions have broken me,
        you try to make peace with words.

NURSE Words are not helping us.
      Yes, I was indecent and stupid,
      but I can still save you, child.

PHAIDRA That's as much as I'll listen to.
        You gave me evil advice, you acted evilly,
        and would have made me act so.
        You leave me now.
        Use your wits to save your own life.   1070

49

As for my life, I will take hold
of it and make it straight again.

Exit NURSE *into the palace.*

Troizenian friends, do this for me.
Let nothing of what you've just
witnessed ever be known.

LEADER We swear in Artemis' presence and in her name,
none of your troubles will be known
through any of our words.

PHAIDRA Thank you.
I have one final thing to tell you.   1080
I see my way clear to securing—
despite this catastrophe—
an honorable future for my children,
salvaging from my wrecked condition
as much as I can. I will never
humiliate my native Krete.
I will not stand before Theseus
and hear him accuse me of incest—
never—merely to save one life.

LEADER What will it be—this last desperate act?   1090

PHAIDRA To die. But how?
That I must now decide.

LEADER How can you speak so calmly—of such things?

PHAIDRA Calmly? Think of a better plan—
then death will frighten me.
On this day, gone from my life,
I will at last delight you, Aphrodite.
But I was beaten by a poisonous love,
and in death I will touch with this venom
someone else—he'll not be able   1100
to smile with complacent hauteur

when news of my misfortune comes,
because he will then share with me
this sexual sickness unto death;
then he will learn that chastity in all things
cannot survive its own arrogance.   *Exit.*

CHORUS   It would be good to arrive in the mountains,
poised in a secret recess on the rock face—
a god there might give me airborne lightness,
make me a bird among the other high   1110
floating creatures;
from there I could sail west
out over the Adriatic shoreline,
the surf swelling up as it pounds in,
below me the river Eridanos,
by whose black current
live black poplars, sisters endlessly tearful,
echoing in exquisite deliquescence
the plunge of Phaëthon their brother, sending
into the seas their amber tears'   1120
fallen radiance.

My flight will at last touch down
on the Hesperian shore, that gentle
garden where apples thrive and girls sing,
where the sea lord, from his dark
ominous shallows,
commands venturesome sailors to turn back
because here he has set
the outer limits of the sky, and placed
that sacred weight on Atlas' shoulders.   1130
Ambrosial vale!
I love your fountains pouring through banks
where Zeus and Hera first made love—
for it is here that Earth, lavish
with her gifts, swells into endless rapture
the lives of the gods.

A ship with soaring white sails made the crossing
from Krete with Phaidra on board,

51

from her tranquil home launched into the world,
and the salt sea threw up waves   1140
booming against the bow timbers.
It was to fulfillment that ship carried our queen,
but of a marriage whose joy drained cruelly
away, for omens had alarmed us twice—
when first she embarked from Minos' country,
then at her landfall in mainland Greece.
When the hawsers were fast in Piraeus
she walked without luck toward her life in Athens,
where Aphrodite—without flinching—broke her spirit,
using reckless love as a deadly infection.   1150
Hopelessness now climbs over her head
like mammoth waters, and reaching up
Phaidra finds the beam of her bedroom,
makes fast the noose which she slides snug
against the whiteness of her throat.
Convulsed by loathing for her own
inexorable conduct, she escapes, leaping
into whatever solace comes from a chaste
repute. Her heart is released from that
dead weight: unbearable desire.   1160

NURSE (*within*) Help me!
          Who is out there? I need your help!
          Please come! Our queen is dead.
          Theseus' wife has hanged herself.

LEADER She's ended it,
          her body is lifeless,
          it sways heavily at the end of her rope.
          Our queen is gone.

NURSE (*within*) Quick! Bring me a sharp tapered blade
          to free her neck from this huge knot.   1170

1ST WOMAN Should we do it?
          Should we go in and free our queen
          from the rope that killed her?

2ND WOMAN Let's stay out here.
There are plenty of house
servants inside. Let's not
join that hysterical confusion.

NURSE (*within*) Lay her poor body down gently,
gracefully. Her bitter vigil ends in this.

3RD WOMAN She's surely dead. That's what those sounds mean.   1180
Listen: they are already preparing
Phaidra's body—giving it
the decorum of death.

Shouts from inside the palace. Enter THESEUS,
wearing a crown of flowers.

THESEUS Women, what are the house servants
shouting about? Their keening carried to me,
it's still echoing through the house.
And the house doors are shut tight,
no one stood waiting by the road
to swing them open for me,
though it's from Delphi I'm returning,   1190
full of god's favor, and ready to enjoy
the cheerful welcome my journey deserves.
Nothing alarming has struck Pittheus?
He's very old now, and yet
if he's gone the hurt would be deep.

LEADER It's not the old who are dying, Theseus,
it's the young. Look there for your grief.

THESEUS My children?
No! Who would wish
to rob me of their lives?   1200

LEADER They're living, Theseus, but in wretchedness
because their mother is dead.

53

THESEUS What are you saying? Phaidra is dead?
         How is she dead?

LEADER She made fast a knotted rope
         and hanged herself.

THESEUS Did the coldness and grief of our long
         separation get to her heart?
         Or something more violent?

LEADER We know very little, Theseus.   1210
         Like you, we just arrived,
         to mourn. To bear this agony with you.

          THESEUS *removes the entwined flowers on his head.*

THESEUS A crown of flowers! Why am I wearing it?
         To show my mind still glows with the god
         Apollo's advice? Because I come home
         to this deadly good luck?
         Slide back the bolts and open the door.
         Let me look at my wife, though the sight
         has fangs, and her death
         seeps bitterly into mine.   1220

CHORUS Your sorrows, Phaidra, are beyond
         understanding by us. All we sense
         is what you have done, an act
         so enormous it dooms this palace.

               The doors open to reveal PHAIDRA's *body.*

         How desperate you were, comes over us now.
         You threw your life violently away,
         defiant of everything divine,
         the victim of a stranglehold you placed,
         like a merciless wrestler, on your own neck.
         Who bled your life into such   1230
         vanishing frailty?

54

THESEUS My people, I am thinking deep through my life's
         wanton miseries. There were many.
         This blow dwarfs them all.
         It was struck by my personal Fate,
         insidious adversary!
         In my own house we come to grips:
         you crush me there, taking the shape of some
         insane spirit of revenge,
         inflicting an invisible contagion   1240
         upon me, whose carnage
         leaves me less than alive.
         I see troubles around me in an endless expanse,
         as though I were awash in mid-ocean—
         I can't swim back to my old life
         or climb with bare thrashing arms
         over this swollen disaster.
         I don't know anything, Phaidra,
         not what to say to you,
         or what the cause of your death was.   1250
         I feel your life as vanishing
         from my cradling hands,
         leaping like a pulse of feathers,
         a bird alighting in the underworld.
         This miasma has blown over me
         out of some black swamp of history
         because a god had hate left unexpended
         for some remote dead man of my race
         who had hugely sinned.

LEADER   My lord, other men have lost good wives.   1260
         Others have faced this sorrow.

THESEUS I see myself on a bed in my dark house
         dying into the greater dark under the earth.
         Will one of you tell me exactly
         what drove Phaidra to her death?
         Or do I keep in my palace
         a mute contingent of fools?
         I must keep going through this grief,

55

though her death makes no sense,
though my mind can't accept it,   1270
or frame words to speak of it.
The truth is—I have nothing left.
My palace is a lifeless shell,
my children motherless.
And you, Phaidra, so dear, so vital,
have disappeared.
                        How I loved you!
You were lovely beyond any woman
this sunlight ever saw
or night's glistening lustful face of stars.

LEADER Evil grips this house.   1280
        We can't see through our tears.
        And we are crying
        because of what that evil
        did to you, Phaidra.
        But I am shaking now
        at what comes next.

THESEUS Look! This tablet, still gripped tensely
         in her dear fingers.
                        Can it carry, I wonder,
         even worse news.

He removes tablet from her dead hand and examines it.

Or is the poor girl silently begging me   1290
to honor her marriage and her children?
Phaidra, child. Let nothing upset you in death.
No woman ever will take over this house
or sleep in my bed, where you slept.
That is her signet, set in an arc
of hammered gold, inviting me
to open it, a gesture full of her charm—
I'll unravel the windings and crack
the seal. Let me just take in
her last words to me.   1300

LEADER Only a god could inflict
        a progression so cruel.
        As one evil shock sinks in
        another more savage strikes home.
        Our line of kings is wiped out—
        where it stood I see nothing.
        Spirit of death, I feel in my bones
        more murder at hand. Spare this house!

THESEUS Ahhh! Sorrows in infinite waves
        break over me.

LEADER   Tell us this news, King,   1310
        if it is right that we know it.

THESEUS This tablet is screaming at me,
        all our agony wells up within it.
        Evil in all its tonnage
        is stone upon my body.
        There is no way to get free.
        I don't live in myself now—
        I am nowhere, nothing!
        When I look down at it,
        God help me, her writing   1320
        sings out in her own
        melodious tortured voice.

LEADER Feel the ruin in his words.

THESEUS The truth is hideous. It sears and wrenches
        and will not stay clenched in my throat.
        To speak it excruciates me,
        but it must come. Ahhh!
        Hear it, men of my city!

                    His voice rises to a roaring shout.

        My wife was raped—by Hippolytos!
        And the implacable light of Zeus   1330

57

has seen it and is sickened. You are my father,
Great God Poseidon, and once you gave me
three mortal curses. I use one, now,
and with it ask you to murder my son.
You must not let him
escape alive from this day—
if I can trust your promise.

LEADER Don't do it, Theseus! Call off your curse.
How mistaken you are
soon will be horribly clear.   1340
Believe us!

THESEUS There's no chance. And add to that curse, this one:
I banish him beyond our borders.
Whatever happens now, he will be broken.
Either Poseidon will back my curse
and drive my son dead into Hades' swamp,
or this land will never see him again,
as he drifts, begging his way
into an alien existence,
where he will drink this pain   1350
until his life itself is bone dry.

LEADER Your son is nearly here, Theseus,
the moment is crucial—shake off
your murderous rage. Take some thought
for the survival of your royal house.

                                          Enter HIPPOLYTOS.

HIPPOLYTOS I heard you shout the alarm,
Father, and ran here.
I don't know what the trouble is—
I'd better hear it straight from you.
Lord, what's this? Father, there's your wife—   1360
lying dead. I can't believe it.
Moments ago I was near her,
she stood alive in the sunlight.
What happened? What killed her?

Father, will you tell me?
Why won't you speak?
Silence is not in your interest now.
It won't soften pain. It's not right, Father,
to shut your friends out of your grief
and turn sneering away   1370
from those who love you!
More even than friends.

THESEUS O humankind, there's nothing to match
         your pride, your absurd presumption.
         Your history is all creative mastery—
         blazing imagination and technical skill—
         but you have not perfected,
         or even been much concerned with,
         the most essential art of all:
         teaching good sense to moral idiots!   1380

HIPPOLYTOS What's this? It would take
            a very clever man
            to make wisdom take root
            in minds where it can't grow.
            Father, why should your thoughts
            be tied in subtle knots—now,
            with grief all over you?
            Your tongue runs wild
            because of what you've suffered.

THESEUS Ahhh, if only we men had command   1390
         of an infallible instrument, and with it
         could probe our dearest friends' sincerity!
         We need a perfect path
         into the heart, one that could tell,
         as clear as a heartbeat, a faithful
         loving friend from one who is false.
         And our speech ought to have two
         distinct registers, one for truth's
         perfect pitch, and another
         that always grates when you lie.   1400

Unjust accusations could no longer
hide in suave eloquence;
they'd be exposed, because
our ears would always recall
the sweetness of a person's truthful voice.
We'd never again be deceived.

HIPPOLYTOS Tell me this: is there some "friend," one
close to your heart—whom you deeply
trust—speaking slander about me?
Though there is *nothing* in me to blame,   1410
because you suspect me, I feel diseased.
Don't you see that, Father? Your words
are so far from coherent sense, I'd be
amazed if you understood mine.

THESEUS I pity mankind's driven intellect,
always racing beyond its own foresight.
Are there no limits to callous audacity?
If all this wickedness wells up
even in the lifetime of one man,
and each generation outdoes   1420
the previous in criminal acts,
the gods will need to provide us
another land mass, which will soon
swarm like a rotten fruit with sinners—
breeding more lewd and vulgar men.
Take a close look at this man. Though
I fathered him, he forced his way
into my wife's bed. And if you want
proof this maniac has raped her,
she gives her dead body as proof.   1430

HIPPOLYTOS *plunges his face into his cloak.*

Don't hide your face. Your eyes
have already polluted me.
Look at me straight.

HIPPOLYTOS *removes cloak.*

The gods, you tell us, are your close friends,
because you are a man of virgin holiness.
And you have given yourself in lust
neither to women nor to sin of any kind?
There is no chance I would take
seriously your applause for yourself.
What an affront that would be to the gods,   1440
to believe them so clumsily duped.
You're highly pleased, aren't you,
with your initiation into orgiastic cults.
You're a promoter of weird ideas: taking
such pride in your vegetable banquets.
Your current hero's Orpheus, your days
are spent inhaling holy aroma
from books of arcane absurdity.
I have caught up with you, son.
To everyone within earshot I say: 1450
shun this man, and all those like him
who speak in the accents
of clean-living ascetics, while
their minds race conniving and they
close in on the foulest pleasures.
Because she lies there dead,
speechless, you imagine that clears you?
Her stillness convicts you, you killer.
Nothing you plead or swear
could be more overpowering   1460
than she is in voiceless quiet. You'll claim,
I would imagine, that she hated you
because there's natural resentment
between bastards and the true-born.
You really think her capable
of striking such an insane bargain
as this: to throw away
the sweetest thing she owned, her life,
merely to quench the malice she held for you?
Maybe you'll take this line: lechery   1470
is not a masculine trait at all,
but is as peculiar

to females as their wombs.
Listen: male blood is as warm as theirs,
and you aren't any more in control
when lust sends its pulse toward the crest;
the very suppleness of the male sex
thrusts you into trouble
and gets you out again.
So . . . but why should I grapple   1480
with any of your arguments? Her corpse
disposes of them all, and drives home your guilt
each time my eyes touch her body.
Listen to my curse,
and may it smash your life.
Get out of Troizen. Use all your proud speed.
And in your exile stay clear of that city
imagined by the gods, Athens;
cross no frontier into those provinces
commanded by my military power.   1490
If I resigned myself to this outrage from you,
old Sinis would feel free
to jeer from his isthmus that I never killed him,
that I'm a boastful liar; and in their turn
the Skironian Rocks will shrug
when asked how heavy was my fist
on the bandit I dashed in their surf.

LEADER How can I speak for the good luck of any mortal?
        Even the great fall from the heights they reach.

HIPPOLYTOS Father, I can't match your fury, or outwit   1500
            all your convoluted vehemence.
            But if you could listen calmly to the facts,
            if something could silence
            your eloquence, you'd see.
            Your hard cold words would lose their force.
            I'm too plain spoken to persuade a crowd.
            I'm more at home pursuing rigorous
            enlightenment with a few wise friends.

There's rough justice in that, since
men who falter among the brilliant   1510
are often charismatic
in their hold on the mob.
But since this crisis is forced on me
I must find the will to speak out.
There is one charge I must meet first,
the annihilating one you hoped
would break me down and stun any reply.
Look out through the light of heaven
and the vast country surrounding us.
You couldn't discover in all that space   1520
a man more completely honest than me.
I see your face is hard with doubt.
I respect our gods, and I choose friends
whom sin doesn't tempt, who wouldn't
dream of corrupting others, or
tolerate in themselves an unclean lapse
to pay a friend back for his shady help.
I don't betray my friends, Father.
I am as loyal to those close to me
when we're together as when they're gone.   1530
There is one practice I have never touched,
though it's exactly what you attack me for:
physical love. To this day
I've never been to bed with a woman.
All I know about sex is what I hear,
or find in pictures—and those I'm not keen
to see, since I keep my inner life
as calm and clean as I can.
My innocence doesn't impress you,
that I can see, so let it go.   1540
Try instead to imagine the reasons
I would trade innocence for depraved lust.
Was your wife's body more sexually
attractive than any living woman's?
Was getting into bed with her some scheme
so I could take over your palace—
a marriage into power? If I thought that,

it would show a warped mind,
in fact, no brains whatever. Or will you
argue that peaceful dispositions   1550
like mine are power-mad? That's
preposterous, unless the thrill of kingship
has eaten into the minds of us all.
I'll tell you what I wish most in life:
to win a race in the Olympic games,
then come home to live gracefully,
drawing friends from the best men in town,
but in political life to come in second.

Granted such a career, success
would lie within my power.   1560
Danger would leave me alone.
A relaxed way of life would have
more appeal than a king's.
I'll add one last point to my defense.
If a single witness to my feelings
could describe my conduct these last hours,
and if your accusations had come
while Phaidra was alive,
you'd see these facts in their true pattern,
you'd see the face of those who have harmed others.   1570
The only chance I have left
is to swear before Zeus,
who judges the truth of all human oaths.
Zeus, I swear by you
and by the earth that holds us,
that I did not touch Phaidra,
never wished to make love to her,
couldn't hold that thought in my head.
If I am a malignant liar in this
I am willing to face annihilation: let   1580
my name and my accomplishments
be forgotten, let neither the sea nor
the earth give rest to my corpse.
What seizure of remorse drove
Phaidra to suicide, I cannot say...

because I have sworn not to.
There was honor in her death
but none in her, and because my honor
is stronger than hers, it is useless.

LEADER   Your words have thrown up a staunch   1590
blockade against this charge—
no one makes lightly
a sworn oath to Zeus.

THESEUS   We have a born wizard on our hands—
whose magic would banish
his recent scorn of me:
he thinks gestures of mild openness
will disarm my hatred.

HIPPOLYTOS   I am just as amazed at your blandness,
Father. Were you my son, without one qualm   1600
I would have had you killed, not exiled,
if you had raped my wife.

THESEUS   Your death will not come so opportunely
as in the sentence you impose on yourself.
A swift annihilation erases
suffering, but you'll have your share:
a restless alien cut off from your homeland,
surrounded by strangers,
your acrid life will be
forever lifted to your lips.   1610

HIPPOLYTOS   What will you do? At least
won't you let time lay the facts
before you on my behalf? Time
is our only incorruptible witness.
So you will force me out of my
own country and into exile?

THESEUS   I would drive you beyond the confines
of the known world—the Black Sea,

the Pillars of Herakles—if I had power
enough, my son, I hate you so much.   1620

HIPPOLYTOS Then you will throw me out?
Without a trial? Without looking hard
at my oath, without waiting to hear
advice from men who can read god's will?

THESEUS This tablet, without resort to any
oracular ambiguity,
accuses you with absolute conviction.
If birds of omen want to fly
over my head, let them.

HIPPOLYTOS O gods, can you tell me why   1630
I don't speak the words
that would free me?
Here I am, revering you, gods,
and yet it's you who force my ruin.
I cannot say it. Even if I did speak
I couldn't persuade the one who counts.
I'd betray my sworn oaths—
for nothing.

THESEUS Your sanctimony turns my stomach.
Get out! Right now!   1640
Go anywhere—but leave this country.

HIPPOLYTOS Who will my wretchedness touch?
Is there one man in all Greece
who'd take me into his house, once
he hears the charge against me?

THESEUS   Yes—
whoever is salacious enough
to urge his guests to fornicate
with his women. Oh you'll
find room as a resident
orgiast and master of defilement.   1650

66

HIPPOLYTOS   Father, what you say feels like a spear
             driving through my body.
             It fills me with tears—
             to see myself as a lustful killer
             when I look through your eyes.

THESEUS   The time for groaning and forethought
          should have come sooner—before
          you thought it venturesome
          to rape your father's wife.

HIPPOLYTOS   If only this calm lifeless house   1660
             could speak for me, and say fairly
             if there's anything so vile in my blood.

THESEUS   You're fond of calling witnesses
          who can't speak a word. But there are
          facts which don't need speech
          to expose your vile nature.

HIPPOLYTOS   If only I could manage
             to see myself from out there
             perhaps I'd be permitted tears
             for all this unbearable squalor.   1670

THESEUS   The truth is, my son, your self-regard
          took more of your devotion
          than your own parents ever did.
          A good man would have honored us.

HIPPOLYTOS   I came bitterly from your womb,
             O my cruelly wounded mother.
             Let no one I love ever
             enter this world a bastard.

                              THESEUS *turns to his servants.*

THESEUS   Drag him from my sight.
          Has my meaning eluded you   1680

67

all this time? I've ordered
banishment for this man!

HIPPOLYTOS The man who touches me will regret it.
I want you, Father, yourself,
to drive me from our country—
if that is your grim will.

THESEUS I will do it, if obedience
to my commands doesn't come now.
That pity which you hope
will weaken me is not there.   1690

HIPPOLYTOS Your decision, I can see, is sealed.
The worst has come,
yet I am blocked from speaking truth.
Daughter of Leto, you who were
closest to me, my friend, my hunting partner,
now I will go in exile
from radiant Athens.
I say goodbye to my city,
and this domain of Erektheus,
and to the plains of Troizen   1700
so filled with the bright pleasures
my childhood devoured. Goodbye.
This is the last time I may
survey you and bless you.

Come, my friends, who have played out
my youth over these hills, make me
your parting salutes, escort me
to the frontier, for never will you find
a man who loved moral beauty
so much, and who was granted it,   1710
though my father has no eyes for it.   *Exit.*

                                   THESEUS *goes into the palace.*

CHORUS When we imagine ourselves in the gods' care
our troubled souls are immensely reassured.

But when deep inside us we struggle
to make rational sense of our lives
frustration strikes from all the erratic
crisscrossing paths of reality:
man's life is volatile; it will not
run clear and reveal its essence.

If fate is friendly to my prayers   1720
life will be rich and secure for me,
my heart will endure unscathed.
I hope my approach to experience
is neither rigid and willful
nor its best principles diluted;
but always keep me in pliant resilience
so that the colors of my thought and feeling
will blend and join every morning
with that day's blessed necessities.

The peaceful clarity of my mind is gone,   1730
its confidence shattered by what I see:
the brilliant Hippolytos,
the clearest light of Athens,
we have seen driven estranged and headlong
into exile by his own raging father,
leaving to their sorrows
the sands along our city's shoreline
and our mountainous timberland, where
reveling in the speed of his hounds
and in the guidance of Artemis the Hunter   1740
he tracked down and killed wild game.

Hippolytos, you will not feel
that surging momentum—
a team of Veneto stallions
gaining ground as they race on our tidal flats.
Nor will the lyre respond to your touch,
blowing music at strange hours
through the quiet of your father's palace.
No more will wildflower crowns for Artemis

be placed where she sleeps in the green shadows.   1750
All ended. Because you are gone,
our maidens no longer
are rivals to glide through a marriage
with you, into your passionate arms.

My tears for you are ones I won't outlive,
my helplessness will always match yours,
Hippolytos—your mother's agony, as she gave
you life, earned you no luck.
What the gods did to you
fills me with rage.   1760
O Graces, goddesses
of beauty and kindness,
you have given—why did you do it?—
a hard life to an innocent man.
You cut him off from his home and country
to travel depressed and alone.

LEADER One of Hippolytos' men
is now coming up to the palace
on the dead run, his face full of pain.

Enter MESSENGER.

MESSENGER Women, where can I find Theseus,   1770
the king? If you know, please tell me.
The palace—is he inside?

LEADER There is the king, coming now through the doors.
Enter Theseus

MESSENGER I have some news, Theseus, grave news,
for you and the people of Athens and Troizen.

THESEUS Tell it. Is it possible that fresh
trouble has hit both towns at once?

MESSENGER Hippolytos is gone—as good as dead.
He breathes, but just on the brink of death.

70

THESEUS Who did this to him?   1780
         Surely there's not some man whose wife
         Hippolytos has already raped,
         just as he did his father's wife?

MESSENGER His chariot, at speed, killed him,
           that, and the curses of your mouth
           when you asked your father the sea lord
           to act against your son.

THESEUS O gods! Poseidon, you really are my father,
         and you have driven home my curse.
         How did he die?
                         Tell me exactly how   1790
         justice closed its iron jaws upon that son
         who violated his father's honor.

MESSENGER We were down on the rocky beach,
           combing our horses' sides with stiff brushes,
           and we were in tears.
                                 A man had just told us
           Hippolytos couldn't range through these hills
           any more because your orders exiled him
           beyond us into a miserable life.
           Hippolytos soon himself came up
           beside us on the shore,   1800
           his own voice breaking with the news.
           A great army of friends followed him down.
           He wept, but soon commanded his pain,
           saying, "What use is raving? I must accept
           my father's will. Grooms,
           yoke up four horses to my chariot,
           for this has ceased to be my city."
           Instantly, each lad bore down on his job
           and with remarkable speed the harnessed team
           was ready for our master.   1810
           He lifted the reins off the rail into his grip,
           then slid his feet into their slots.
           Stretching his arms high, he prayed:
           "Zeus, if I am guilty, let me die.

71

But make certain Theseus learns
how wrong he is, whether I live or die."
His strong arm hauled back the goad
and smacked the horses' flanks.
We servants jogged beside our master,
heads bobbing near the reins,   1820
out the straight road to Argos and Epidauros.
As we plunged through that desolate country,
we saw a headland rising beyond our borders,
far out in the Saronic Gulf.
At that moment a subterranean undertone
gathered volume like Zeus thundering,
or an earthquake's massive tremors—
a thoroughly chilling sound.
The horses slashed their heads,
their ears shot straight up.   1830
Our fear grew violent as we tried
to locate the source of that sound.
Eyes scanning the shoreline
swarmed over by the loud surf,
we saw this huge uncanny wave
frozen against the blue sky, wiping out
our sight of the Skironic coast,
the Isthmus, and Asclepius' rock.
The wave bulged ever higher,
a mass of seething foam, geysers shot clear,   1840
and then it charged the land
taking dead aim for the racing chariot.
Just as the wave's tremendous peak
broke loose its waters, it disgorged
a mammoth bull, savage and crazed.
The whole earth swelled as the bull bellowed
and answered with a counter-roar.
Our numbed eyes, hit by these wonders,
blacked out—
At that instant the horses panicked.   1850
Hippolytos, instinctively skillful with horses,
seized the reins in both fists,
leaning backward against their live weight

as a sailor puts his back into an oar.
The horses clenched the fire-hardened bits in their jaws
and tore free of their master's control,
no longer feeling the harness
or the chariot's weight.
Hippolytos tried to reach safer terrain
but as he veered the bull would cut him off,   1860
spooking the horses sideways,
out of their minds with terror.
But when they bore down insanely on the rocks
the bull closed silently in,
harassing the chariot's outer edge,
which struck the cliff, the whole chariot rocking up
and over into chaotic, sliding wreckage.
Axles, spokes, linchpins sheared off,
exploding into space.
Our wounded lord was trapped as the reins   1870
lashed him into a terrible snarl—
he was dragged thrashing and his head
smashed rocks, flesh coming off in skeins.
I never heard more tortured screams:
"Stop! You mares," he was saying.
"I fed you! Don't kill me! I'm a good man!
My father's curse destroys me!
Help me, friends. Cut me loose!"
We were all willing and sprinting,
but it was hopeless. We were so winded   1880
the horses outran us.
                                        When he did
somehow roll clear of the leather thongs
we found him just barely breathing.
What happened to the horses
and that grim monstrosity of a bull
I don't know—they must have
vanished somewhere among those rough cliffs.
King, I am your slave, but don't ask me
to believe that your son was guilty.
I couldn't, not if the whole female sex   1890
hanged itself, and all the timber on Mount Ida

were sliced up to write suicide notes.
I know he was a good man.

LEADER New evils still
pour into this catastrophe.
There's no way out
when the will of fate and his own luck
converge to destroy a man.

THESEUS I hated him. His suffering, while you told it,
filled me with satisfaction. Now,   1900
I know I should not feel this. It shames me
in the gods' eyes and in my son's
because he is my child.
I give up any pleasure
in his destruction.
But I can feel no grief.

MESSENGER Your orders, King? Shall we carry him
here to you? How would you like us
to care for this badly wounded man?
Consider it, Theseus. Isn't it time to end   1910
your bitterness toward your dying son?

THESEUS Bring him. I want to see his eyes,
the ones that denied he befouled
my marriage bed with bestial rape—
to see him face an argument
he can't refute, one I and the gods use
against him—his own death.

Exit MESSENGER.

CHORUS Aphrodite, with a flash of your power
you caress the hard minds of humans and gods—
as Desire in his bright imperial plumage   1920
overwhelms them with huge fast wings.
On your radiant golden sorties,
cruising inland or riding the loud salt sea,

swift Eros, you inflict your mad beat
on the pulsating hearts of us all.
O Goddess, you inflame
beasts in the mountains, fish in the seas,
all creatures the earth raises to life,
all the sun burns down upon—
and over men, O Queen of everything,   1930
you alone hold absolute power.

                              ARTEMIS *suddenly appears.*

ARTEMIS You! Powerful, high born man!
         Theseus, it is time now to listen,
         to let my words sink in,
         mine, for I am Artemis, the child of Leto.
         How can you find
         any joy in this hour, atrocious man?
         You are a killer, and the one
         you killed was your own son.
         That you were utterly taken in   1940
         by your wife's lies is now as clear
         as the vengeance that strikes you down.
         You ought to damn your loathsome body
         where it belongs, into the gutters of Hades.
         Get wings, fly off into a bird's safe life,
         to keep your feet from miring
         in this polluted anguish.
         There are no men
         who would ask you to share their lives.
         Theseus, listen.   1950
         You must hear from me the straight truth—
         how your grief reached this aching size.
         Nothing I say will help you.
         It will deepen your pain.
         My purpose is to illuminate
         the honesty of your son's mind,
         so that the honor he deserves
         will come to him as he dies.
         I will reveal and you must face

75

the sexual passion of your wife,   1960
though what she did, seen in its own strange light,
burns with her soul's nobility.
Kypris' sensuous fingernails
cut into Phaidra and aroused her,
driving her into love with your son.
We hate that goddess,
all of us who have found
virginity beautiful.
Counting upon her own self-mastery
to contain her animal passion, Phaidra   1970
instead was wrecked by an intrigue
designed by her nurse.
Phaidra was ignorant
of what the nurse did,
which was to offer your wife's
erotic frenzy to your own son,
once she had sworn him to silence.
Like the honest man he remains
Hippolytos was not moved,
his goodness was so deep and sure.   1980
But Phaidra, dreading exposure,
wrote out those lies which maddened you,
and because you were taken in,
her savage ruse murdered your son.

                                THESEUS *cries out.*

Does that hurt, Theseus?
Keep still awhile. The rest of what I say
will need all the voice you have left
to speak its agony.
Poseidon gave you three implacable curses?
You used the first to crush your son.   1990
Had your enemies grown so scarce,
you loathsome man?
Your father provided that curse in good faith
and he made good its violence.
But such a stupid hateful use of it
leaves you evil, in his thinking and in mine.

Too headstrong to respect a man's sworn oath!
Or call in a prophet to this crisis.
You could have made a just,
deliberate investigation, or simply   2000
waited for passing time to clear things up.
But no. You launched with mindless reflex
the curse that wrecked your son.

THESEUS Goddess, let me die.

ARTEMIS Your crimes could not be worse—
even so, you may be forgiven.
She who lusted for these things
to happen was Kypris alone.
She satisfied her rage.
Since we gods have agreed   2010
not to frustrate each other's cherished purpose,
we always stand aside. If Zeus did not
command otherwise, you can be sure
I would never have been so abject
as to let this man die. I loved him.
You were more ignorant than wicked.
When Phaidra died, her voice
went with her, and all chance
her story would change under questioning—
your mind had no defense against her lies.   2020
Now, the brunt of this anguish falls on you,
I know, but I, too, am cruelly hurt.
When a man dies who pays the gods
lifelong respect, no god enjoys his death.
Blasphemous men, of course, we ruthlessly crush—
and then crush their children, their homes,
and their dynastic pride.

LEADER Look at the ruined lad now
helped toward us
sustained by friends, in great pain,   2030
his blond head bloodied, his strong young limbs

77

bruised and disfigured.
Twice has grief from the hand of god
seized and shaken the beams of this house
and filled it with sorrow.

Enter HIPPOLYTOS, *on the arms of his friends.*

HIPPOLYTOS Ahhh!
My father asked a god to kill me.
My body's a frail ruin,
ravaged by his command—
his unjust magical words.   2040
Pain shoots up my spine, it's
pulsing fire through my brain.
Men, stop! Right here.
My tired body needs to rest.   *Sharp cries.*
O you horses, I fed you, trained you,
with all my skill. Now you have
hurt me and I die cursing you.
For god's sake, men, move my broken
body with care. Whose arms are holding
up my right side? Lift me gently,   2050
keep your arms firm as you lift—there.
I am a man whose own father
wrongheadedly cursed him to death.
Look at me, Zeus! I'm the man
who honored all the gods.
See what happens to your
world's most virtuous man?
I see death closing over me.
My life's wasted; all the good I
did men through my whole god-loving life,   2060
has been entirely useless.
Aii!
Agony has me. Men, let go,
relax your hold. Death, have you come
at last? To cure my life? My pain?
I want a spear's razoring edge
to tear through my body so I can sleep.

O Father, what inspired your curse?
It must have been murder,
one ancestor killing another,   2070
so our past pollutes our present.
But why did it strike me?
I am guilty of nothing.
Ahhh! Words lead nowhere.
All I ask is to go free of pain.
Let the compulsion of death,
dark and nocturnal, lay my body down.   *He lies down.*

ARTEMIS Poor man, you drew the luck of the damned,
yoked to a Fate like a crazed beast.
You had a noble generous mind   2080
and it wrecked you.

HIPPOLYTOS That voice has heaven's fragrance in its sound!
I feel your presence blowing through
these wounds—my body's pain
is lightened.
                    She's come down! Artemis! Goddess!

ARTEMIS She's with you, gallant man, your dearest goddess still.

HIPPOLYTOS Mistress, can you see how badly I am hurt?

ARTEMIS I see. But a goddess may not be in tears.

HIPPOLYTOS You have lost your hunter and servant.

ARTEMIS I lose you, but my love stays with you as you die.   2090

HIPPOLYTOS I'll no more go racing your horses
or guard again your statues and gardens.

ARTEMIS That lascivious criminal,
Kypris, arranged all this.

HIPPOLYTOS I know my killer. I feel her power.

79

ARTEMIS   Your nature was incorruptibly pure.
          She felt that as a bitter
          insult to her honor.

HIPPOLYTOS   All three of us owe our ruin
             to that lone goddess.   2100

ARTEMIS   Yes. You, your father, and a queen suffer.

HIPPOLYTOS   I pity my father
             for what he suffers.

ARTEMIS   He had no chance, so subtly did Kypris
          twist his actions into her plot.

HIPPOLYTOS   All this must sink you in misery, Father.

THESEUS   There's nothing to salvage, child.
          I take no pleasure in living.

HIPPOLYTOS   Your grief is worse than mine, Father,
             because you must live with your mistakes.   2110

THESEUS   Child, I would take your place in the grave.

HIPPOLYTOS   Poseidon's gifts were deadly largesse.

THESEUS   I wish my lips had never given them life.

HIPPOLYTOS   Father, you were angry enough
             to have killed me outright.

THESEUS   Yes, I would have.
          The gods had so deluded me
          I acted in a blind daze.

HIPPOLYTOS   I wish we men could curse gods—
             curse and destroy those killers from our graves.   2120

ARTEMIS Hush, lad. Even with you
in the black world of the dead,
there will be reprisal.
For never could Kypris in her anger
at your innocence and honor
attack your body without our revenge
mauling her interests.
I will choose some great favorite of hers
and drop him with the flex of this bow,
a shower of arrows no man can dodge.   2130
That's how much I regard
your love of me and your honorable heart.
I will try to redeem your sorrows,
brave lad, by making you forever
a hero in this town of Troizen.
Girls in their thoughtful hours before marriage
will clip their locks and offer you
rich folds of hair, and as time's seasons
change, you will receive their tears
in a sad and generous harvest.   2140
And the maidens' spontaneous songs
will dwell on you with endless care.
And fame will find musical words
for Phaidra's terrible love of you,
and that, too, will be known.
Theseus, child of an old man, Aigeus,
hold your son in your arms and draw him near.
You killed him with your mind darkened.
When gods blind a man, he goes wrong.
Do not hate your father, Hippolytos.   2150
I wish you not to.
                            You know what great part
the powers beyond played in your death.
Now, I must go. Goodbye.
It is forbidden gods to see death
come to a man. We must not be touched
by pollution from last agonies and gaspings.
I believe you are close to this.

HIPPOLYTOS To you, too, lucky maiden, a serene goodbye.
            You take leave lightly of our long companionship.
            I grant your wish and relinquish   2160
            bitterness toward my father. As always
            I am ruled by your words.

                                             ARTEMIS disappears.

            Ai!
            Darkness has tracked me down
            and alights on my eyes.
            Father, raise me up.

THESEUS Child, what are you doing to me?

HIPPOLYTOS I'm letting go now and see
            the gates of the dark world below.

THESEUS You go, and my hands still   2170
         hold the guilt of your murder.

HIPPOLYTOS Father, you are no murderer.
            My blood will not ask for your blood.

THESEUS Are these your words?
                                Can you forgive me,
         free me from your murder?

HIPPOLYTOS Yes. By the deadly arrows of Artemis I swear it.

THESEUS What a radiance of noble spirit, son,
         you show to your father.

HIPPOLYTOS I hope you will pray for and find
            that noble radiance in your legitimate sons.   2180

THESEUS I lose your good and gentle soul.

HIPPOLYTOS Goodbye to you, Father.

82

THESEUS Live, son. Stay and fight.
         Don't slip from me.

HIPPOLYTOS The fighting is over. Death is here.
            Father, darken my face in my cloak.

THESEUS Athens,
         you will have your splendor, but never again
         the splendor of this man you lose.
         Aphrodite, I have no heart for your graces.   2190
         I remember forever only your savagery.

CHORUS This blow that struck out of the blue
        touches everyone in our city;
        it will inspire tears far into the future,
        for when the great are destroyed, their
        stories are the ones that move us the most.

                                        All leave in silence.

NOTES

1–193 / 1–120 *Prologue*

1–5 / 1–2 *The power I possess...Aphrodite* Lit. "Powerful and not nameless among mortals, as well as in heaven, am I; I am called the goddess Kypris." To stress the range of significance of the goddess's name, Kypris, I have translated it twice, first using its common popular meaning, sexual activity ("sexual passion"), and then as "Aphrodite," the cult name most familiar to modern readers. The play's first word, *polla*, "great" or "abundant," intensified by its placement, stresses the impact of the goddess's power, the worldwide scope of which—Black Sea to the Atlantic—is established by lines 6–7 / 3–4.

17 / 10 *Amazon mistress* Theseus, in some versions of the myth, raped a hostile Amazon, Hippolyte, by whom he had his illegitimate son, Hippolytos.

19 / 11 *Pittheus the Pure* In his father's absence Hippolytos was brought up by his great-grandfather, the "pure" Pittheus.

50 / 31 *a stone temple* On the Acropolis Phaidra had constructed a temple to Aphrodite, possibly to persuade the goddess to quiet the passion she felt for Hippolytos. Such a temple did in fact exist in Euripides' time.

55 / 35 *a hated rival's sons* Pallas' sons, rivals for the Athenian throne, whom Theseus killed.

59 / 37 *his exile year* Such banishments for homicide were intended to protect a city from the defiling presence of the killer. This invention is introduced not only to explain Theseus' absence from Athens; it also helps contrast the son's purity and the father's defilement.

72 / 46 *curses* A curse was originally a prayer, "in vernacular Attic a maleficent prayer" (Barrett). The god Poseidon, according to legend, gave Theseus the right to use three such "prayers." Theseus in the present action will use two curses; after the first, that Hippolytos die, is fulfilled, the second, that Hippolytos suffer a miserable exile, becomes irrelevant.

106 / 73 *this green crown* Of flowers and leaves, a traditional mark of favor given by a devotee to his goddess, usually placed, as here, on her statue.

109 / 74 *a meadow* A precinct sacred to the goddess, a place whose freshness and unspoiled beauty symbolize Artemis' chastity.

116 / 78 *Restraint* *Aidos*, sometimes translated "Reverence." The goddess who prevents a man from breaking a taboo, who inhibits self-assertion that might violate morality. See note on **588–95**.

120 / 80 *the instinctively good* Lit. "those who are by nature possessed of *sophronein*"—"wisdom," or "virtue," or "superiority to sexual desire" (see Introduction 1)—contrasted with those who are "pure" only because they obey outward ceremony and constraints. Hippolytos asserts that inner purity was officially required of those entering the sanctuary.

122 / 81 *the vulgar* The "base" or "evil" (*tois kakoisi*)—any who lack the innate *sophrosyne*.

131 / 87 *the turning-post* The "halfway post" in a race, around which the horses or runners turn back toward the finish line.

136 / 90 *thoughtless* Lit. not *sophoi*, "unwise."

138 / 91 *fact* Lit. "law" (*nomos*). The context suggests something universally understood to be right rather than cultural legislation.

140 / 93 *arrogance* Lit. "pride," (*to semnon*) suggesting stand-offishness, indifference to the customs of right-thinking people. But see note on "holy force" (160 / 103) which translates the same word.

148 / 98 *inner logic* Lit. "laws." (*nomoisi*).

156 / 101 *Kupris* This alternative name for Aphrodite (from the story that after her birth from the sea she was wafted ashore on the island of Cyprus) is also the commonest Greek word for sex.

160 / 103 *her holy force Semnos*, here "holy" (since it applies to a god) rather than "pride" as above, when applied to Hippolytos. See the passage quoted from Guthrie (Introduction III).

187 / 116 *your icon* The statue of Artemis on stage.

190 / 118–19 *insane blasphemy* Lit. "empty and reckless words."

192–93 / 120 *possess / more tolerance* Lit. "be wiser."

194–252 / 121–169 *Parodos* (choral entry song).

195 / 121 *the River*, not our "ocean," but in ancient geography, the stream that circles the world.

214–16 / 142–43 *Pan . . . Hekate . . . Korybantes* Gods capable of possessing mortals, thus causing madness.

217 / 144 *the Great Mother of beasts* Kybele; the Korybantes were her divine ministers.

220 / 147 *honeyed sacrifice* A cake offered to Artemis in periodic rituals.

224 / 148 *the lagoon* It is possible that the Chorus means the body of water that separates Phaidra's present home from her native Crete.

243 / 162 *poorly composed* Lacking *harmonia*, proper order; according to one Greek prejudice (expressed by Aristotle), the male's was the more perfectly designed human body; thus a woman's body was considered innately faulty. The Chorus may be wondering if Phaidra is pregnant and has morning sickness.

253–807 / 170–524 *First episode*

286 / 195 *the strange drench of a new life* A disputed passage. I suggest the Nurse perhaps has in mind the mystery religions of her age, which offer their initiates rebirth into a new life.

333 / 231 *the plains of Venice Enetias*, the region in Italy now called the Veneto, famous for its horses. Cf. **1744 / 1131**, where "Veneto stallions" are explicitly associated with Hippolytos.

390–91 / 264 *excessive anything* Lit. "nothing too much"—the motto on Apollo's temple at Delphi.

471 / 316 *you've had . . . crime* Lit. "Your hands are clear of blood, I suppose?"

473 / 317 *clean* Lit. "pure" (*hagnai*, the same word Hippolytos uses to describe his sexual purity).

474 / 317 *crime* Lit. *miasma*, stain, a religious pollution. The Greeks normally assumed that *acts*, not intentions or desires, caused pollution; *miasma* is usually translated as a "stain," but the intensity of shame Phaidra expresses here indicates she's *thinking of the crime she has desired to commit*, not the damage to her honor that has not yet been inflicted.

476 / 318 *Are you caught in some psychic spell?* The Nurse would not understand such an internalized "crime of the heart," so she asks if some witchcraft has caused Phaidra's inner damage.

478 / 319 *blood-close Philos*, "kin," a person with blood ties.

486 / 325 *. . . my hand?* The Nurse seizes it in supplication, an act which gives her temporary power over Phaidra. (See note on **913**.)

488 / 326 *your knees* Body parts also vulnerable to supplication.

509 / 337 *Pasiphaë* Phaidra's ancestor who so lusted for a bull that she hired Daedalus to disguise her as a cow. He built a cow-shaped structure that incited the bull to mount her. Their offspring was the Minotaur.

513–14 / 339 *Ariadne, / wretched bride* In the version of the myth Euripides probably alludes to here, Ariadne deserts Dionysos, using the crown he gave her to guide Theseus out of the Labyrinth. For this impious defection she dies prematurely. The point is that Ariadne, like Phaidra, is not merely sexually driven, but sinful.

520 / 343 *a compulsion* Phaidra alludes to disastrous instances of lust in the female side of her family.

587 / 384 *daydreaming* Lit. "leisure."

588–95 / 385–88 *shame Aidos* (also the goddess Holiness with whom Hippolytos is completely in tune). The exquisite difficulty of distinguishing between the appeal of external religious scruples and a higher, inner sense of the right thing to do is very important in the decisions of both Phaidra and

NOTES

Hippolytos. See C. P. Segal, "Shame and Purity in Euripides' *Hippolytos*," *Hermes* XCVIII (1970), 278–99.

610 / 399 *modesty* *To sophronein* (see Introduction I), a quality Hippolytos also claims for his own.

713–14 / 467 *To spend your life in a mad craving for perfection* Lit. "nor should mortal men take too great pains to perfect their lives."

725 / 474 *conceit* *Hubris*, the will to violate; in this case to violate what the gods have ordained for her.

749 / 489 *honor* *Eukleia*, an external reputation, rather than inner self-approval. See note on "shame" (**588–95**).

750 / 490 *sanctimony* *Semnomytheis*, lit. "You talk (*mytheis*) in a way that makes an absurd pretension to virtue and holiness (*semnon*)."

763 / 499 *degrade* Lit. "most shameful," "execrable" (*aiskhistous*).

766–67 / 501 *the act / itself* *Ergon*, i.e., whatever will win Hippolytos to return Phaidra's love.

768 / 502 *good name* *Onoma*, i.e., reputation for chastity.

780 / 509 *medicine* *Pharmakon*, "drug," with potentially the negative as well as positive connotations of the English word. The passage maintains an additional ambiguity: is the medicine meant to cure Phaidra by quieting her lust or by making Hippolytos fall in love with her?

785 / 514 a *token* To involve Hippolytos in her charm by obtaining some material bit of his person or property.

793 / 517 *I'm not sure* The Nurse is evasive. She has no drug; what she intends is a much simpler approach.

806 / 524 *a certain young friend* Lit. "dear ones," *philois.*, using a vague plural. The Nurse plays on the ambiguity of this word, which could mean "friend" or "relative."

808–57 / 525–64 *First stasimon*

848 / 556 *Dirke* Here to be pronounced *Dirsee*.

851–53 / 559–62 *a pregnancy /.../ cut short* When Zeus' wife, the goddess Hera, discovered that he was in love with Semele, the daughter of Kadmos and Harmonia, Hera decided to end the affair with extreme prejudice. Disguised as an old woman, Hera persuaded Semele to ask Zeus to make love to her in his full splendor, just as he did with his wife. After Semele was killed by the lightning released by his divine ejaculation, Zeus hid their unborn son, Dionysos, in his thigh, from which the child was eventually born.

856–57 / 563 *sifting /... her savage pollen* Euripides is not explicit on the point of whether the distribution of love is uniformly bitter. "Savage pollen" is my intrusion, to convey the tenor of the whole song, which suggests that sexuality is both a blessing and a curse.

858–1106 / 565–731 *Second episode*

890 / 595 *your own treacherous, intimate friend* (again a vague plural, *philôn*, "ones dear to you"). The Chorus presumably refers to the Nurse, but the audience may understand the friend to be Hippolytos. See note on 806.

912 / 605 *by your... right arm* As at 486–88 / 325–26, when a suppliant accompanies a plea with a gesture such as seizing the arm or knee, it was an unholy act for the one supplicated to refuse. (At least "unholy" in the external sense; see note on 588–95).

924 / 613 *a loving friend* *Philous*, plural again, but here clearly referring to Phaidra.

983–84 / 656 *my religion* Hippolytos, like Phaidra, cannot distinguish clearly between inner and outer religious compunction. See note on 588–95.

997 / 665 *Some say* Lit. "if anyone says."

998 / 666 *lewd* *Kakai*, "evil."

999 / 667 *chaste decency* *Sophronein* (see Introduction 1).

1000 / 668 *stomp on them* *Epembainein*, lit. "trample," a savage declamation.

1007–8 / 673 *to shake that noose sliding toward my throat* Barrett paraphrases more literally, "to undo the knot words have tied."

1011 / 674 *hideousness* Pema, "hurt"; she clearly has in mind her disgraced honor.

1087–88 / 720–21 *stand . . . accuse me of incest* Lit. "face Theseus with dishonor done"; she feels herself guilty of the desire she is trying to suppress.

1104 / 730 *sexual sickness* Lit. "illness," "disease."

1105 / 731 *chastity* Sophronein (see Introduction 1).

1107–60 / 732–75 *Second stasimon*

1115 / 737 *Eridanos* Sometimes refers to the river Po in Italy; but Euripides may not intend any very exact geographical reference.

1120–21 / 740–41 *Their amber tears' fallen radiance* When Phaëthon dashed the chariot of his father the sun god to earth, his sisters the Helides wept amber tears as they were changed into poplars. Euripides does not mention the poplars.

1126–29 / 744–47 *here he has set the outer limits of the sky* A reference to Poseidon's prohibition of sailing beyond the land of the Hesperides.

1144 / 759 *omens had alarmed us twice* Lit. "with ill omens."

1147 / 761 *Piraeus* Lit. "the shore of *Mounikos*"; Euripides refers to an older port of Athens than the Piraeus, which his audience would have recognized as an anachronism.

1157 / 772 *inexorable conduct* Lit. "cruel daimon." The *daimon* was a divinity that ruled a person's actions, for good or ill. *Daimon* could refer to one's presiding divinity, one's luck, one's character, one's immortal self. Here Phaidra fears what she will be forced to do by her daimon.

1161–1711 / 776–1101 *Third episode*

1190 / 792 *though it's from Delphi* Theseus refers to himself, without mentioning Delphi, as a *theoros*, one who goes on an expedition to see a god. He went to the shrine of Apollo at Delphi to purge the guilt caused by his murder of Pallas' sons.

1239 / 820 *insane spirit of revenge* Alastor, a spirit of revenge which pursued and maddened its victim. "Insane" because Theseus knows no cause for the "revenge."

1255 / 830–33 *miasma* The word does not appear in the text, but I use it to summarize Theseus' sense of ancestral taint. (See note on 474.)

1287 / 856 *tablet* Probably two wax-coated boards containing writing bound with ribbons and tied to her hand.

1307 / 871 *Spirit of death* *Daimon*, here in its meaning of an indistinctly conceived divinity. Barrett suspects the authenticity of these lines.

1328 / 884 *Hear it, men of my city* Theseus here yells out a formal alarm to rally townsmen in an emergency. The call brings Hippolytos as well.

1333 / 888 *three mortal curses* The three maleficent prayers which Poseidon promised to fulfill. See note on 72.

1372 / 914 *friends* *philoi*, "kin," as usual "loved ones" as well as "intimate acquaintances."

1375–76 / 917 *creative mastery—blazing imagination* Lit. "innumerable arts."

1380 / 920 *moral idiots* Lit. "those without any mind."

1386 / 923 *be tied in subtle knots* Lit. "making niggling distinction."

1388 / 924 *Your tongue runs wild* My metaphor; lit. "your tongue has burst the bounds of rational speech."

1391 / 925 *instrument* Lit. "token," or "sign."

1392 / 925 *our dearest friends'* *Philoi*; here the meaning is wide enough to be general and refer ironically to Phaidra.

1395 / 927 *as a heartbeat* My simile.

1397–1405 / 928–31 *And our speech . . . a person's truthful voice* A cryptic passage I've elaborated to clarify. Barrett believes it means: "Every man ought to have an honest voice in addition to the one he would have had anyhow (which might be dishonest or not)."

1407 / 933 *some "friend"* *Tis philôn*: i.e., someone of the household. He realizes he has been betrayed by Phaidra or the Nurse.

1411 / 934 *diseased* Lit. "afflicted in body, fortune, etc."

1424 / 942 *like a rotten fruit* My simile.

1431 / 946 *Don't hide* ... Hippolytos covers his head with his cloak presumably in mortification at his father's accusation. The gesture may recall Phaidra's request that the Nurse cover *her* head.

1431–32 / 946–47 *Your eyes ... polluted me* Greeks believed that a murderer could pollute others just by looking at them, or touching them. Theseus misreads Hippolytos' purpose in hiding his face.

1435 / 949 *virgin holiness Sophron* (see Introduction I).

1443 / 952 *orgiastic cults* Like those of Orpheus and Dionysos. An unjust charge.

1445 / 952 The vegetable diets Theseus scornfully attributes to his son were known in Euripides' era by the term "macrobiotic," which means "life extending." His charge is false; Hippolytos, a hunter, is, as the play's first scene implies, carnivorous.

1446 / 953 *Orpheus* His followers believed man's soul resided only temporarily in the body, was punished or rewarded after death, and could be reborn in other bodies. An Orphic purified himself by ritual, by a vegetable diet, by reading sacred texts. Hippolytos does not reveal any real attraction to these beliefs.

1473 / 967 *as their wombs* My addition.

1492 / 977 *Sinis* A monster, as is the bandit of the *Skironian Rocks* (**1495** / 979); Theseus killed both these monsters in his youth. See Glossary.

1539, 1542 / 1007 *innocence to sophron* (see Introduction I).

1568 / 1022 *a single witness* Phaidra.

1587–89 / 1034–35 *There was honor ... it is useless* Lit. "She acted with *sophrosyne*, not having it. I who have it make no good use of it." The words are cryptic, partly because the inner and outer kinds of purity are not distinguished clearly (see note on **588–95**), partly because Hippolytos, under oath to the Nurse, cannot tell all of what he understands.

1619 / 1053 *Pillars of Herakles* Lit. "Atlantic limits." The Pillars were the Rock of Gibraltar and the mountains across the strait on the African side; for the limitation, see note on 1126–29.

1654 / 1071 *lustful killer Kakos* "base," "evil"; the word here implies guilt as well as a corrupt nature. Throughout the exchange whether Hippolytos is *kakos* is at issue.

1662 / 1075; **1666** / 1077 *vile Kakos.*

1670 / 1079 *squalor Kaka.*

1709 / 1100 *a man who loved moral beauty / so much* Lit. "more *sophron*" (see Introduction 1).

1712–66 / 1102–1150 *Third stasimon*

1752–53 / 1140–41 *maidens ... marriage* The very idea of Hippolytos marrying seems odd in this play, but Euripides was, in his usual manner, inserting a reference to a known cult ceremony—in this case one involving brides, grief, and the spirit of Hippolytos. The Chorus assumes that, had Hippolytos lived, he would have outgrown his resistance to the attractions of women.

1754 / 1141 *passionate* My adjective.

1761–62 / 1146 *goddesses of beauty and kindness* Lit. *Kharites*, "Graces." I specify their attributes, which are only implied in the Greek.

1767–1917 / 1151–1267 *Fourth episode*

1788 / 1169 *Poseidon, you really are my father* Since the curse proves effective, Theseus assumes Poseidon was his true father, rather than Aigeus.

1791 / 1172 *iron jaws* Lit. "deadfall"—a trap for animals. Scholars are not agreed on this reading.

1861 / 1229 *spooking* The bull never actually hits the horses or chariot. It may be a phantom, an apparition, or a hallucination; in any case it is supernatural.

1889 / 1251 *guilty Kakos*, "evil," "guilty."

1893 / 1254 *good esthlos*, "noble," "virtuous."

1897 / 1256 *the will of fate . . . his own luck Moira, khreōn*: these terms are used here as virtual synonyms.

1918–1931/ 1268–82 *Fourth stasimon*

1932–2196 / 1283–1466 *Exodos*

1957 / 1299 *honor Eukleia*: "good renown," the admiration of all men.

1960 / 1300 *sexual passion Oistros*, lit. "gadfly," but often used metaphorically to suggest an unpleasant stinging sensation that drives one to unwanted behavior.

1963–64 / 1303 *fingernails . . . aroused her* Lit. "bitten by Kypris' goads."

1968 / 1302 *beautiful* Lit. *hedone*, "sweetness, pleasure."

2030 / 1342 *sustained by friends* That Hippolytos is walking is implicit in the verb *steikho*, "come" or "go" under one's own propulsion, and in his remarks to his attendants.

2057 / 1365 *virtuous* Lit. "with *sophrosyne*" (see Introduction I).

2086 / 1394 *gallant man Tlēmon*, the same word translated in 2078 / 1389 as "poor man." Artemis' tone implies gallantry while suffering.

2096 / 1402 *incorruptibly pure* Lit. "having *sophrosyne*."

2097–98 / 1402 *She felt . . . her honor* Lit. "She found fault with you because of (lack of) honor (for her), and was annoyed with you because you were chaste (*sophronounti*)."

2119–20 / 1415 *I wish we men could curse gods* The following line is my intrusion to convey here the full implication of what "curse" meant to a Greek. Hippolytos means that if men could effectively curse the gods that have caused their deaths (as the Greeks believed men could do to each other) that curse would pursue and destroy the god. Artemis' reply may include some disapproval of Hippolytos' wish.

2135 / 1424–25 *a hero* A hero was a dead man to whom a half-divine status was awarded and to whom such honors described here were paid. The word "hero" does not appear in the text.

2137 / 1426 *will clip their locks* The maidens will do this as a token of grief.

2154 / 1437 *It is forbidden* Lit. "it is not *themis*." *Themis* was the generic word applied to all ancient customs whose observance procured the blessing of gods and ancestors.

2158 / 1440 *a serene goodbye* Perhaps a note of irony in the resignation of this farewell. Does Hippolytos sense a fundamental indifference beneath Artemis' *pro forma* grief for him? See Introduction i.

2177–80 / 1452–53 *noble spirit . . . legitimate sons* The word for "noble" and the word for "legitimate" are from the same root but distinct in meaning.

2190 / 1461 *I have no heart for your graces* My intrusion. Theseus is implicitly turning his back on those graces of the goddess he once valued.

2192–96 / 1462–66 I translate the final words of the Chorus, although many scholars, including Barrett, believe them spurious. In their favor is the somewhat unusual word *pitulos*: "a repeated rhythmic movement." Barrett notes passages in which *pitulos* appears in Euripides' surviving plays as possible but insufficient evidence for the passage's authenticity. In my view these lines undercut by their triteness and aristocratic presumption the final intense harmony of the play. Literally they say: "This common grief has come unexpected. There will be an outpouring of many tears. Tales that are prevalent concerning the great deserve greater grief (than those of ordinary citizens)."

CHILDREN OF HERAKLES

Translated by

HENRY TAYLOR

and

ROBERT A. BROOKS

INTRODUCTION

I

The *Herakleidai*, or *Children of Herakles*, is an extraordinary play. It is even more extraordinary if we conceive it, as Greek plays too rarely are, in terms of action in the theater before an audience. It is at once rapid, fabulous, noble, and common to the point of comedy. It pursues concepts of deep moral grandeur and perplexity in the environment and often the language of the marketplace, the barracks, and the courts. It ends with a denouement of astonishing physical and ethical brutality. It may not be wholly success- ful. One could say the same about *Troilus and Cressida* or Ionesco's *Amedée*. But like them, it is remarkably alive because the playwright is pushing brusquely and with passion at the boundaries of his art.

II

The plot of the play is part of the complex of legends dealing with Herakles and his descendants. The legends, and the tangled dynastic relationships they involved, would be familiar to the audiences of Euripides' time, and the particular incidents depicted in the *Children of Herakles* would strike them with an overwhelming ironic force.

Herakles was the greatest and most universal hero of Greek legend. He was not constrained, like most of the other heroic figures, by time and place, but ranged over the entire Mediterranean world from the far west of Spain and Morocco (and perhaps beyond) to the fleshpots of Asia, encountering Titans from the pre-heroic world and begetting sons to fight in the Trojan War at the end of the heroic cycle. His exploits drew upon his superhuman strength, often for the benefit of lesser men endangered by the savagery or obstacles of man and nature.

For all his strength, Herakles was cursed from his birth with misfor- tune and subjection to other men. He was the son of Alkmene by Zeus, and since his mother was of the royal house of Argos and Mykenai, he was the expected heir to the throne. Hera, however, with her usual jealousy of Zeus' liaisons, managed to delay the birth of Herakles and hasten that of Eurystheus, his cousin, so that instead of becoming king, Herakles became Eurystheus' subject. To enforce this subjection and keep the hero afield, Eurystheus imposed on him the famous twelve labors. Herakles in fact was one of the few Greek heroes whose legend did not include a triumphant homecoming to his native land. For Oedipus, Theseus, Perseus, Odysseus, even Agamemnon, the return home was the summit of their story, even though terrible events might follow. For Herakles "home," in the person of Hera (patron goddess of Argos) and Eurystheus, her human agent, was his bitter enemy, never overcome, manipulating him like a slave in distant lands.

Herakles died in agony upon a pyre in Trachis, and according to the received legend was translated to become one of the gods. His tale of banishment and frustrated homecoming continued in a different mode with his children. Eurystheus sought to kill them, and they went into exile accompanied by their cousin Iolaos. Eurystheus continued to hunt them down, forcing each place where they took refuge to drive them out again, until at last they came to Attika.

Here Euripides' play begins. It was one of the boasts of Athenians that their city had given refuge to the children of Herakles, had settled them around Marathon, and with the help of Iolaos and Hyllos, Herakles' oldest son, had defeated Eurystheus' army and killed the king himself. The role of Athens as protector was a familiar one in legend. Oedipus (Sophocles' *Oedipus at Kolonos*) and Medea (Euripides' *Medea*) found refuge there, and Herakles himself was received earlier by Theseus (Euripides' *Herakles*). It was an easy theme for self-congratulation if Euripides had chosen so to use it.

The continuation of the Heraklid legend, however, had a bitter meaning for the Athenians. After Eurystheus' death, which closes Euripides' play, the children of Herakles and their descendants continued their effort to return home. Following a first abortive campaign to the Isthmus of Korinth which cost Hyllos his life, their descendants in the third generation marched south at the head of a Dorian army and overcame most of the Peloponnese including Argos, Mykenai, Sparta, and Messene. Their legendary conquest reflects the fact of the destruction of Mykenaian civilization in the twelfth century B.C. and the subsequent mastery of southern Greece by Dorian Greek tribes. Herakles' "homecoming," so long delayed, was accomplished at last in a tidal wave of violence and destruction.

Most of the nobility of the Peloponnese in historic times regarded themselves as descended from Herakles. In particular, the Spartan kings

traced their ancestry to two of the Heraklid conquerors of the Peloponnese. At the probable time of the play's production, one of the kings was
preparing to march on Athens at the head of a Spartan army.

III

Children of Herakles is not datable from external evidence, nor do we
know the other plays which Euripides produced with it. Most commentators assign it to the early years of the Peloponnesian war, between 430
and 425 B.C. This is a reasonable dating on all known grounds. Unquestionably it is a play about war, and the effects of war within the state. In
incidents and theme, it works upon the background provided by the
great struggle between the Athenian and the Spartan alliances which
began in 431 B.C.

Between them the two alliances controlled most of the Greek world
except for Italy and the West. Thucydides tells us that "the growth of the
power of Athens, and the alarm which this inspired in Sparta, made war
inevitable." Inevitable or not, it was an appalling disaster. The war was to
go on for a generation and end with the enfeebling of Greece, the defeat
of the Athenian democracy, and the discrediting of its ideal of the free
citizen. No one foresaw the catastrophe at first, but neither did any one
doubt the significance of the conflict. There was patriotic exhortation on
both sides, and mutual accusations of past sacrilege involving the murder of suppliants under religious protection. Once the war began, there
was an almost hysterical reaction to the slightest reverses, particularly on
the Athenian side. Perikles' strategy was to retain command of the sea,
withdraw his land forces behind the walls of Athens, and let the superior
Peloponnesian armies move virtually unchecked through Attika. This
they did five summers in a row, ravaging farms and villages and probably
by 427 B.C. sacking Marathon, the symbol of Athenian military heroism
against the Persians and the location of Euripides' play. The outrage of
the citizens, cooped up in Athens and helplessly watching their posses-
sions being destroyed, put Perikles' leadership in jeopardy and led to his
being fined by the Athenians before his death in 429.

The tensions of the war led also to a series of small but vicious
atrocities, increasing with the progress of hostilities. A band of Thebans
who had broken into the town of Plataia, an Athenian ally, early in 431 B.C.
in the first act of hostilities, were killed by the Plataians after surrendering
with a promise of safe-conduct. In 430 the Athenians captured by
treachery Peloponnesian ambassadors to the king of Thrace, brought
them to Athens, and murdered them without trial, although by custom
the persons and ambassadors and heralds were sacred. They alleged
retaliation for the murder of Athenian traders caught in the Peloponnese

at the outset of the war. In 427 the Athenians voted to kill the entire adult male population of Mytilene in Lesbos and enslave the women and children for having revolted against them. Fortunately, they had second thoughts the next day and stayed the order, killing "only" about a thousand of the leaders. Meanwhile, the Spartans, taking Plataia after a two-year siege, killed all the surrendered Plataians who had been promised "the form of law" and destroyed the town. The events of this year culminated in the savage civil war at Kerkyra which Thucydides vividly summarizes (III, 81):

> Death . . . raged in every shape, and, as usually happens at such times, there was no length to which violence did not go; sons were killed by their fathers, and suppliants were dragged from the altar or slain upon it; while some were even walled up in the temple of Dionysos and died there.

It is not necessary to read specific topical reference to such events into the *Children of Herakles*. It is essential to understand that both Euripides and his audience were involved in them, whether in battles and killings or in the debates and decrees on military expeditions, judgment of leaders, and punishment of rebels. The climate of Athens in the years when the play was produced was an increasingly volatile mixture of bravado, sophistry, rage, and horror at the progess of a vicious conflict. Thucydides, writing later, saw at this point the crumbling of an essential element in Greek life: the relations between man and man, class and class, city and city (III, 83): "The ancient simplicity into which honor so largely entered was laughed down and disappeared; and society became divided into camps in which no man trusted his fellow."

A sense of this decay, and of what was being destroyed, is at the core of Euripides' intention in the *Children of Herakles*.

IV

The first impression of the play in action is one of compression and breakneck speed of development. It is one of the shortest plays in the existing Greek repertoire, running for about an hour and fifteen minutes, but it contains enough incident for two or three plays of normal length.

Iolaos appears first with the young sons of Herakles at the altar before the temple of Zeus at Marathon. He explains his position as companion and kinsman of Herakles, and after his death, as guardian of his children with Alkmene, Herakles' mother, who is inside the temple with her granddaughters. He tells of their pursuit by Eurystheus, and has barely finished when Eurystheus' herald bursts upon the stage. Kopreus is the spokesman and agent of force.[1] After a brief angry exchange with Iolaos, he lays hands on the children and attempts to drag them from the altar. Iolaos intervenes and is knocked down. Another hasty entrance follows: the Chorus of citizens of Marathon. They prevent the herald's design and interrogate Iolaos, who enters his group's claim to sanctuary as suppliants. Kopreus argues with the Chorus but breaks off at the entrance of the king of Athens, Demophon, son of Theseus. All this has taken about seven or eight minutes on stage.

The rapid development continues in argument. The herald and Iolaos present their cases to Demophon, who decides for the suppliants. Kopreus, undaunted, offers the king a slippery excuse for giving them up to him, fails, and tries again to seize one of the boys. Demophon is prevented from striking him down only by the Chorus, and Kopreus goes off threatening Argive retaliation. After a short ode, Iolaos and the children offer formal thanks to Demophon and the Chorus. Demophon leaves to prepare the city for war. Iolaos remains at the altar to pray for victory.

Up to now the plot of the play has been the formal equivalent of the whole *Suppliants* of Aeschylus, which tells a similar story with parallel incident. It is condensed to one-third the length of Aeschylus' play. Euripides rushes on. Demophon returns with an oracle requiring a virgin's sacrifice, which he refuses to impose on his city. Iolaos futilely offers himself to buy off Eurystheus. Makaria, Herakles' daughter, comes out from the temple and insists upon being the victim. She goes off with Demophon. A servant appears to announce to Iolaos and Alkmene the return of Hyllos, Herakles' oldest son, with an allied force to join the Athenians. Iolaos suddenly decides to enter the battle, obtains arms and struggles off with the servant. After another ode, a messenger runs on to report the battle, the bravery of Hyllos, the cowardice of Eurystheus, the victory of the Athenians and Heraklids, the miraculous rejuvenation of Iolaos, his pursuit and capture of Eurystheus, and the imminent arrival of Eurystheus as prisoner. In an extraordinarily complex and condensed final scene, Eurystheus is brought in; Alkmene vengefully demands his death and meets opposition from the Chorus and messenger who tell her that Athenian law requires prisoners taken alive to be spared. Eurystheus answers with fortitude, composure, and a prophetic vision that his grave will help Athens against the descendants of the Heraklids when they

---

1. His name is not given in the play. It means "dung man." He was traditionally the herald of Eurystheus.

invade Attika. Alkmene browbeats the Chorus with this new argument for executing him. It agrees. The play ends abruptly.

The movement of the play seems all the more brusque because no single character occupies a dominant role. The children of Herakles, who are the characters of the title, are on the stage and highly visible throughout, but do not say a word. They maintain an enigmatic silence at the center of the turbulent action. Among the other characters, Kopreus, Demophon, Makaria, Iolaos, and the messengers appear, disappear, and are not seen again. Alkmene enters the action late, and Eurystheus, the presumed villain, at the very end. Dramatic attention is continually being shifted from one character-grouping to another. None of the individual parts has time or mental room within the play to develop or to internalize the dramatic action.

External action is plentiful. The play is full of physical activity; the use of physical objects (wreaths knocked from the altar, Demophon's staff, Iolaos' armor) and physical contact between the characters (Iolaos and Kopreus, the servant and Iolaos, Alkmene and Eurystheus) tend to insist upon a realistic and almost a knockabout environment. The language matches this. Though recognizably the language of tragedy, it is plain and spare for the most part, and some of the most striking images are common, even crude. Kopreus compares the effect of war to stepping into the bilge of a ship. Demophon says (**253** / 246) that if he were to give up the suppliants to Argos it would be a "hanging crime." Other more traditional images are sometimes used ironically. When Iolaos in the prologue (**13** / 10) says that he has Herakles' children "under the dwindling shadow of my wings," he is using a phrase from Aeschylus, where it signifies divine protection, but he obviously means to contrast the confidence of that image with his present feeble and powerless condition (**14** / 11): "I defend them—though I need defenders of my own."

The institutional furniture of the play, too, is deliberately contemporary and everyday. The talk is of law-courts, legal claims, jurisdiction over runaways. Demophon is chosen king by lot like an Athenian archon; he marshals his army like an Athenian *strategos*; his soldiers are Athenian heavy infantry of the fifth century. The whole question of refugees and sanctuary on which the play turns is one of intense topical interest to the Athenians of the time.

The play presents itself initially then as a rapid, almost bewildering series of actions, played out in an environment immediately familiar in important ways to its audience—the rush of public business in a democratic state, and specifically in a democratic state at war for its life. Events are not generated by the participants; they press in upon them. Decisions must be made on the spot; once they are made new crises and alarms arise; public reaction is instantaneous and must be dealt with. The business is not ended even with a victory; there are the issues of the aftermath. Under the pressures of such a time, people do not behave with composure and gravity; they scuffle, they grab weapons, they collapse in despair.

The familiarity is intentional. Euripides, of course, was to write several plays with a comparable wealth of incident and activity, for instance the *Orestes* and the *Iphigeneia at Aulis*. He was to write others which deliberately emphasized a contemporary and everyday environment or characterization, like the *Elektra*. But in no other play did he combine and compress these two devices to such effect as in the *Children of Herakles*. His intent is to hold a mirror to the spectators, and in the absence of a commanding dramatic hero, to involve his audience in the significance of the play and in the deep questions which work through its troubled action. The play generates such questions, and thrusts them outward to the watching community.

v

It is fair to ask: are there in fact any deep questions or problems of the human condition developed in the *Children of Herakles*? Or is such a hurly-burly play merely intended as an exciting wartime diversion, catering to the natural desire for images of Athenian courage against the Peloponnesian enemy, Athenian nobility in protecting suppliants, and the pious assurance of ultimate divine favor and protection for Athens? The weight of critical opinion about the play is affirmative to this last question. Ours is opposed.[2]

Within the turbulent action of his play, Euripides sets himself at first to develop the theme of an ideal nobility of action which is accessible to the free citizen and brings him into harmony with the divine order. Moral complications are stripped away in order to clarify his proposition. The Chorus and Demophon are confronted with a ready-made act of violence, both civil and religious, on the part of the Argive herald, the attack on suppliants in a sacred precinct, so that their judgment is never in doubt. The herald's arguments for giving up the suppliants rest ultimately on force and nothing else, the superior power of Argos to enforce its decrees anywhere in the Greek world (272–73 / 262–63):

2. It is not the function of this Introduction to engage in detailed critical polemics. We should like to cite two commentaries on the play which have provided especially sympathetic and useful insights: G. Zuntz, *The Political Plays of Euripides* (Manchester, 1955), and P. Burian, "Euripides' *Heraclidae*: An Interpretation," *Classical Quarterly*, LXXI (1976).

DEMOPHON This is my country. Here, I am king.
KOPREUS So long as you don't provoke the Argives.

His thesis would be familiar—and not merely as a denunciation of the
attitude of Athens' current enemies. Thucydides was to put a similar
sentiment into the mouths of the Athenian ambassadors to Sparta before
the outbreak of the war, in defense of Athens' own imperial policy (I, 75):
"... it has always been the law that the weaker should be subject to the
stronger." In any case, the argument is uncomplicated, and the risk is
vividly presented by Kopreus. It is nothing less than death, destruction,
and the reduction of Athens to a subject status. The city can avoid the
first two only by accepting the third. Demophon responds without
hesitation; he will protect the Heraklids come what may.

Demophon's reasons and the way in which he states them are vitally
important. Greatest, he says, is Zeus, since the suppliants are at his altar
and under his protection. Next is kinship between the Heraklids and
himself, and his father Theseus' debt to Herakles. Finally, with a curious
reversal of priority, he says (**249–52** / 242–46):

> Third, dishonor—which should be the first of my considerations.
> If I allow strangers to desecrate this altar,
> men would charge that Athens was no longer free,
> that I had betrayed a suppliant out of fear of Argos.

The ambiguity is crucial to the theme of the play. Demophon and the
other characters accept religious obligations (the protection of suppliants) and injunctions (the oracle) with conventional piety. They never
question them, but do not feel them as a personal spur to action. The
relationship of the action to the gods is largely placed in the mouths of
the Chorus. The real motivation, Demophon says, for himself, is the
sense of disgrace before the human community at large in showing fear
and abandoning his city's freedom. Iolaos has already introduced this
theme as a reason for his faithful guardianship of the children of
Herakles after their father's death. If he failed them, he says, people
would speak of him with contempt. Again, in countering the herald's
arguments, Iolaos assures him that Athens will respect the same standard
(**208** / 200–201): "Brave men fear dishonor more than death."

Against the herald's arguments of power, therefore, both Demophon
and Iolaos are appealing to that sense of restraint from viciousness and
impulse to decency which has its roots in the opinions and expectations
of the surrounding community, and which often goes under the un-
translatable Greek term *aidōs*. Iolaos in fact uses the word almost at the

beginning of the play, as furnishing the motivation for his whole career. The concept is older than Homer, and is often linked with an aristocratic outlook and ethos, but remained powerful among the Greeks of the fifth century. Perikles, in Thucydides' account, gave it a preeminent place in his funeral oration over the Athenian dead in the campaigns of 431 B.C. (I, 38):

But all this ease in our private relations does not make us lawless as citizens. Against this, fear is our chief safeguard, teaching us to obey the magistrates and the laws, particularly in regard to the protection of the injured, whether they are actually on the statute book, or belong to that code, which, although unwritten, yet cannot be broken without acknowledged disgrace.

We need not assume that Athenians of the Periklean age always acted on the precepts of *aidōs*. But it remained important in men's minds and emotions, along with the complementary sense of confidence that their interests and standards were shared by others in the community. It was precisely this kind of unwritten standard of trust that Thucydides saw beginning to break down with the strains of war, to be replaced by the justification of deceit and atrocity. At this point in his play, Euripides is saying with Perikles that despite the pressures and within the democratic institutions of his city, there is still room for the "ancient simplicity."

Demophon's determination is soon overturned by the oracle which demands the sacrifice of a girl of noble family to Persephone. He accepts the oracle's injunction without question, as do all the characters in the play. But it leaves Demophon at a loss (429–31 / 411–13). There is no noble solution for him. In justice,

> I will not kill my own daughter,
> nor will I compel any Athenian to such an act
> against his will.

He appeals to the Heraklids for help. Iolaos again without hesitation offers himself, but the king declines with realism as well as courtesy. On cue, Makaria comes in. She is the most idealized picture of nobility in the play. As soon as she learns the situation, she demands to be sacrificed (518–19 / 501–2): "I'll be your sacrifice. Unforced, of my own free will, / I volunteer my life."

A few lines later, she firmly rejects Iolaos' proposal that the lot be used to choose among her and her sisters. In doing so, she recalls to us the similar choice made by Theseus, Demophon's father, who had volunteered among the young people normally chosen by lot to be sent to Crete and sacrificed to the Minotaur. By her action, Makaria, too, saves

Athens, but there is no question that she does it as a Heraklid and to safeguard the seed of the house of Herakles. Almost her last words, spoken to her brothers around the altar, are (608–9 / 591): "In the place of children / I will never have, these are all my treasures . . ."

The noble decision by Athens is not enough; it needs a reciprocal gesture from the strangers it protects to save both city and suppliants. In providing it, Makaria appeals to the same sense of *aidōs* and the opinion of men that motivates Demophon and Iolaos. Like Iolaos, she imagines vividly what others will say if she shirks her duty to die and wanders once more to seek refuge. Surely other cities would expel her for such cowardice. In her mind, outraged opinion would be even stronger than the religious injunction to protect the suppliant.

The whole character of her appearance makes her a kind of apparition. There is a curious anonymity throughout this scene. Makaria is not called by her name (it is known only from the list of characters and other sources of the legend), and after her exit disappears entirely from the play.[3] She comes, she acts, she does what is necessary for "my father's daughter," (546 / 527) and she departs.

One further action completes the theme of nobility; it is gratuitous and not prompted by outside events like those of Demophon and Makaria. In the next scene, Iolaos hears of the arrival of Hyllos with an army and questions the messenger with growing excitement. As the man breaks off to return to the battle lines, Iolaos cries out (706 / 680–81): "We think alike. I'm going with you. Friends help friends." The play has emphasized Iolaos' old age and feebleness. He has spoken of it himself. The herald has thrown him to the ground, and he has just been seen collapsed and almost insensible with grief at the sacrifice of Makaria. He now proposes to go into battle from a simple sense of honor and duty, again motivated by a respect for the world's opinion (725–26 / 700–701): "Only a coward would stay here, safe behind walls, / while others do our fighting for us."

The effect is first one of pathos, like the picture of old Laertes preparing to fight with the suitors at the end of the *Odyssey*, or Priam at Troy, or the blind king of Bohemia at Crécy. But the ridiculous, too, is not far away, and Euripides stresses both to a point almost unparalleled in extant Greek tragedy. He has established the framework of common life earlier, and here the everyday world, in the person of the servant-messenger, answers by mocking the impulse of nobility which presents itself in such unlikely decrepitude (707–11 / 682–86).

---

3. Except for a brief reference to human sacrifice in the messenger's speech reporting the victory.

SERVANT Sir, this is no time for foolishness.
IOLAOS Foolishness? To fight in my own cause?
SERVANT Sir, you're not the man you used to be.
IOLAOS I'm still man enough to handle a spear.
SERVANT Man enough—provided you don't stumble.

Up to this point we have been given images of nobility acting in harmony with democratic ideals and institutions (Demophon), then appearing from among the refugees in a savior role (Makaria). But Iolaos' extreme and quixotic intention seems too much. The play's environment and its theme are placed in confrontation. We are invited to laugh, but the laughter is almost painful. A few minutes later, Iolaos leaves on the servant's arm. He stops to appeal to his lost strength (766–69 / 739–42):

> Oh, gods, give me back
> the strength of this good right arm of mine!
> Make me what I was when I was young
> and at Herakles' side, I took the city of Sparta!

We realize that he, too, is perfectly aware of his weakness but is still determined to take his place in the war.

The denouement of this action is against all expectation. Another messenger returns to report to Alkmene the victory of Athens and the Heraklids. Nobility is justified, the suppliants are saved, and the words of the Chorus in the ode just before the battle link the human success to a divine endorsement. Then the messenger goes on to report a miraculous change in Iolaos. In Hyllos' chariot, he has pursued Eurystheus from the battlefield. In answer to his prayer for strength (880–87 / 854–58),

> Suddenly, two stars, all blazing fire, settle down
>   on the horses' yokes, hiding the chariot
>   in a kind of cloud or shadow.
> Men who understand these things said those stars
>   were Hebe and your son, Herakles.
> Then, out of that darkness in the air came Iolaos—
>   young, his strong shoulders straining on the reins,
>   a man in all the vigor and freshness of his youth.

Even if the change is only for one day, as Iolaos has asked, it goes far beyond any expected divine justification and enters the realm of fantasy. But it is a fantasy that transforms the perceptions of everyday life. Everything that Iolaos in seeming folly has said he will do, he has done; everything that the common-sense servant has ridiculed, that the

Chorus has decried, that Alkmene has called madness, has come to pass. A key to Euripides' meaning is found in another play, the *Madness of Herakles*. There the Chorus, speaking of old age and youth, says (655–59):

> If the gods were wise, and understood
> what human wisdom understands
> second youth would be their gift
> to seal the goodness of a man.[4]

In that play, the Chorus denies the possibility of such a gift. Here the gods have bestowed it. The earlier scenes show human characters pushing the values of "human wisdom" to their limit. Their choices are simply made, by the old standard of *aidōs* and from the impulse to satisfy the expectations of their community and mankind. They accept the framework of necessity established by events and the gods, and do not appeal to it for justification. There is no theodicy in their minds. But the choices they make are by no means easy, entailing the risk of destruction, self-sacrifice, and death in war. At this point, as if in recompense, the gods adopt human standards. They show that they understand "what human wisdom understands" and glorify the hero with the gift of youth, while justifying the other sacrifices with victory.

VI

The play seems complete. But there is one more turn, a short scene of a hundred-odd lines that totally reverses all that has gone before and closes the drama with brutal shock instead of heroic fulfillment.

Immediately after the news of Iolaos' rejuvenation, the messenger relates the epic capture of Eurystheus by the new hero, and his imminent arrival in chains as Iolaos' spoil of war. It is most probable that Euripides invented this incident. In the more usual version of the legend, Eurystheus died in the battle at the hands of Iolaos or Hyllos. Euripides' intention is soon clear. Eurystheus has been the most powerful king in Greece, but also the ultimate source of violence and evil throughout the play. The vicious herald Kopreus has been only Eurystheus' creature. Alkmene asks with some amazement why Iolaos spared his life. In the messenger's answer, Euripides begins to show his audience a more repulsive side of their popular ethos (913–18 / 883–87):

---

4. Translated by William Arrowsmith, to whom we are also indebted for suggesting this passage. Euripides used the theme of rejuvenation and a second life elsewhere, as in the *Suppliants* (1080–87). It must have played a major part in his lost play *Daughters of Pelias*, which was his first production in 455 B.C.

> He was thinking of you.
> He wanted you to see Eurystheus yourself—
> see him subject to *your* will, *your* slave.
> Eurystheus, of course, resisted—so they used
> force, they yoked him. He had no wish
> to meet your eyes and suffer your revenge.

This is audacious. Euripides is using one of the most popular and most obscene tricks of the stage: to build up fear and hatred of a powerful and evil character, then to show him helpless and humiliated to the audience and to invite them to gloat righteously over his physical torture and mental agony. There is more than a frisson of that suggested pleasure in the messenger's speech. When Eurystheus is dragged on in chains, Alkmene fulfills the expectation. She abuses Eurystheus verbally and physically (there is no question of this from her language), rehearses her old grievances against him, and finally pronounces his death sentence. In the fetid atmosphere of this setpiece of revenge, there is nothing so far unusual in this.

But both the servant in charge of Eurystheus and the Chorus intervene. She cannot kill him, they say; the Athenian rulers have decreed that Eurystheus, having been taken alive, must be kept alive. Hyllos has agreed. We are suddenly reminded of what the play has been about, the achievement in action of honor and just dealing among men, and we realize that Eurystheus and Alkmene have changed places in a particularly menacing way. She is now the agent of unbridled violence; he is the intended victim under the protection of the same Athenian state. But is the popular will still allied to lawful action and compassionate behavior? Certainly the Athenians who had seen the Spartan ambassadors dragged through the streets to the death-hole or perhaps had voted for total vengeance on the surrendered Mytileneans, might be of two minds.

Alkmene responds to this check with fury. She insists that she will kill Eurystheus with her own hands. She specifically and scornfully rejects the claim of community opinion and female *aidōs* (1006–8 / 978–80):

> Call me what you like, call me cruel,
> say I'm more arrogant than woman ought to be—
> but this man *must* die, and *I* will do it.

Here Eurystheus himself speaks for the first time, and produces yet another reversal within the play. He has been described as tyrannical and cowardly, owing all his success to good luck, but his speech is that of a brave man, facing death with indifferent calm. He will not beg for his life. He defends his behavior by casting the blame on Hera, but he recognizes that it was a sickness, and generously praises Herakles. He tells Alkmene that in his place, she would have acted exactly as he did, and we recognize a deadly truth in this. He asserts the religious nature of the decree which spared him, and the religious pollution that will fall upon his executioner. Eurystheus does not clear himself of his crimes, but his whole bearing is a moral confirmation of the decision to save his life. It is not merely now a question of keeping an enemy prisoner alive but also of killing a man of courage and sensibility.

But the Chorus, representatives of the Athenian will, has already begun to waver. It has told Alkmene that her anger is understandable. Now it "advises" her once more to let Eurystheus go (as though she were the ruler of Athens), but when she offers a way to satisfy both the law and her lust for killing Eurystheus, the Chorus grasps at it eagerly (1053 / 1021): "That would be best." Her proposed solution turns out to be a horrid sophistry: she will kill him, then "obey the city" by delivering his body back to the Argives. In this she echoes Kopreus who has used a similar play on words in demanding that Demophon give up the sup-pliants. There Demophon angrily rejects the proposal. But here the Chorus says nothing in reply. From this point, there is no doubt of the complicity of the Chorus in Alkmene's actions.

Instead, Eurystheus speaks once more. In recompense for Athens' clemency (literally, a derivative of *aidōs* is the word he uses) he will present it with an ancient oracle: his own body buried at Pallene will be Athens' savior and the enemy of the Heraklids when they return as invaders (obviously referring to the current war with Sparta). In Eur-ystheus' words there is a translation from the human theme to that of the sacred hero, whose body and burial place retain an immortal power to influence human events. The hero is addressed by cult words supplied by Eurystheus himself: "avenger" and "noble." He places himself be-yond the sphere of common mortality, like Oedipus, who was also buried in Attika at Kolonos. But Oedipus did not die by human hands. Within the framework of this play, the oracle offers to the Chorus and Athens a pragmatic and political excuse for closing their eyes to Eur-ystheus' murder. Alkmene seizes upon it and characteristically pushes it even further. "What are you waiting for?" she cries (1079–81 / 1045–47); "Kill him. *Now*." She draws the Chorus into the act that she said earlier she would do herself, and in her rage disregards the fact that her own descendants will suffer from it. She even tells the guards to throw Eurystheus' body to the dogs, an injunction so shocking and so at variance with the prescription of the oracle that some editors have sought to emend the text. But to all this the Chorus merely replies in the last speech of the play (1087 / 1053), "We agree," and go on to assert that the Athenian rulers are free of pollution. The play ends on this note of self-serving exoneration.

It is inconceivable that Euripides shared this view, that he wanted to present Alkmene as some evil and alien will, embodying perhaps the hated Spartans of the time, and the Chorus' action as merely prudent and reasonable in securing Athens' future. He has shown Alkmene along with the Heraklids taken under the protection of Athens and received into the Athenian community, in part through their own courage and self-sacrifice. Her participation is emphasized several times by Iolaos, and she is the only one of the group whose name Makaria actually uses with affection and reverence in her final speech. Whatever her significance, she is a member of the community.

Euripides has also taken care to present the episodes of Makaria and Eurystheus in parallel and contrast. In both, an oracle has defined the conditions of action, and in neither do any of the characters question the validity of this definition. But in the first case, one of the Heraklids themselves comes forth with the purest nobility to offer herself to death and thereby save Athens as well as the suppliants. In the second, another of Herakles' family, also a woman, comes forth with repulsive savagery to insist on murdering a man who is under Athens' protection. After the first act, the Chorus shows a full if conventional appreciation of Makaria's sacrifice in almost Periklean terms (**644–48** / 621–26):

> Even as she dies, this girl discovers
>> deathless honor and glory in giving up her life
>> for her brothers, for us all.
> The glory she leaves behind her will shine forever,
>> as noble actions outshine the darkest pain.

After the second, the Chorus can only say "we agree." Euripides leaves us with this appalling reversal of judgment, and of the communal ethos which underlies it. Cold-blooded advantage has triumphed, *aidōs* and the loving fantasy of harmony between gods and noble men which it has brought about have been blotted out. The play in its completeness creates and springs from an almost unbearable sense of loss, the wasting away of that "ancient simplicity" which was recognized by Thucydides, too, at the moment of its departure.

VII

In the final scene, the Chorus emerges as the central figure of the play, responsible for decisions that are crucial to the action and its meaning. If the *Children of Herakles* fails, it is in this respect. For Aeschylus, the Chorus could be full participants, even principal characters, in both external and internal action; he used them as such in his *Suppliants, Eumenides,* and *Agamemnon.* Both Sophocles and Euripides abandoned not only the dramatic device but the whole style and dramatic concept of which it is a part. Their Choruses occasionally take part in the external action as *ad hoc* partners or opponents of the principal characters,[5] but never in a decisive role and far more usually as lyric commentators upon the action. Euripides, even if he had wanted to, could not return to the Aeschylean model, and in this play he did not perfect a new technique answering to the role which he thrust upon the Chorus.

It is worthwhile to recapitulate the Chorus' function in the *Children of Herakles.* If there is a key to production of this tense and difficult play it is in the interpretation of the Chorus as a subliminal "role-player," and in the relations thus established with the central theme.

The Chorus first appears in swift, disciplined intervention in the action, just as Kopreus has thrown Iolaos to the ground and is attempting to lay hands on the children at the altar. One part of the group interposes between Kopreus and the children; the two leaders question Iolaos, ascertain his case, assert religious prohibition and their own civic freedom against Kopreus' violence, and announce the arrival of the Athenian kings. In the next scene, the leader again intervenes to prevent Demophon from committing a sacrilegious act by striking the herald. Immediately then the Chorus establishes a participating role as civic representatives and active guardians of secular and religious standards in the state. As the play continues, the Chorus relinquishes this direct intervention and develops its theme principally through a succession of choral odes. The first follows the expulsion of the herald and the adoption of the Heraklids into the Athenian community. It is a simple, almost balladlike defiance of Kopreus, Eurystheus, and the Argives. It has been called "jingoistic," but it does not spring from mindless patriotism; it rests on an appeal to decent common opinion which is outraged by violence offered to suppliants in a free community. This is exactly the reason that Demophon has given earlier for his decision to protect the Heraklids. City and king are united in their stand, and the play emphasizes the voluntary and essential nature of this sympathy.

The second ode follows Makaria's departure. It has been called "flat" and "unoriginal." But again we have seen how the tone and even the language grow from the Chorus' civic role. It does not represent the lyric reflection of the poet, but rather the restrained and formalized expres-

---

5. Such plays are the *Iphigeneia in Tauris* and the *Orestes* of Euripides, the *Oedipus at Colonus* of Sophocles, and the *Rhesus.*

sion of condolence and praise appropriate to the city's funeral oration over the heroic dead. It is clear that the Chorus is being "characterized" in these odes as within the sphere of action, rather than "characterizing" the action from an outside point.

The third ode follows Iolaos' fantastic and seemingly foolish departure to the battle. The three odes therefore relate to and complement the three principal stages in the "noble action" of the play. The third takes a bold step beyond the others. It is a battle-ode like the first. The Chorus has already presented the arguments of common sense against Iolaos' resolve, but the first strophe of its ode strikes a new chord, more lyrical than anything that has gone before and more in tune with the old hero's fantastic enterprise. It calls upon all nature—earth, moon, sunlight, to shout to heaven in an actual summons to the gods. "I"—the city, the Chorus—will now go into battle (779–81 / 755–58):

> We're ready, ready to take up shining steel, ready to fight
> for these guests of ours, for Athens,
>   for glory, and home.

In the mouths of the Chorus, this is startling and essentially unparalleled in Greek tragedy. It implies direct participation in the battle, and it would not seem out of place to have some members of the Chorus arm and follow Iolaos off stage. At the same time, there is none of the sturdy defiance of the first ode here, or of the bravado that casually places Athens' strength equal with Argos'. Rather (782–84 / 759–62),

> Oh, day of shame when Mykenai,
> arrogant in her swelling power,
> came breathing hatred against our city.

The rest of the ode grandly develops the theme that human justice and right action, placing themselves in such peril, demand the support of the gods (794–95 / 775–76): "Our justice, our courage deserve / their home, deserve to hold and keep this land forever." The Chorus carries the justification of the actions of its city, and of the suppliants whom the city has taken in, beyond the realm of common opinion, to the level of divine order. The Chorus goes into battle looking for a sign from the gods, as if it were the protagonist within the drama.

In the next episode, the Chorus receives it, in the form of victory and the miracle of Iolaos' rejuvenation. The last choral ode follows, celebrating the victory and the revealed divinity of Herakles. It is an extraordinary composition. The first words (923 / 892), "Sweet, the dance is sweet," speak of the Chorus' own role (generically, not as a dramatic chorus) as a celebrating group of singer-dancers—but as it were from the outside, as though they were the citizens watching a performance. The following language and the whole structure of the ode suggest the performance of another form of lyric: the choral odes celebrating victories in the Olympian and other pan-Hellenic games. Pindar, the greatest lyricist in this form, had died about ten years before the play's production, but others were still composing. Euripides' ode here suggests the structure often used by these poets:

1. The comparison of glorious or beautiful things to the present occasion: "A is great (lovely), and B, but it is most joyful to celebrate this victory." Compare Pindar, *Olympians,* I and XI.
2. Praise of the victor and his qualities, in this case the city. The victory is related to divine favor.
3. A mythic reference, often critical of other versions, and appropriate to the victor—here the marriage of Herakles and Hebe.
4. A moral or gnomic sentiment closing the ode.

The Euripidean Chorus transforms itself for this occasion into a group performing a rite of celebration for victory which would suggest a noble, aristocratic, and faintly archaic character. On the stage, concerted with the music and movement of the dance, this could have a stunning theatrical effect. The democratic city and its representative Chorus, the same people who argue on street-corners, go to court or to battle, and bustle about the city's business, finally lay hold upon a world in which individual human excellence arising among them is paid supreme honor, and nobility consorts easily if transiently with divine favor.

It is from this world that the Chorus is wrenched into the horrors of the final scene. The last gnomic words of its ode are (951 / 926–27): "May such passionate ambition never be mine." It is immediately confronted with the insatiable rage of Alkmene. It protests, wavers, and collapses into acquiescence. It is perhaps too much, too rapid, too brutal for an "acceptable" dramatic framework. Perhaps this was Euripides' intent. The assumption of individual responsibility to the community which brings forth the purest heroism under the press of events in war can also incorporate the arbitrary will, the assumption of individual license which bring forth unbridled cruelty, vengeance, and self-interest. If the play ends with a hero in defeat and moral disintegration, that hero is the civil body of the city, and not only the Chorus as its representative, but also the real community, strained to a danger point under siege, the spectators in the Theater of Dionysos.

VIII

It remains to provide some notes on characters and on the production of the play for an audience. We have dealt with the characters as they advance the themes of the play and have noted that in the compression of action and multiplicity of actors there is little room for depth of character explanation and development. There is no Medea, no Hippolytos, no Herakles here (though all these plays date from the same period of Euripides' dramaturgy). But neither are the characters mere busy and lifeless puppets. Euripides illuminates each one swiftly and surely, enriching dramatic function with personality. Even the messenger roles have this individuation. Alkmene's slave who brings the news of the victory is supple, quick, and flamboyant in his vivid descriptions. At the end of the scene, he takes a lewd enjoyment in Eurystheus' desperate struggle for death against his capture and bondage, only to become a slave in Alkmene's hands—then quickly and brashly reminds Alkmene that she has promised him his own freedom for the news. He is an able, outspoken soul, deeply poisoned by his servitude. The other messenger is Hyllos' servant who tells Iolaos of his master's arrival with an army. He is probably the same as the messenger in the last scene who brings on the captured Eurystheus. This is a wholly different personage, a bluff, loyal countryman, familiar and laconic in his description of war and princes, and nonplussed to the point of derision by Iolaos' sudden resolve to join him in the battle.

The young king, Demophon, not only is the perfect nobleman in his dissection of his royal responsibilities, but also shows the necessary touch of inexperience and uncertainty when confronted with the oracles. He wants very much to be a good king, to enjoy mutual dealing in justice with his people. But he sees no way to do it while obeying the oracles, and at last turns to old Iolaos with the confession (**491** / 472–73): "I've seen the oracles; and I'm afraid."

Even Makaria, that isolated figurine of nobility, makes a quick and intense impression of intellectuality as well as virtue. Every one of her speeches is a kind of public reasoning with herself, from her first entrance, stating and then rebutting her own reluctance to come out in public, through her rapid enumeration of all the unacceptable contingencies if she shirks her duty, and her instant rejection of the choice by lot proposed by Iolaos, to her last speculation on the possibility of an afterlife. Her presence conveys little pathos and much power; in her brief appearance she overshadows the other characters.

The most expanded character in the play, and the most fascinating, is Iolaos. He is the old nobleman, maintaining the same code as Demophon, but no longer having the power to enforce it. And yet he is very far from being simply a pathetic study in feeble old age. From his appearance at the beginning of the play, his words have an ironic bite and mastery in each situation (1–2 / 1–2): For a long time now, I've lived by this law: / the good man is born to serve others. It is the central theme of the play, but as Iolaos develops it here, we understand his implication: the good man does himself no good at all, in the vulgar sense of the word. He describes his guardianship of the children ironically with an Aeschylean phrase. He understands why other cities have driven them out (27–28 / 25): "they wilt / in the face of power." He is quick to grasp the implication in Demophon's appeal for help in the face of the oracle; it is that the Heraklids should voluntarily leave Athens once more, and spare the king the agony of choice. Iolaos creates an impression of self-knowledge and knowledge of others which inform his prickly sense of honor, his impetuousness, and his feeble physical strength. It is of course the Greek kind of self-knowledge, not of psyche and motivation, but of one's position in the scale of powers, one's mortality, one's degree of subjection and that of others to the conditions of life, fate, and necessity, that is comprehended in the phrase *gnōthi seauton*, "know thyself." Iolaos' knowledge is unflinching, and it extends in time. He knows what it is to have been a hero, and he knows what he is today. It leads him to offer Herakles' children to Demophon even as slaves; it would be better than the obliteration of their race forever. From such a base his passion and fantasy spring up with increased power and credibility. When he speaks of praising Demophon to Theseus his dead father, and we realize that for all his ironies he accepts quite simply the underworld of the Homeric age, the dead heroes walking the fields of asphodel in converse with each other, the effect is moving. Again, he speaks with a terrible and human truth (623 / 607), after Makaria has gone out to her death with his praises in her ears: "This is a cruel deliverance." And in his last scene, as he struggles with the armor and stumbles on his way to war, we cannot help but hope that somehow that piercing knowledge is still with him.

Alkmene has been Iolaos' partner and twin marshal in all their trials and wanderings. They are of the same age, at least for the purposes of the play.[6] Although she does not appear until late in the play, her name and the fact that she is nearby in the temple are kept constantly before the audience. When she comes forth, it is soon clear that she is Iolaos'

6. Actually, in the usual version of the myth, Iolaos was the son of Iphikles, Herakles' mortal twin, and therefore the grandson of Alkmene, like the Heraklids. For Euripides' purposes this was impossible. He therefore avoids all mention of Iolaos' specific relation to Herakles' family and refers only to a general kinship. See the genealogy in the Note to 213.

opposite in every sense. She is a model of irredeemable ignorance—of self, of others, of the situation. She does not wait to be told who the messenger from Hyllos is, but is ready to fight him as a herald from Eurystheus. Her words are those of non-comprehension, and she soon retires from the animated dialogue between Iolaos and the messenger. So far she might seem good-hearted if dull-witted. But later in the scene when Iolaos leaves her finally to the protection of Zeus, she says with scorn (**745–47** / 717–19),

> Zeus?
> Zeus will never hear a word of reproach from my lips,
> but Zeus knows best how he's treated me.

Something perhaps may be permitted to one who has been Zeus' consort, but in the play this is a jarring and vulgar note. No other character speaks of the gods or their actions in this spiteful tone. In her ignorance of the human station, the menace of Alkmene begins to show. It bursts forth after the victory. She assumes that Iolaos' sparing of Eurystheus' life is a clever trick. This is the level of her understanding. It is never raised. Her lust for vengeance, when Eurystheus comes before her, reduces every inkling of thought to an animal cunning which serves her only goal. Her position as a suppliant taken into the community of Athens, the laws of the country, the opinion of man, even the safety of her own descendants, go by the board. Her stated sufferings simply do not justify it. She is the demon of self-ignorance and self-interest, raised up out of Euripides' dark apprehension of his time, and coming only too vividly true in reality as his play came to the stage.

The difficulties and possibilities of the Chorus as "character" have already been outlined. Chorus members are usually described as old men of Marathon. They are certainly at Marathon, the scene of the play, and Demophon addresses their leader as "old." Beyond this the Chorus is not characterized, nor does it, like many other Greek dramatic choruses, describe its own composition and status. Also, Euripides does not make much of the possible association with Marathon, still a rich symbol of heroism for the Athenians. After an initial fix on the location, the Chorus and characters refer to their city exclusively as Athens. It is most tempting, therefore, in the light of the different *personae* assumed by the Chorus in its odes to think of it as a diverse group representing the range of the Athenian citizen body—young and old, city men and country men, rich and poor, soldiers, assemblymen, traders. Such a composition would at once provide a comprehensive frame for the "noble action," not limited to a single class or place, and would help to explain the final helplessness of the Chorus in the face of Alkmene's demands.

A significant question of staging, finally, is the relationship of the silent children of Herakles to the other characters and to the developing action of the play. Their presence alone must create a certain tension; it would be impossible to forget that the descendants of these boys created the Spartan state and the Spartan kings. Their interaction with Iolaos, Kopreus, Demophon, and Makaria is fairly well suggested by the language of the play. But how do they react to Hyllos' messenger, to Alkmene, to Eurystheus, and finally to the Chorus, especially in the last scene? Euripides left no stage directions here; but it is impossible to think that, as the play's producer, he neglected the silent force that these characters could give to his theme.

IX

We have based the translation upon the Budé text edited by Louis Méridier, as providing the best overall guide among the considerable textual difficulties of the play. Departures from that text are signaled in the Notes.

We are grateful to Donald C. Goertz, who assisted in the preparation of early drafts of the translation. The playwrights David Kranes and Thomas Phelps read an early draft, and made many valuable suggestions. The National Translation Center made a small but indispensable travel grant at a crucial stage of the composition. William Arrowsmith, the Herakles of his time, has expended enormous amounts of energy in advising and encouraging us; we are deeply grateful for his criticism, and for his example. Our wives, Frannie Taylor and Jane Brooks, have made many suggestions, typed many pages, endured many spirited readings of odes and speeches, and have in countless other ways earned more of our love and gratitude than we can express. We dedicate this book to them.

ROBERT A. BROOKS
HENRY TAYLOR

CHILDREN OF HERAKLES

Translated by

HENRY TAYLOR

and

ROBERT A. BROOKS

CHARACTERS

IOLAOS   guardian of the children of Herakles

SONS   of Herakles, half a dozen boys, seven to sixteen years old

KOPREUS   herald of Eurystheus

CHORUS   of citizens of Marathon

LEADER   of Chorus (a second chorister acts as "Second Leader" in one scene)

DEMOPHON   king of Athens

AKAMAS   brother to Demophon

MAKARIA   daughter of Herakles

ALKMENE   mother of Herakles

SERVANT   of Hyllos, Herakles' son

MESSENGER   slave of Alkmene

EURYSTHEUS   king of Argos and Mykenai

GUARDS   two spearmen who escort Eurystheus

Line numbers in the right-hand margin of the text refer to the English translation only, and the Notes beginning at page 163 are keyed to these lines. The bracketed line numbers in the running heads refer to the Greek text.

The scene is Marathon, near the eastern coast of Attika. The stage building represents the temple of Zeus; it has one entrance, in the center. Before the temple stands a simple altar: a waist-high rectangular block of stone, placed on a stone base a few inches thick and some eighteen inches longer and wider than the block itself. A few simple wreaths, made from leafy branches, have been placed on the altar.

As the play opens, IOLAOS, *an old man, stands near the altar. The* SONS *of Herakles are grouped around the altar, sitting or kneeling on the base.* IOLAOS *addresses the audience.*

IOLAOS For a long time now, I've lived by this law:
        the good man is born to serve others.
        The man who devotes himself to his own advantage
        is a dead weight in any common enterprise,
        a useless burden, good for nothing but himself.
        This, years of hard experience have taught me.
        I could have left the world alone,
        living a life of privacy and peace in Argos;
        but compassion—compassion, and the bond of blood—
        compelled me to become Herakles' only partner   10
        in his great labors, when he was still with us.
        Now that he's gone among the gods, he leaves
        his children under the dwindling shadow of my wings.
        I defend them—though I need defenders of my own.

        After Herakles had left this world,
        Eurystheus wanted us dead, so we ran away.
        We lost our country, but we saved our lives.
        Now we wander like fugitives, hounded

from town to town. Outrage after outrage:
after all our suffering, he still pursues us.   20
He discovers our whereabouts, and then immediately
dispatches a herald after us, demanding
we be surrendered, like runaway slaves.
So our would-be allies are forced to choose
friendship with us, or war with Argos. No choice there.
They look at us, a handful of wretched orphans
with an old feeble guardian, and they wilt
in the face of power, and drive us out.

Now I share exile with these children here—
exile, hopelessness. I can't betray them.   30
People would say, "You see,
now that their father is dead, look how quickly
Iolaos, their only kinsman, has deserted them."
Now we're outcasts, everywhere. So in the end
we came here, to Marathon, as suppliants
seeking asylum at this altar of their gods,
asking protection one last time. We know
that this country is now ruled by Theseus' two sons,
who inherited it when the descendants of Pandion
divided the kingdom. They are our cousins.   40
And so, our wandering has ended here
at the boundaries of Athens. Shining Athens.

Two old, unlikely marshals lead this march of ours
to nowhere. Myself, worn out from fending
for these boys; and Alkmene, their grandmother,
who's minding the girls inside the temple there.
It would be a shameful thing for young girls to stand here
outside, exposed to public crowds before this altar.
Hyllos and the older boys have gone ahead
to look for still another sanctuary.   50
Even here, we might be refused—
                                        Quick, boys,
here! I see Eurystheus' herald, on his way
to make us fugitives again.

The SONS *assemble behind* IOLAOS *as* KOPREUS *enters.*

                              Gods,
how I detest you—you and your king!
When I think how many times you came to Herakles
mouthing your demands, threats—humiliation on
        humiliation—

KOPREUS   So here you are. You think you're safe, do you?
          You think the people of Athens will fight for *you*?
          Madness.
                    No sane man would choose your helplessness
          when he might choose the power of Eurystheus.   60
          (*moving toward* IOLAOS) On your feet.
          No more stalling. On your feet and come with me.
          You'll get the justice you deserve in Argos—
          death by stoning.

IOLAOS   Not to Argos.
          This altar of the gods will protect me.
          So will this earth on which we stand.
          This earth is free.

KOPREUS   Must I use force?

IOLAOS   You won't take me or these boys. Not by force.

KOPREUS   Then you're no prophet.   70

          Tries to seize one of the SONS; IOLAOS *struggles with him.*

IOLAOS   Not while I'm alive.

KOPREUS   Out of my way!
          (*knocks* IOLAOS *down*) These boys are going back
          to Eurystheus. Back where they belong.

IOLAOS   Help! Men of Athens! Help! Look—suppliants
         at Zeus' altar—forced away—our wreaths trampled—

125

an outrage to your city—sacrilege to your gods—

Enter, from right, CHORUS *of citizens of Marathon. In dress, height, style, and age, they represent various types of citizenry. In this scene two men divide the* LEADER's *speeches.*

LEADER What's going on here?

2ND LEADER Why this brawling at the high altar of Zeus?

LEADER Look, an old man, knocked down, lying here—
this is shameful . . .   80

2ND LEADER (*to* IOLAOS) Who did this?

IOLAOS (*indicating* KOPREUS) That man. He did it.
He dragged me from the altar, insulted your gods.

> *Members of the* CHORUS *confront* KOPREUS, *interposing between him and the suppliants. The two* LEADERS *continue to question* IOLAOS.

LEADER You, sir—who are you? Where are you from?
How did you get to Marathon?

2ND LEADER Or did you come here by boat, from Euboia?

IOLAOS We're not island people, strangers.
We come from Mykenai.

LEADER Your name?

IOLAOS Iolaos. Squire and companion of Herakles.   90
You may have heard of me.

LEADER Yes, I remember hearing your name in the old days.
But who are these boys?

IOLAOS The sons of Herakles. We came here

(*motions to* SONS, *who kneel before* CHORUS)

as suppliants to you and your city.

LEADER Why are you appealing to the people of Athens?
        What is your request?

IOLAOS We want protection. We ask for sanctuary.
        We ask not to be returned by force to Argos.

KOPREUS (*to* IOLAOS) I warn you: it won't sit well with your   100
                masters,
         if they find you here. They have power over you.
         Even in Athens.

LEADER (*to* KOPREUS) Stranger, the rights of suppliants must be
                respected.
        There can be no violence at the altar of the gods.
        Here, justice rules. Violence is forbidden.

KOPREUS Surrender these children to Eurystheus,
         then there'll be no question of violence.

LEADER I tell you, it would be sacrilege
        to ignore a suppliant's appeal to our city.

KOPREUS I warn you once more. You're risking trouble.   110
         In this case, prudence would be best.

LEADER Practice your own prudence. My advice to you is this:
        explain to our king why you've acted
        as badly as you have here. Don't outrage
        our gods by tearing suppliants from sanctuary.

KOPREUS Who's king here?

LEADER Demophon, son of Theseus.

KOPREUS Then I'll take my case to him.
         Talking to you is wasting words.

LEADER Here's King Demophon now—Demophon and his brother
            Akamas.   120
         They'll hear your charges.

         Enter, from right, DEMOPHON *and* AKAMAS. *Both are*
         young men, simply dressed. DEMOPHON *carries a staff.*

DEMOPHON (*to* LEADER) Old man, I commend your vigilance.
         You were prompt—quicker than our young men, I see—
         to answer a cry for help. Now,
         why are these people kneeling here at the god's altar?

LEADER My lord, these are the sons of Herakles.
         This is Iolaos, Herakles' friend and squire.

DEMOPHON But why all this brawling?

LEADER That stranger there, the herald, tried
         to drag them from the altar. They shouted for help.   130
         Then he knocked the old man down. It was pitiful.

DEMOPHON In dress, in style, this man looks Greek.
         His behavior is barbarous.
                                        (*to* KOPREUS) All right,
         stranger, who are you? Where are you from?

KOPREUS Since you ask, I am Argive, from Mykenai.
         King Eurystheus dispatched me here
         with orders to return these fugitives to Argos.
         I am provided, sir, with legal claims to present.
         I have authority to act. I am here as an officer of Argos,
         empowered to take formal custody of Argive runaways,   140
         fugitives from Argive jurisdiction.
         They have been condemned to death by Argive law.
         As a sovereign state, Argos has the right

to execute the verdicts decreed by its own courts
against its own subjects. Again and again these runaways
have sought sanctuary at altars throughout Hellas,
but our position has been consistently the same,
and no Greek city has dared to risk the reprisals of Argos.
Either they thought that Athens was mad,
or they themselves were mad with desperation,   150
ready to stake all on this last appeal;
in any case, they have sought asylum here.
How, otherwise, could they have dreamt that Athens—
Athens alone, of all cities in Hellas—
could let compassion outweigh the claims of common
          sense?
Compare; then decide whether it's wiser
to harbor these fugitives, or surrender them to us.
This is what you gain from us: the power of Argos
will be yours; the great strength of Eurystheus, your ally.
But if you soften, swayed by their sorry tale,   160
hard steel will be our answer.
Don't suppose that Argos will concede without a fight.
And what pretext would Athens have for war?
That we had robbed you, annexed your land,
attacked your allies? And when you bury your dead,
for what great cause will you claim your soldiers fought
          and died?
Imagine the gratitude of your citizens,
if, for the sake of one doddering fool—
this walking charnel house, this ancient zero—
and this clutch of miserable brats,   170
you and your city founder in the bilge.
Your only argument is hope—a hope
worth far less than what lies in your hands.
Perhaps you like to think these boys will grow up
and fight for you. But even then,
they could never cope with the army of Argos. Meanwhile,
the Argives will have ample time to conquer you.
Believe me. Do as I suggest. Concede me nothing,
simply let me have what is mine by right,

and, by so doing, gain Mykenai's friendship.
Abandon your old way of siding with the oppressed.   180
Why choose weak friends when you could have strength?

LEADER   No case can be judged, not
         until both sides are presented and debated.

IOLAOS   Here, in this place, my lord, I have the right
         to speak, not only the right to listen.
         You will not drive me away, as others before you have,
         not until I present my case to you.
             I have no legal argument with this herald here.
         These children and I ceased to be Argives   190
         when our sentence was decreed, when we went into exile.
         So how can he claim that we are Mykenaians still?
         How can they banish us, then hunt us down?
         We are aliens, outcasts.
                              (*to* KOPREUS) Or is it your argument
         that exile from Argos means exile from Hellas?
         Surely Athens is open to us still.
         The men of Athens have no fear of Argos;
         they'll welcome, they'll protect the sons of Herakles.
         Athens isn't Trachis, or some small Achaian town.
         Athens is none of those places from which you've driven   200
             us before—
         driven us, not because you had a right, but because
         you flaunted your Argive strength, exactly as you're doing
             now.
         Everywhere you showed contempt for the rights of
             sanctuary
         afforded by the altars of the gods.
         If that can happen here, if Athens can be cowed by Argos,
         then Athens is not the city, the free city I have known.
         But I do know the Athenian spirit; they'd rather die
         than yield this point. Brave men fear dishonor more than
             death.
         I say no more. Excessive praise, I know, is tiresome.

         (*to* DEMOPHON) My lord, let me explain why, as leader of   210
             this country,

it is your duty to protect these boys.
First, they are your relatives by blood.
Pelops' son was Pittheus. And Pittheus had a daughter,
Aithra. She was the mother of Theseus, your father.
Now Herakles, the father of these boys, was the son
of Zeus by Alkmene, granddaughter of Pelops.
So, Demophon, your father and their father were cousins,
which means you're bound to them by blood.
But you have other obligations, too.
Once, as Herakles' squire, I sailed with him and Theseus   220
to win the belt of the Amazon queen.
Many brave men died on that expedition. And all Hellas
knows how Herakles brought your father Theseus
home alive from the blind world below.
In return for Herakles' help then, his sons ask you now:
Do not surrender them. Don't let them be driven
from the altars of your gods, expelled from Athens.
You would be disgraced before all Athenians
if homeless suppliants, your own cousins—
look, look at these boys!—were hauled away by force.   230
(*kneeling*) I beg you,
by your knees, your hands, your beard,
protect the sons of Herakles.
Adopt them as your own sons. My lord,
make yourself their friend. Be kind. Be their cousin.
Be their father, their brother. Be their master, even,
before you hand them over to the Argives.

LEADER My lord, when I hear what these people have suffered,
I pity them. I have never seen nobility
so abused by fortune. What they suffer,   240
they should not suffer. It is wrong.

DEMOPHON Iolaos, three considerations compel me
to honor your request.
                        The first argument
is Zeus, before whose altar you now kneel
with this holy gathering of god-protected children.
Second, old debts and ties of blood

demand that I protect them—
they are the sons of Herakles.
Third, dishonor—which should be the first of my
        considerations.
If I allow strangers to desecrate this altar,   250
men would charge that Athens was no longer free,
that I had betrayed a suppliant out of fear of Argos.
A disgrace, a hanging crime.
I wish you had come on some happier mission. . . .
But courage. Don't despair. *Here* you and these boys
will be safe from all violence, I promise you.
(*to* KOPREUS) As for you, stranger herald,
go back to Argos, give Eurystheus my answer.
Tell him, if he thinks he has a legal claim
against these people, our courts will give him fair hearing.   260
But I will not surrender them. Not to you. Never.

KOPREUS Even if I prove my claim is just?

DEMOPHON Just? How can force be just?
        Or driving suppliants from an altar?

KOPREUS The disgrace and risk are mine, not yours.

DEMOPHON It would be disgrace to hand them over.

KOPREUS Then banish them. I'll seize them at the frontier.

DEMOPHON Fool, do you think you can outwit the gods?

KOPREUS Criminals, it seems, find asylum in Athens.

DEMOPHON All men find asylum at the altars of the gods.   270

KOPREUS The Argives may disagree.

DEMOPHON This is my country. Here, I am king.

KOPREUS So long as you don't provoke the Argives.

DEMOPHON Better anger the Argives than the gods.

KOPREUS War with Argos, then? An ugly prospect.

DEMOPHON Agreed. But I will not abandon these suppliants.

KOPREUS So you say.
But they're mine to take, and I'll take them.

DEMOPHON Then you'll find your homecoming hard.

KOPREUS (*attempting to seize a child*)

Let me put your courage to the test.   280

DEMOPHON (*raising his staff to strike* KOPREUS)

Touch them, and you'll regret it. Now—

LEADER In the name of god, don't strike a herald!

DEMOPHON I will if he forgets he's a herald.

LEADER Leave, stranger.
My lord, his person is sacred.

KOPREUS (*moving away*) I'm leaving. I am not strong enough,
or fool enough, to fight you all.
(*from a safe distance*) But I'll be back, and with me
an army of invincible Argive soldiers.
Even now, at the frontiers of Megara, ten thousand men,   290
under arms, Eurystheus at their head, are drawn up,
waiting to learn the outcome of my mission here.
When Eurystheus hears your insolent answer,
a tide of iron will sweep over Attika,
destroying everything you have—
your people, your land, your crops, everything you have.
If we failed to take revenge,
all the martial vigor of Argos would flourish for nothing.

133

DEMOPHON Be damned to you! I'm not afraid of Argos.
You won't take these children. Or my honor either.   300
Athens is a free city, not a colony of Argos.

Exit KOPREUS, *followed by* AKAMAS. *As they leave, the*
CHORUS *members* turn to each other, speaking
individually and excitedly.

CHORUS —Now is the time to make ready,
now, before the Argive army reaches our border.
—The war god of Argos is savage, brutal,
more brutal now than ever before.
—You know how heralds bluster, always the same.
—Their reports always magnify the facts.
                              —Twice as large!
—Imagine his lies.
                  —Imagine what he'll tell his king.
—The outrage,
            —the insult to his person,
how he barely,
            —barely,
                  —escaped
                        —with his life.   310

IOLAOS The best, the finest heritage a son can have
is a noble and courageous father.
In the hour of hardship, when ordinary men weaken and
      fail,
nobility stands firm. Look where *we* stood:
we thought we had no hope. And then
we found allies, found kinsmen here in Athens—
the only city in Hellas willing to take us in.
Come, boys, give your hands to these men of Athens,
(*gently pushing* SONS *toward* CHORUS, *and beckoning to
individual choristers*)
and you, gentlemen, give them your hands.
                              —Boys,
we've tested this city's friendship.   320
Now, if someday you see your home in Argos again;

if someday you inherit your father's house and honors,
remember Athens, remember these friends.
They saved your lives. Think of this day,
and swear eternal peace between yourselves and Athens.
These men have earned your loyalty, your love.
They readily accepted the burdens we brought with us,
even the vengeance of the Argives.
Remember what they did.
They saw we were helpless exiles, wanderers,   330
but refused to surrender us or drive us out.
(*to* DEMOPHON) In life, and in death, when at last I come
        to die,
I'll honor your name, my lord Demophon. And when at
        last
I stand with Theseus, I'll bring him news to make him
        proud,
proud to hear how courageously you welcomed
and protected the sons of Herakles,
how splendidly you upheld his fame and honor.
You are your father's son, Demophon, no less great than he
in nature, in action. Most men are faint reflections
of their fathers. Sons like you are rare, King Demophon.   340

LEADER Athens has always defended the oppressed
        when their cause was just. For friends like these
        we have suffered greatly in the past.
        Now another trial lies before us.

DEMOPHON (*to* IOLAOS) Well spoken, sir. I know that these boys
        will remember your words, and the actions of Athens.
        Now I'll go and mobilize the citizens
        so I can meet the Argive attack with my forces
        fully mustered. I don't want to be caught off guard,
        so first I'll send out scouts to reconnoiter.   350
        Count on it—the Argives are disciplined and ready.
        Then I'll have the priests prepare the sacrifice.
        You, Iolaos, leave the altar and go to my house.
        My servants will take care of you while I'm away.
        (IOLAOS *does not move*) Go inside, old friend.

135

IOLAOS I'd rather stay here, here at the altar. Let us stay
where we can offer prayers for the city's success.
We'll join you inside after the Argives are defeated.
(DEMOPHON *hesitates*)
My lord, now we have gods to call upon, gods as great
as any gods of Argos. Hera is *their* champion; *ours*   360
is Athena. Success means having stronger gods,
and honoring their strength—or so I hold.
Goddess Athena will never know defeat.

> *Exit* DEMOPHON. IOLAOS *and the* SONS *assemble at the
> altar. A trumpet sounds.*

LEADER Boast away.
What do we care for your bluster?

CHORUS (*speaking individually*)
—Your Argos is nothing here, stranger.
—You won't frighten me with your bragging threats.
—This is Athens.—This great city
has no fear of you.

LEADER Not Athens,   370
where the wheeling chorus
weaves the lovely mazes of the dance.

CHORUS (*speaking individually*)
—You're mad.
—Mad as your master, Eurystheus of Argos.
—You come to a city as great as Argos—

LEADER You lay violent hands on helpless wanderers
who sought asylum here
at the altars of our gods.

CHORUS (*speaking individually*)
—You flouted our king's authority.
—Offered no justification.   380
—How can such arrogant madness win approval

from sane and prudent men?
—We are peace-loving people.
                                        —And now, herald,
take our message home to your lunatic master.

LEADER Tell Eurystheus this: King,
        if in your rage, your frenzied anger,
        you think to seize this city,
        I warn you: It will not be,
        nothing will happen as you dream.

CHORUS (*speaking individually*)
        —There are swords in Athens, too,   390
        Athens has shields of shining bronze.
        —You love war, you and your Argos.
        —But keep your lust for war, your turmoil,
        —keep them to yourselves, keep them at home in Argos.
        —Here, they have no place, they are strangers here,
        —here where the Graces live,
        —at peace, at peace in shining Athens.
        —King, in the name of the graces, then:
        —hold back.

            Enter DEMOPHON, *accompanied by three or four armed*
                                            men.

IOLAOS What is it, son? You must have news   400
        of the enemy. I can see it in your eyes.
        Are they on the move, or already here?
        That herald of his wasn't simply bragging.
        The gods have always smiled upon Eurystheus,
        and now, glowing with confidence, he's marching here,
        where Zeus, who punishes all arrogance of mortal thought,
        will bring him down.

DEMOPHON   The Argives are here,
        Eurystheus at their head. Rather than rely on scouts,
        I observed them at first hand, with my own eyes,

137

so I can give responsible orders to our army.   410
The enemy hasn't moved to occupy the plain. Instead,
Eurystheus has taken a temporary position
on high ground, along the ridge. He'll be looking,
I think, for the safest means of bringing his troops down
before making camp in Attika. And we'll be ready for them.
The city's fully mustered. The sacrifices
have been prepared as required by the gods receiving them.
Everywhere in Athens the priests have made offerings
intended to repel the enemy and save the city.
I've summoned all the seers; I've questioned them,   420
every prophetic voice in Athens, about the ancient oracles—
those in common domain, those that circulate in secret.
No detail bearing on our safety has been omitted.
In many small matters, the oracles disagree,
but in one essential point, Iolaos, they all concur.
They command me to sacrifice to Persephone. To sacrifice
a virgin, a girl of noble birth.
    You know the good will I bear you, Iolaos, but this new
requirement is too much. I will not kill my own daughter,
nor will I compel any Athenian to such an act   430
against his will. What man would be so mad
as to kill his own child? Now, all over the city,
people are gathered in small groups, arguing whether
we ought to protect the suppliants, or whether I'm mad
in promising to help you. If I order such a sacrifice,
civil war will be the consequence.
So now I need your help. Help me find some way
of saving you, these children, and this city,
without subjecting me to the city's bitter anger.
I am no tyrant, no barbarian.   440
If I act fairly, others will be fair with me.

LEADER   Are the gods opposed to helping these strangers?

IOLAOS   Poor children, we're like sailors at sea.
They escape the savage anger of the gale,
they reach out to touch the land, and an offshore wind,

gusting hard, drives them back out to sea again.
That's how it is with us—driven from this land
when we were almost there, safe ashore, or so we thought.
Hope, hope. Why was I allowed the joy of hoping
only to have its promise torn from my hands?   450
I understand Demophon's decision not to kill
his people's children. He has done what he could—
and should. My lord, even if the gods oppose me,
my gratitude to you remains the same.
                              —Boys, I don't know what to do.
Where can we turn? Is there any god we haven't invoked?
Where haven't we turned for shelter and protection?
We'll be surrendered to Argos, and we'll die.
My life doesn't count, doesn't matter,
except that by dying I delight my enemies.
It's you I pity, boys—   460
you and your old grandmother, Alkmene.
Poor woman, to have lived so long, only to come to
        this . . .
I pity you, pity myself—all my sufferings and trials,
all for nothing.
                    No way out.
We were fated to fall into Eurystheus' hands,
fated to die in dishonor and shame.
(to DEMOPHON) No, wait. There's still a chance, one
        chance,
of saving these boys. You can help me, Demophon.
Surrender me to the Argives in their place.
You risk nothing, and the boys will be safe.   470
To have Herakles' friend in his power—to humiliate me—
there's nothing Eurystheus would like more.
The man is brutal. Civilized men should pray
for enemies like themselves, not brute savages.
Then, even in defeat, there'd be respect,
there'd be compassion.

LEADER Old sir, your suggestion dishonors this city.
The charge of failure to defend a suppliant

is false, yet it's a shameful accusation.
It brings disgrace.   480

DEMOPHON Noble words, but no solution.
It's not for you Eurystheus brings his army here.
What does Eurystheus gain from an old man's death?
He wants to kill these boys. Why not?
They're the sons of Herakles. They're nobly born;
grown to manhood, they'd be bound to avenge their
          father's wrongs.
They'd be dangerous to him. Eurystheus knows that;
he has to act before it happens. Now,
if you have some better idea, some effective plan,
let me hear it. For my part,   490
I've seen the oracles; and I'm afraid.

> MAKARIA *appears in the temple doorway, and pauses before*
> *approaching* IOLAOS. *She is about fifteen.*

MAKARIA Strangers, please don't think my coming out
is brashness. I ask your pardon. I know
that women are honored most for silence, for knowing
and keeping their proper place at home.
But when I heard that anguish in your voice, Iolaos,
I couldn't stay inside. I had to come out.
I'm not head of this family, I know that.
Still, I should be here. I love my brothers.
I'm here for them. For them, for myself,   500
I have to know what's happened.

IOLAOS Daughter, of all the children of Herakles, it's you
I've always admired the most. And how right I was.
Just when I thought all was well, suddenly
everything turned hopeless. According to King Demophon,
the oracles demand a living human sacrifice.
Not a bull, no sheep, but a girl, a virgin
of noble birth must be sacrificed to Persephone
in order to save this city and ourselves. There's no
          other way,

no way out. Demophon refuses absolutely   510
to sacrifice his own child, or any other man's.
Either we must extricate ourselves on our own,
or we seek asylum elsewhere. Those aren't his exact words,
but the meaning is clear. His first priority
is the safety of Athens.

MAKARIA   Then our lives depend
          upon this sacrifice?

  IOLAOS   Yes, provided other things go well.

MAKARIA Then you needn't fear the Argives any more.
          I'll be your sacrifice. Unforced, of my own free will,
          I volunteer my life.
          (*stopping* IOLAOS' *protest*) The people of Athens have   520
               risked their lives for us.
          So how can we, who imposed our burdens on them,
          shrink from dying, when by our dying we give them
          life? What could we say in our defense?
          Not a word.
                    It would be cowardice, contemptible,
          if we who, weeping, sought asylum at the altars of their
               gods,
          who boast ourselves to be the children of Herakles,
          should cringe from death. Every decent man
          would laugh us to scorn.
                              No, far better
          this city should fall—the gods forbid!—   530
          better the enemy should take me prisoner, treat me
          with outrage and abuse me, daughter of a hero though
               I am,
          and, in the end, send me down to Hades just the same.
          And what if I'm banished?
          What could I say for shame when people ask me
          why I come to them with suppliant branches, imploring
               their help,
          but show a coward's love of life? They'd drive me out,
          saying, "Cowards get no sanctuary here."

141

And suppose my brothers die, leaving me
alive, alone, what hope of happiness would I have?
Many men have sacrificed family and friends   540
to their own happiness. I couldn't do it.
Who would want a wife without family or friends?
What man would want my children? Better, far better,
          to die
than live so empty a life. It might suit
another woman, but it will not do for me.
I am my father's daughter.
                              I am ready.
Take me to the place of sacrifice,
wreathe my head with garlands, perform your rite.
Then go fight. Fight and win. Of my own free will,
unforced, I give my life. Tell the world   550
I'm dying for my brothers, I'm dying for myself.
It's not life, not *my* life, that matters.
And knowing that, I've found a better thing
than life itself, by bravely leaving it.

LEADER What can I say to such noble words—
              this girl's offer to die for her brothers?
              No man could speak so well or act so bravely.

IOLAOS Your spirit reveals your birth.
              You are the true daughter of your father Herakles,
              son of highest Zeus. I'm proud of you, proud
              of your words, but there's bitterness in what you say.   560
              Let me propose a fairer solution:
              we'll ask your sisters to come outside,
              we'll draw lots. The sister chosen will die
              on behalf of her brothers. It's the fairest thing
              to decide the issue by lot.

MAKARIA I refuse to let my death depend on chance.
              It has no grace of freedom. Not another word.
              If you accept my offer, if you stand ready
              to make use of me, I am ready, of my own free will,
              unforced, to give my brothers the gift of my life.   570

142

IOLAOS Dearest child.
Your earlier words were unsurpassable,
but these words surpass them. In bravery,
in generosity, you outdo even yourself. I cannot order
you to die, I can't prevent it. But by dying
you save your brothers' lives.

MAKARIA   You speak wisely.
Don't fear my death will taint you. I die of my own free
      will.
    But go with me, Iolaos. Be there to hold me
when I die, cover my body with my dress.
My father was Herakles, but I'm still afraid. I need you   580
      there
beside me, Iolaos, when I face the knife.

IOLAOS I couldn't bear it, standing beside you, watching
you die.

MAKARIA   Then ask the king to see to it
that I die with women around me, not men.

DEMOPHON Granted. I pity you. It would be disgrace and shame
for me to refuse you these last honors
so clearly required by your generosity, your bravery,
and what is right. I have never seen,
never, a woman of greater courage. Now,
if you have any last words for your brothers   590
and Iolaos, speak, child. It's time to go.

MAKARIA Goodbye, old friend. Farewell.
                              Teach these brothers of mine
to be like you. Make them wise and kind
in everything, like you. That's all; I want nothing more.
Protect them. Cherish them. I know how well
you love them. We're your children. You cared for us,
you brought us up. And now you see me go
unmarried, to death, dying for my brothers
clustered here around me.
                              —Brothers, I wish you

143

all success and happiness, every good thing   600
of which my death deprives me.
                                Honor Iolaos, honor
your grandmother, Alkmene. Honor these men of Athens.
And if someday the gods send you release
from your wanderings and give you back your home
in Argos, remember me, remember the funeral honors
due the sister who saved you.
                               Let my honors match
my gift: I stood at your side when you needed me,
I gave my life for you.
                        In the place of children
I will never have, these are all my treasures,
these are my reward,
                       if anything goes with us underground.   610
Nothingness is best. If even after death
we endure the troubles which burden us here on earth,
there's no escape. For human suffering,
the strongest medicine, I think, is death.

IOLAOS Generous, courageous girl, you are the noblest
woman I have ever known. Living and dying,
you will have our reverence and honor, always.
Farewell . . . I am afraid to speak ill-omened
words of goddess Persephone, to whom your body
is consecrated.

                Exit MAKARIA, *escorted by* DEMOPHON.

                Boys, this is too much,   620
too much pain, I need to sit . . .
Help me rest my back
against the altar. Cover my head with my robes.

            SONS *place* IOLAOS' *cloak over his head.*

This is a cruel deliverance.
We had this choice: to obey the oracle, or die.

Your death would have been a worse grief even than this,
but the choice we made is anguish, torture.

CHORUS (*speaking individually*)—Man's mind and hands, without
            the gods, can devise no triumph—not even failure.
        —Success vanishes, does not return.
        —Will not grow again in the same field,   630
            will not return with the seasons.
        —One fortune crowds out another, uprooting
            a man from his place in the sun,
            planting him again in stony darkness.
        —Or suddenly veers, shifting direction—
            as when a poor man stumbles on shining gold.
        —The gods hold us, caught fast in the torrent.
        —The man who tries to change the course of this current
            by stubbornness, by craft,
            struggles in vain.   640

        —Bear your burden.
        —Whatever the gods may send, do not falter.
            Endure it, unembittered.
        —Even as she dies, this girl discovers
            deathless honor and glory in giving her life
            for her brothers, for us all.
        —The glory she leaves behind her will shine forever,
            as noble actions outshine the darkest pain.
        —What she does today is worthy of her birth,
            worthy of her father Herakles.   650
        —Whoever you may be, if you kneel in reverence
            for human bravery;
        —if you kneel in honor of nobility, and in
            sorrow at its dying;
        —you will find me here, kneeling at your side,
                                (*the speaker of this line kneels*)
        —as I kneel now.

    Enter SERVANT *of Hyllos. He does not at first see* IOLAOS.

SERVANT Boys, where are Iolaos and Alkmene?
         Have they left the altar?

IOLAOS   Here I am—what's left of me.

SERVANT Why are you sitting there, staring at the ground?   660

IOLAOS   Sorrow for this family. Grief.

SERVANT Stand up. Lift your head.

IOLAOS   I am too old, too old. I have no strength.

SERVANT My news is good news.

IOLAOS   Who are you?
         Do I know you? I can't remember.

SERVANT Hyllos' servant. You know me now?

IOLAOS   Welcome, friend. Good news, you say?

SERVANT Glorious news.

IOLAOS   (*calling toward the temple*) Alkmene, come outside!   670
         I have good news!
         (*to* SERVANT) Poor terrified woman. She's the mother of
             Herakles,
         and yet a lifetime of concern for Hyllos and the other
             children
         has nearly broken her.

         Enter ALKMENE *from the temple. She is a very old woman,*
                        darkly and shabbily dressed.

ALKMENE Why all this shouting, Iolaos?
         Is this another herald? With more threats?
         (*to* SERVANT) I'm a weak old woman, stranger, but I
             warn you,

146

touch these children, you'll have to kill me first,
or I'm not the mother of Herakles. Touch them,
and you'll have a shameful struggle with two old people.

IOLAOS Stop, Alkmene. Don't be afraid.   680
This is no herald bringing threats from Argos.

ALKMENE Your shouting frightened me.

IOLAOS I was calling you to come out and see him.

ALKMENE I don't understand. See who?

IOLAOS A messenger. He says that Hyllos is back.

ALKMENE (*to* SERVANT) Then welcome, friend! You and your
                      news are welcome.
But where is Hyllos? I want him.
Why isn't he here?

SERVANT He's reviewing his troops, assigning them their positions.

ALKMENE I don't understand these military matters.   690

IOLAOS I do. Tell me.

SERVANT What do you want to know?

IOLAOS How large is the allied force under Hyllos' command?

SERVANT Strong. I don't know the exact number.

IOLAOS The Athenian generals have been informed?

SERVANT Yes. They've stationed Hyllos on the left flank.

IOLAOS Is the army drawn up in battle formation?

SERVANT Drawn up, and the sacrifice is ready.
The animals have been driven up to the front lines.

IOLAOS How near is the Argive army?   700

SERVANT Near enough so we could see Eurystheus clearly.

IOLAOS What was he doing? Marshalling his men?

SERVANT I think so. We couldn't hear the words.
But I must go, sir. I can't desert my commander.
Not when the battle's about to begin.

IOLAOS We think alike. I'm going with you. Friends help friends.

SERVANT Sir, this is no time for foolishness.

IOLAOS Foolishness? To fight in my own cause?

SERVANT Sir, you're not the man you used to be.

IOLAOS I'm still man enough to handle a spear.   710

SERVANT Man enough—provided you don't stumble.

IOLAOS One look at me, and the Argives will take cover.

SERVANT Looks don't draw blood, sir. I wish they did.

IOLAOS If I go, that's one more man on our side.
That changes the odds.

SERVANT Not very much.

IOLAOS Enough talk. It's time for action.

SERVANT Action, sir? Wishing would be more like it.

IOLAOS Call it what you like. I'm on my way.

SERVANT How can you fight without armor?   720

IOLAOS There's captured armor hanging on the temple walls.
I'll use that. If I live, I'll return it.
If I die, the god won't want it back.
Take it off the pegs and bring it here.

Exit SERVANT.

Only a coward would stay here, safe behind walls,
while others do our fighting for us.

Members of the CHORUS *approach* IOLAOS *and speak
individually to him.*

CHORUS —Time has not weakened your spirit.
Your will is as young as ever.
—But your body, your strength, are gone.
—Why these useless efforts,   730
these struggles to help our cause?
—They only hurt you,
        and do our cause no good.
Remember your age. Let these fantasies go.
—Your youth is gone. —Your strength is gone.
—Gone forever.

ALKMENE Have you lost your mind, Iolaos?
Are you deserting me and these children?

IOLAOS War is man's work. You mind the young.

ALKMENE But if you die, what will become of me?

IOLAOS Your grandchildren will take good care of you.   740

ALKMENE But what if something should happen to them?

IOLAOS The Athenians will protect you. Don't be afraid.

ALKMENE Then they're my only protection, my only hope.

149

IOLAOS Zeus knows your troubles. Zeus cares.

ALKMENE Zeus?
Zeus will never hear a word of reproach from my lips,
but Zeus knows best how he's treated me.

> ALKMENE *sits on a corner of the altar-base as the* SERVANT
> *returns from the temple, carrying armor.*

SERVANT Here's your armor. Quick, on with it.
The battle's begun. Ares hates a straggler.

> IOLAOS *struggles unsuccessfully with the armor.*

Let it be. If it's too heavy, go as you are.   750
Put it on when we reach the ranks. I'll carry it.

IOLAOS Good. Carry it, but keep it handy.
Now put the spear in my hand. Take my arm. There.
Brace me. Steady, steady.

SERVANT Are you a soldier, or a schoolboy?

IOLAOS Don't let me stumble. A bad omen.

SERVANT I wish your legs could match your zeal.

> *They begin to move off.*

IOLAOS Move! I don't want to miss the fight.

SERVANT Move, is it? You only imagine you're moving.

IOLAOS Can't you see how fast I'm going?   760

SERVANT The speed is all in your mind.

IOLAOS Wait till you see me in action.

SERVANT Action, you say.

> IOLAOS *stumbles; the* SERVANT *holds him up.*

> I wish you luck, sir.

IOLAOS I'll split their shields, I'll shatter them!

SERVANT If we ever get there. Which I doubt.

> IOLAOS *stops.*

IOLAOS Oh, gods, give me back
the strength of this good right arm of mine!
Make me what I was when I was young
and at Herakles' side, I took the city of Sparta!
Give me back my youth, let me crush that coward   770
Eurystheus now. He couldn't face my spear.
When men succeed, we wrongly assume they're brave;
we wrongly think they're clever.

> *Exit* IOLAOS *and* SERVANT. *The* CHORUS, *from watching them
> go, turns toward the audience, looking above and beyond it.*

CHORUS Now may earth, and the nightlong moon, and sunlight
shafts of the shining god whose radiance reaches down,
touching all mortals, be our messengers.
Let the word go soaring up to the high throne,
and echo through gray-eyed Athena's halls:
We're ready, ready to take up shining steel, ready to fight
for these guests of ours, for Athens,   780
    for glory, and home.

Oh, day of shame when Mykenai,
arrogant in her swelling power,
came breathing hatred against our city.
And this, too, oh Athens, would be a thing of shame,
to drive away these suppliants at Mykenai's demand.
Our ally is Zeus. We are not afraid.

151

Zeus will be just with us; and we, in what we do,
will make his meaning clear: no mortal power
      can compete with god.   790

Lady Athena, this land, this city, are yours.
You are our mother, our mistress, our shield.
Rout the arrogance of Argos! Drive this army
far from this holy place! Our justice, our courage deserve
their home, deserve to hold and keep this land forever.
Great Athena, honor and sacrifice have always been yours.
Our city remembers always the waning of the moon,
when songs of children rise and chanting voices
glorify your name, and on your windy rock
voices lift in praise, with the sound of maidens dancing   800
as the bright moon sets toward morning.

                  Enter MESSENGER, *a slave of* ALKMENE.

MESSENGER Mistress, my message is brief and glorious.
          We have beaten our enemies, their armor is our trophy.

ALKMENE Then you're welcome! Welcome. For bringing me this
            news,
          dear friend, I give you your freedom. Now free me
          from my fears. Is Hyllos alive?

MESSENGER Alive, and acclaimed a hero.

ALKMENE And Iolaos, is he alive?

MESSENGER More than alive. Thanks to the gods, he performed
          miracles.

ALKMENE Iolaos? You mean he fought bravely?   810

MESSENGER No, it was a miracle, lady.
          There he was, an old man. And suddenly he was young
          again.

ALKMENE A miracle indeed, if true.
                              But tell me first about the battle
          and how it went. I want to hear how our men won.

MESSENGER I'll tell you the whole story, from start to finish. Listen:
          There we were, drawn up in battle formation, each
                army ready, impatient to get at the other.
          Then Hyllos, dismounting from his chariot, walked out
                alone, the spears bristling all around him,
                and shouted to the Argive king: 820
          "I challenge you, Eurystheus. Leave this land at peace.
                Why risk hurting Argos, or any Argive soldier?
                Meet me yourself, alone, in single combat.
          Kill me, and the sons of Herakles are yours
                to do with what you will. But if you lose, give me
                back my father's honors. Give me back my country."
          Men on both sides cheered. They heard a brave man
                speaking, and they saw a way to avoid
                a terrible battle.
          But nothing could shame Eurystheus, nothing.   830
          There he stood, the supreme Argive commander, proven
                a coward in the presence of thousands
                of watching soldiers,
          and still he refused to accept Hyllos' brave
                and generous challenge.
          And this is the man—this proven coward—who
                wants to capture the sons of Herakles!
          So Hyllos returned to his place in the ranks,
          and the priests, knowing that the battle was inevitable,
                swiftly sacrificed the victims   840
          and drew the human blood whose shedding made
                our victory certain.
          Then the cavalry mounted their chariots,
                the foot soldiers raised their shields,
                lapping them together into a wall of iron.
          The king of Athens addressed his army
                as though he had been born a general:
          "Fellow Citizens, this mother earth that gave you life,

this sacred earth of Attika that nourishes us all,
now summons you to her defense!"   850
On the other side, Eurystheus implored his troops
not to disgrace Argos and Mykenai.
The trumpets sounded the charge, and the massed armies
crashed against each other. Lady,
try to imagine it—the clanging of metal shields,
and the sudden, final cries of dying men!
First, the shock of the Argive charge broke our ranks;
then the Argives pulled back. Then, toe to toe,
in the second charge,
they fought hand to hand, desperately, and many   860
brave soldiers died.
You could hear men shouting from both sides:
"Hold on, men of Athens!" "Sons of Argos, charge!"
"Save your country from disgrace!"
At last, with all our strength, with heavy losses,
we drove them from the battlefield.
Then, suddenly, Hyllos' chariot broke through the lines.
Iolaos hailed him down and begged to have
the chariot for himself.
So Iolaos picked up the reins and drove, fast and hard,   870
straight after Eurystheus.
That much I saw myself, but I only heard reports
about what happened next.
Iolaos had just passed Athena's sacred hill at Pallene
when he saw Eurystheus' chariot ahead,
and he prayed aloud, to Zeus and Hebe, asking
to have his youth restored for this one day,
so he could take revenge on his old enemy.
Now, this was the miracle:
Suddenly, two stars, all blazing fire, settle down   880
on the horses' yokes, hiding the chariot
in a kind of cloud, or shadow.
Men who understand these things said those stars
were Hebe and your son, Herakles.
Then, out of that darkness in the air came Iolaos—
young, his strong shoulders straining on the reins,

a man in all the vigor and freshness of his youth.
There, right by the rocks of Skiron, he caught his man
 and threw him into chains. Now,
 he is bringing Eurystheus here—   890
Eurystheus himself, once a king, the greatest man
 in Argos, almost a god; now, nothing at all,
 a prisoner of war, a man in chains.
The meaning is clear, lady, clear to all who see.
No human fortune lasts. Glory dies, greatness fades.
Call no man happy until he dies.

LEADER   Oh, Zeus,
god of victory, now I see the dawning day
whose sunlight sets me free of fear at last!

ALKMENE Oh, Zeus, you took your time, watching me suffer.
Still, I give you thanks for what has happened here. 900
I never really believed my son had become a god
among the gods in heaven. But now I know it's true.
 At last you boys will be free of your trials,
at last you'll be free of that damned tyrant,
Eurystheus. You will see your father's native city
of Argos, you will walk your native earth again,
 make sacrifice to your father's ancestral gods,
all those good things from which you've been excluded,
 boys,
to live as fugitives, your wandering unhappy lives.
(to MESSENGER) But why did Iolaos spare Eurystheus' life? 910
What was his real purpose?
        Answer me.
It makes no sense to me to take your enemy
and not take your revenge.

MESSENGER   He was thinking of you.
He wanted you to see Eurystheus yourself—
see him subject to *your* will, *your* slave.
Eurystheus, of course, resisted—so they used
force, they yoked him. He had no wish

to meet your eyes and suffer your revenge.
And now, lady, I take my leave. Remember
what you said when I started to speak—   920
that you would set me free. In matters like this,
noble tongues should keep their word.

Exit MESSENGER. *Slowly and reverently, as the* LEADER
speaks, the CHORUS *assembles to offer a prayer of gratitude.*

LEADER Sweet, the dance is sweet when with it comes
the high, clear song of the flute,
and goddess Aphrodite graces the feast.

CHORUS But sweeter than all dancing
is the coming on of good fortune, against all
          expectation,
touching the lives of those we love.
All things come to pass, all converges at the touch of Fate,
and the strong persistence of Time.   930

LEADER Oh, city, honoring the gods, your road is justice.
Never leave this path.

CHORUS Who could say of Athens
that she swerved from the path of justice? Only a fool
          could say it,
given the vindication of this day. Always, always
the gods curb the high ambitions of arrogant men, always
they make their meaning clear, for all to see.

LEADER The story is true, lady. Your Herakles is a god.

CHORUS They lied, they lied, who said
that Herakles descended to the world below,   940
his body consumed in the agony of fire.
With Hebe at his side
in a bed of shining gold, he lives forever in the golden
          house
of his father Zeus, and Hymenaios joins two gods in love.

LEADER   All things converge at last. This is the pattern.

CHORUS   They say Athena once appeared
         and rescued Herakles. And now,
         in turn, this Athens of the goddess
         has saved the sons of Herakles
         and mastered a man who chose not justice but violence.   950
         May such passionate ambition never be mine.

         *Enter Hyllos' SERVANT from the right, with two spearmen
         who escort EURYSTHEUS in chains, his upper arms bound
                                   to a yoke across his shoulders.*

SERVANT Mistress, you can see for yourself, but give me the joy
                 of saying:
         we've brought you Eurystheus. There he is.
         A sight you never thought to see. No more
         than he ever dreamed of being your prisoner,
         when, with such huge effort and expense, breathing
         arrogance, outraging justice, he marched from Argos
         to destroy Athens. But the gods prevented him,
         opposing his ambition, reversing his hopes.   960
         In gratitude for victory, Hyllos and brave Iolaos
         have set up an image of Zeus—Zeus of Victory.
         They commanded me to bring Eurystheus here,
         to delight your eyes. There's no sweeter sight
         than to see the enemy you hate in failure and defeat,
         reduced to nothing.

ALKMENE   Monster, is it really *you*?
         Has justice found you out at last?
         Turn your head and look me straight
         in the face. You hate me? Then look at me,
                 monster.

         *Spearmen grasp yoke and twist EURYSTHEUS' face toward
                                                    ALKMENE.*

157

You're *my* slave now, *I* am the master.   970
Are you the same Eurystheus—I can't believe it—
the same Eurystheus who persecuted my son—
wherever he is now—with outrage on outrage?
Was any outrage too much for you, monster?
You sent a living man down to Hades,
you dispatched him all over the world, made him kill
hydras and lions and—but I can't count out
all your atrocities.
                        And even that wasn't enough.
You hounded me, you hounded these poor children
all over Hellas. Young and old alike,   980
you made us seek asylum at the gods' altars
everywhere. But here in Athens you found
a free city, free men who weren't afraid of you.
And now you'll die as you deserve—a slave's death,
and still come out ahead. You ought to die not once,
but over and over and over. I want to see you die
one death for every wrong and cruelty you committed.

SERVANT But you can't put him to death. Not now.

ALKMENE Why else take him prisoner?
What law prevents me from putting this man to death?   990

SERVANT The Athenian authorities. They won't allow it.

ALKMENE Won't *allow* it?
Since when is it wrong to kill your enemies?

SERVANT When your enemies are prisoners of war.

ALKMENE Hyllos agreed to *that*?

SERVANT You want him to disobey the law of Athens?

ALKMENE Eurystheus deserves death. He has no right to live.

SERVANT Then we were wrong to take him prisoner.

ALKMENE Why is it wrong to punish him?

LEADER You won't find anyone to execute him now.   1000

ALKMENE I'm your anyone. *I'll* kill him.

LEADER The whole city will condemn you.

ALKMENE I love this city, who dares say I don't?
But now that this man has fallen into my hands,
no power on earth can take him from me.
Call me what you like, call me cruel,
say I'm more arrogant than woman ought to be—
but this man *must* die, and *I* will do it.

LEADER I know how bitterly you hate this man,
Alkmene. I know, I understand your feelings.   1010

EURYSTHEUS I refuse to grovel at your feet, woman,
or beg you for my life. I won't say one word
to vindicate your charge of cowardice.
I didn't choose this feud of my own free will.
I know that you and I are cousins,
that I'm related by blood to your son, Herakles.
But whether I chose this feud or not, it wasn't I
but the goddess Hera. She yoked me
with this sickness, this affliction. And once our contest
had begun, once I knew I had to persevere   1020
and fight it to the bitter end, I started planning,
scheming. Night after night I stared into the dark,
plotting to get rid of my enemies and destroy them.
I couldn't live my days and nights in terror.
And I knew your son was no cipher, but a man,
a real man. I hated him, but he was great,
a hero—I admit it. When he died,
what choice did I have? His sons hated me;
in them the father's feud remained alive.
I couldn't leave one stone unturned—murder, banishment,   1030

159

plots, anything at all, anything to end my fears.
If you had been there in my place, how would you
have acted? Would you have ignored these vicious cubs?
Oh, *you* would have been more humane, you
would have let them grow up and inherit Argos,
wouldn't you? Absurd.
                              So,
since I didn't die on the field of battle,
where I wanted to die, how do matters stand?
By all Greek law, a prisoner's person is sacred.
My death defiles my killer, it becomes a curse.   1040
This was why Athens, wisely, spared me, believing
in respect for heaven, not mindless revenge.
        You have my answer, woman. Count on it,
if you kill me, I'll take my revenge on you—
the noble vengeance of the dead.
This is how it stands with me: I have no wish to die;
and no great passion to go on living.

LEADER   Alkmene, my advice to you is this:
         do not harm this man. Athens has spared him.
         Respect that decision.   1050

ALKMENE But suppose he dies, and at the same time,
         I respect the city's decision.

LEADER   That would be best, but how can it be?

ALKMENE Simplicity itself. I put him to death,
         then surrender his body to those who come to claim it.
         Where his body is concerned, I obey the city.
         But he dies, and by dying, pays his debt to me.

EURYSTHEUS Kill me. I don't want mercy.
         But since Athens spared me, rightly and humanely
         refusing to kill a prisoner, I now offer this city   1060
         my gift, an ancient oracle of Apollo,
         which in time to come will prove a far greater blessing

than anyone now dreams. Bury my body in the place
    decreed
by Fate, before Athena's shrine at Pallene.
There, an honored guest of state beneath the Attic earth,
I will keep this city safe, forever.
                            And in future years,
when these children's children forget your kindness
and the gratitude they owe you, returning
as armed invaders, I will be their bitter enemy. Traitors,
ingrates—these are the guests you championed.   1070
Why, knowing this, did I choose to ignore the warning
of the oracle, and lead my army here to Athens?
Because I believed the goddess Hera was stronger
than any oracle, that she would stand by my side.
Pour no libations of wine or blood upon my grave.
Let it be, and I will give these children's children
a bitter homecoming. You profit doubly from my death.
It will be a blessing to Athens, and a curse on them.

ALKMENE (*to* CHORUS) What are you waiting for? You heard his
          prophecy.
Put him to death, and you assure your city's safety.   1080
Kill him. *Now.*
He shows you where your safety lies.
Alive, he's your enemy; dead, your ally, your friend.
Take him away, men. Kill him!
Throw his body to the dogs!
(*to* EURYSTHEUS)   Dead,
you'll never drive me from my father's land again.

CHORUS We agree.
        Guards, take him away.
        By our actions here,
        our kings are innocent.   1090

      ALL *exit*; ALKMENE *and the* SONS *first, then the* CHORUS
      and the SERVANT. EURYSTHEUS *and the spearmen are*
                left; they move slowly off after the others.

NOTES

The physical setting of the *Children of Herakles* is in Attika and would therefore be entirely familiar to the Athenian audience. Euripides fills the play with references to the topography of Attika and its neighboring lands, with a specific dramatic intention.

The scene is at Marathon, about twenty-three miles by road northeast of Athens. The marshy plain between Marathon and the sea was the place where the Athenians defeated the Persian army in 490 B.C. In the prologue and the first episode of the play the action, taking place before the temple of Zeus at Marathon, is continuous. It concludes with the departure of Kopreus, the Argive herald, then of Demophon to mobilize the Athenians. Between the first and second episodes, however, and between each succeeding pair of episodes in the play, much action takes place which in normal time would require days or weeks to accomplish. The audience's knowledge of the geographic setting would bring this to their minds, and would reinforce the sense of rapid motion and the pressure of events which is already implicit in the play.

Between the first and second episodes, the herald reaches the Megarian frontier from Marathon, some fifty miles away. Eurystheus marches his army into Attika and takes up his position on a mountain overlooking Marathon (probably Mt. Brilessos), a distance of about forty miles. Meanwhile, Demophon is mobilizing the Athenians from the other towns in Attika, bringing them to Marathon, preparing sacrifices, and inquiring and receiving responses from the oracles.

Between the second and the third episodes, Hyllos arrives at Marathon with an army collected outside Attika, and joins the Athenian forces. The Argives descend to the plain, and both armies array themselves for battle.

Between the third and fourth episodes the battle is fought, and the Argives are defeated. Iolaos pursues Eurystheus via Pallene, past Athens and Megara, to the Skironian rocks (a distance of over sixty miles), captures him and dispatches him back to Marathon.

Between the fourth and fifth episodes Eurystheus completes his journey to Marathon. The Athenian rulers decide that his life must be spared.

The impression of the play against its physical background is that of a swift and vivid chronicle. Each episode represents a reaction by the characters to a new and changed situation. Between the episodes, the choral odes are suspended in a time-movement which is different from that of the dramatic action.

1–76 / 1–72 *Prologue*

9 / 6 *the bond of blood* Iolaos was traditionally Herakles' nephew, and served him as charioteer and shieldbearer in his adventures. See the genealogical table at the note to **213**. Since Iolaos in the play is much older than would be possible for the nephew of Herakles, Euripides does not mention a specific kin-relationship between the two here or elsewhere in the play.

13 / 10 *under the dwindling shadow of my wings* Aeschylus had used the phrase as a metaphor for the divine protection of Athens and its citizens by Athena (*Eumenides*, 1001). The Euripidean character repeats it with conscious irony.

39–40 / 36 *when the descendants of Pandion / divided the kingdom* Choice of certain civic officers, such as archons, by lot was a feature of fifth-century Athenian democracy. The origin of the practice was often referred to the heroic age, in this case to the descendants of Pandion, the great-grandfather of Demophon and Akamas. See the genealogy at the note to **213**.

56 / 54 *mouthing your demands* Kopreus had been Eurystheus' agent in commanding Herakles to undertake his twelve labors.

74 / 69 *Men of Athens!* Iolaos' cry for help incorporates an allusion that is not translatable. Literally he says: "You who have lived in Athens too long a time." The Athenians prided themselves on being autochthonous, that is, on having been the original inhabitants of Attika, rather than migrants from elsewhere. Iolaos is saying with his characteristic ironic force that they have lived too long in one place—that is, they have become senseless clods—if they can allow such outrages to happen.

164

77–119 / 73–117 *Parodos (entrance song of the Chorus)* The Chorus enters hastily, and it is clear from the language that more than one member of the group speaks (77–81 / 73–77). We have assigned these lines alternately to the leader and to a second leader of the Chorus, following with some variation the attribution of the Budé editor. We have then continued the participation of the second leader in the dialogue until the entrance of Demophon and Akamas (122 / 120). The Budé editor assigns all the Chorus' lines after 82 / 78 to the leader alone.

85 / 80–81 *How did you get to Marathon?* The Greek refers to the Tetrapolis, an ancient confederation of four neighboring Attic towns: Marathon, Trikorythos, Probalinthos, and Oinoe. See the Note on the Geography of the Play, at the beginning of the Notes.

111 / 110 The editor of the Budé text suggests that some verses have disappeared between this and the next line. The final lines of the parodos are spoken in standard dialogue meter.

120–363 / 118–352 *First episode*

120 / 119 *Akamas* He was Demophon's brother and shared the kingship with him after Theseus' death. His entrance is puzzling, since he has no words to say and no function in the play. It may be that the tradition of this dual kingship was strong enough at Athens so that the audience would expect to see both. The twin Dioskuri, Kastor and Polydeukes, appear in Euripides' *Helen*, but only one speaks. We have indicated Akamas' departure after Kopreus' scene, but a modern production of the play would not suffer if he were removed entirely.

136 / 136 *King Eurystheus* Kopreus deliberately insults Demophon in this speech. Although he has been told that Demophon is king of Athens, and has reserved his arguments for the supreme authority, he recognizes only Eurystheus as "king" and addresses Demophon as "sir" (138 / 137).

140 / 139–40 *to take formal custody of Argive runaways* Kopreus uses a term here that was normally applied to fugitive slaves. He implies that the Heraklids are subjected to Eurystheus as their father had been, and suggests a stronger claim for their surrender than if they were free citizens. In historic times many Greek states entered into treaties with each other providing for mutual return of fugitive slaves.

191 / 186 *when our sentence was decreed, when we went into exile* Iolaos' own argument is as slippery as Kopreus'. He has already said that Eurystheus decreed the death of the Heraklids (16 / 13), and Kopreus has confirmed this (63–64 / 59–60). The Heraklids took flight in order to avoid the death sentence. Now Iolaos says that the Argives exiled them, in order to substantiate his argument that they are no longer under Argive jurisdiction. We suggest that Iolaos is perfectly conscious of what he is doing. He has seen through Kopreus' sophistry about runaways and is giving him a fine contemptuous piece of flim-flam in return.

199 / 193 *Trachis* This is a city northwest of Athens, on the coast near Thermopylai. Herakles was here with his wife Deianeira and at least some of his children when he died, as told in Sophocles' *Women of Trachis*. Trachis was accordingly the first place to which Eurystheus sent to hunt down the Heraklids. Keyx, king of Trachis, forced them to leave rather than risk war with Argos.

199 / 193–94 *some small Achaian town* All versions of the legend agree that the Heraklids visited many cities in Greece before they were given refuge in Attika, but except for Trachis none of their names has been preserved. Accordingly we do not know which Achaian town Euripides is referring to here, or whether he may be inventing some anonymous place that gave in to the Argive threats. There were two regions called "Achaia" in Greece, one in the northern Peloponnese, on the shores of the Gulf of Korinth, the other, Achaia Phthiotis, north of Trachis on the southern border of Thessaly. Neither grammar nor geography permits the identification which some editors have made of the "Achaian town" with Trachis itself.

213 / 207 *Pelops' son was Pittheus* The dynastic relations traced here and alluded to elsewhere in the play would be generally familiar to the Athenian audience. They are shown in the form of a simplified genealogical table below. The house of Danaos was the ruling house of Argos and Mykenai at the time of the play. The house of Pelops had been established in Elis in the western Peloponnese and, after Eurystheus' death, was to spread its power to Mykenai, Argos, and Sparta with the accession of Atreus and Thyestes, both sons of Pelops, and Atreus' children Agamemnon and Menelaos. The house of Erechtheus was the "autochthonous" ruling dynasty of Athens and Attica.

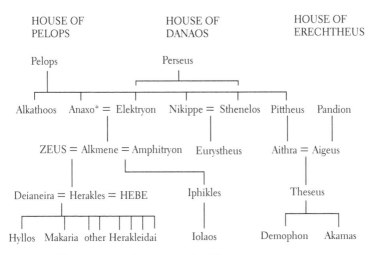

HOUSE OF
PELOPS

HOUSE OF
DANAOS

HOUSE OF
ERECHTHEUS

Pelops

Perseus

Alkathoos   Anaxo* = Elektryon   Nikippe = Sthenelos   Pittheus   Pandion

ZEUS = Alkmene = Amphitryon   Eurystheus   Aithra = Aigeus

Deianeira = Herakles = HEBE   Iphikles   Theseus

Hyllos   Makaria   other Herakleidai   Iolaos   Demophon   Akamas

* In some versions her name was Lysidike.

221 / 217 *to win the belt of the Amazon queen* Traditionally this was the ninth labor imposed on Herakles by Eurystheus. The Amazons lived on the northern shores of the Black Sea. Herakles, assisted by Theseus, Iolaos, and others, defeated them in battle, killed their queen Hippolyte and returned her belt to Eurystheus' daughter. Theseus was awarded Hippolyte's sister Antiope as his share of the spoils. By her, he was the father of Hippolytos. Demophon and Akamas were his sons by Phaidra. Euripides' *Hippolytos*, which tells the story of Phaidra's disastrous love for Hippolytos, was nearly contemporary with the *Children of Herakles*, being dated in 428 B.C. It is perhaps for this reason that Euripides does not have Iolaos mention to Demophon the specific "debt" incurred by Theseus to Herakles in this adventure—the award of Antiope.

223–24 / 218–19 *Herakles brought your father Theseus / home alive from the blind world below* Theseus and Peirithoos descended to Tartaros in an attempt to carry off Persephone, Hades' wife and queen of the underworld, as a bride for Peirithoos. They were caught and imprisoned by Hades. In the course of his twelfth labor, the capture of Kerberos (the monster who guarded the underworld), Herakles found them, and released Theseus to return with him.

231–32 / 226–27 *I beg you, / by your knees, your hands, your beard* A suppliant's touching a person's hands, knees, or beard placed that person under a personal obligation to become his protector.

267 / 257 *Then banish them. I'll seize them at the frontier* Kopreus is proposing a sordid device by which Demophon can give up the suppliants and avoid religious pollution. Demophon rejects it scornfully. But later when Alkmene proposes a similar legalism with respect to Eurystheus (**1054–55** / 1022–24), the Chorus does not object.

281 / 270 *Touch them, and you'll regret it* The physical threat to the herald should be quite real. In one version of the legend, to which Euripides is alluding, the Athenians killed Kopreus, an act of sacrilege, as he tried to drag the children from the altar. Thereafter, we are told, in certain Athenian processions young men wore black cloaks in ritual commemoration of the murder.

290 / 278 *frontiers of Megara* The Greek here refers to Alkathoos, who was king of Megara and a son of Pelops. See the genealogy at the note to **213**.

296 / 281 *your crops* This refers to warfare as it was practiced in the fifth century, and would be a particularly vivid reminder of the devastation of the Attic countryside by the Spartans at the time of the play's production.

302–10 / 288–96 The episode is divided by a short choral passage whose anapestic meter indicates excited movement, and the language rapidly becomes colloquial, even comic, as the members of the Chorus speculate on what the herald will tell Eurystheus.

312 / 299–301 We have omitted three lines following this from the translation. Most editors consider them spurious and a later insertion. They may be translated as follows:

> and to marry nobly. A man blinded by passion,
> who marries beneath him, disgusts me. His selfish lust
> leaves only shame to pass on to his children.

The lines have nothing to do with the situation of Demophon (his mother Phaidra was the daughter of Minos, the greatest king of his time), or with Iolaos' intention in this speech.

333–34 / 320–22 *when at last / I stand with Theseus* Iolaos is expecting to meet with Theseus in the underworld after his death. See the Introduction, p. 24.

339–40 / 327–28 *Most men are faint reflections / of their fathers* Iolaos makes explicit here an important theme of the play: the nobility shown by Demophon and later by Makaria, Hyllos, and Iolaos himself is unusual and not to be taken for granted. In the normal course of events, as depicted by Hesiod in his great parable of the ages of mankind (*Works and Days*, 109–201), and by many Greek writers after him, the sequence of the generations of men is a process of decay and corruption. The characters of the play, until the end, reverse this expectation.

347 / 335 *Now I'll go and mobilize the citizens* It is clear that Demophon is speaking of organizing all Athenians for war, not only the citizens of Marathon or the Tetrapolis. From here on the physical geography of the play remains Marathonian, but the civic environment is that of Athens and all Attika. See the note on geography, p. 163.

359–60 / 347–48 *My lord, now we have gods to call on, gods as great / as any gods of Argos* In Homeric fashion, Iolaos regards the individual gods here as champions in battle, fighting for their partisans. At the time of the play's production, this would be regarded as an old-fashioned and slightly quaint concept, in keeping with Iolaos' quixotic character.

364–99 / 353–80 *First stasimon* This choral lyric has a strong, tight rhythm and popular language suggesting the readiness of the Chorus to participate in military action. We have assigned alternate passages to the leader and to the Chorus, speaking antiphonally.

374 / 360–61 *Eurystheus of Argos* The Greek refers to Eurystheus as the son of Sthenelos, who was in turn the son of Perseus. See the genealogy at the note to **213**.

400–626 / 318–607 *Second episode*

413 / 394 *on high ground, along the ridge* The plain of Marathon is dominated on the west by the ridge and steep slopes of Mt. Brilessos, also called Mt. Pentelikos.

432ff. / 415ff. *Now, all over the city* These lines vividly depict a democratic leader trying to cope with dissent and with criticism of his policies, and create a highly contemporary background to the play's action.

469 / 453 *Surrender me to the Argives in their place* Iolaos' offer to sacrifice himself appears as the one lapse in his otherwise acute knowledge of himself and the situation. Demophon provides a cool and realistic appraisal of his

proposal. But it springs from the same impulses as Iolaos' later effort to join the battle, which is crowned unexpectedly with divine success.

492 / 474 With the unannounced entrance of Makaria (a name not given in our text, which identifies her simply as the Maiden), the resolution of the terrible dilemma facing Athens and the Heraklidae begins. It is not clear whether Euripides invented the story of Makaria or adapted a local tradition. The latter seems somewhat more likely. Pausanias, writing in the second century A.D., relates (I, 32, 6): "In Marathon there is a spring called Makaria, of which they tell the following tale.... An oracle declared to the Athenians that one of the children of Herakles must die a voluntary death, since otherwise they could not be victorious. Then Makaria, daughter of Herakles and Deianeira, slew herself and thereby gave to the Athenians victory and to the spring her name." Makaria's name means "fortunate" or "blessed."

611 / 593 *Nothingness is best* Makaria's rationalistic attitude toward death again sets her apart from the conventions of the other characters and specifically from Iolaos, who has given his own view of the underworld at **333ff. / 320ff.**

618–19 / 600–601 *I am afraid to speak ill-omened / words of goddess Persephone* Iolaos' deliberate abstention from reproaching the gods is characteristic and contrasts with Alkmene's vocal grudges against Zeus. See **745ff. / 717ff.** and **899 / 869.**

627–56 / 608–29 *Second stasimon* A simple ode of sympathy, urging Iolaos to temper his grief. We have divided it among individual members of the Chorus.

627–773 / 630–747 *Third episode*

727–35 / 702–8 Another short choral passage in anapestic meter; like that at **302–10 / 288–96**, we have rendered it as individual speeches.

769 / 741–42 *and at Herakles' side, I took the city of Sparta!* There is an allusion to the current war with Sparta here. Given the superiority of the Peloponnesian land forces over the Athenian, and the formidable reputation of the Spartan soldier, the idea of "ravaging" Sparta would seem as fanciful to the Athenians of the time as Iolaos' prayer for rejuvenation. Herakles' campaign against Sparta was not connected with his twelve labors, but resulted from a feud with Hippokoon, the usurping king of the city. Herakles killed Hippokoon and many of his sons, and restored Tyndareus, father of Helen and Clytemnestra, to the throne.

774–801 / 748–83 *Third stasimon* See Introduction VII for an analysis of this choral ode.

792 / 771 *You are our mother* The appellation of Athena as "mother" here is extremely unusual. Athena had no mother herself, and was always considered as the virgin goddess. Addressing her as mother of the city would lend a unique urgency to the Chorus' appeal.

796 / 777–78 *honor and sacrifice have always been yours* These lines refer to the observance of the Great Panathenaia, a festival in honor of Athena held every four years in the month Hekatombaion, corresponding to June/July. The festival culminated on the 28th, or "waning" of the month, with an all-night vigil on the Akropolis, including song and dance by young girls. This was followed the next day by the great sacrificial procession bearing to Athena's temple, the Parthenon, the *peplos* or embroidered robe as a gift for the goddess. This is the procession represented on the Parthenon frieze, now in the British Museum.

802–922 / 784–891 *Fourth episode*

841 / 822 *and drew the human blood* The lines can refer only to the sacrifice of Makaria. They appear cursory and cold, but are appropriate in the mouth of the messenger, who had seen many die that day, and was looking to his own advantage from his report.

853 / 830–31 *The trumpets* The Greek refers to an Etruscan trumpet, which was a long straight military trumpet, supposedly originating with the Etruscans of northern Italy, and copied from them by the Greeks.

874 / 849–50 *Athena's sacred hill at Pallene* Pallene, on the road from Marathon to Athens, was named after Pallas Athena, and was known in historic times as the site of a shrine of the goddess. Eurystheus was reputedly buried there. See **1063–64** / 1030–31 and note.

884 / 857 *Hebe* was the goddess of youth, daughter of Zeus and Hera. She was an important figure for Iolaos, not only for this reason, but because after Herakles' death and adoption into heaven, Hebe was given to him in marriage (see **942ff.** / 915ff.), sealing his reconciliation with Hera, his old enemy. At this point in the play, Hera abandons Eurystheus.

888 / 860 *by the rocks of Skiron* The rocks of Skiron were in other versions of the story the site of Eurystheus' death at the hands of Iolaos or Hyllos. They were on the seacoast in the territory of Megara, not far from the Isthmus of

Korinth and more than sixty miles from Marathon. Euripides' audience would, of course, be aware of the distance; his intention is to emphasize the superhuman—in fact, Herculean—quality of Iolaos' feat. Skiron had been an outlaw who robbed and killed travelers by hurling them down the rocks into the sea. Theseus, in the course of a series of heroic exploits not unlike those of Herakles, had overcome Skiron and killed him in the same manner.

901 / 871–72 *I never really believed my son had become a god* Alkmene, Herakles' mother, is the only character in the play who doubts that her son has become a god. Iolaos has stated it as a simple fact at the beginning of the play (**12 / 9–10**). Her attitude here is of a piece with her character of ignorance and resentment toward the gods.

923–51 / 892–927 *Fourth stasimon* See the Introduction VII for an analysis of this choral ode. We have suggested alternate assignment of lines to Leader and Chorus.

941 / 913–14 *his body consumed in the agony of fire* The Chorus refers to the story of Herakles' death. Consumed by the poisoned shirt of Nessos the centaur, Herakles ordered that he be placed on a funeral pyre on Mt. Oita near Trachis, and that Hyllos, his son, put the torch to it. The Chorus does not deny this part of the legend (the theme of Sophocles' *Women of Trachis*), but rather that Herakles descended to the underworld after his death.

942–43 / 915–16 *With Hebe at his side / in a bed of shining gold* For the legend of Herakles and Hebe, see the note to **884**.

946–47 / 920–21 *They say Athena once appeared / and rescued Herakles* Athena was represented as providing assistance to Herakles from his infancy, when she tricked Hera into feeding the baby Herakles at her breast, thereby ensuring his immortality. She helped him in his struggles with the Lernaian hydra (the second labor) and the Stymphalian birds (the sixth). She fought alongside him against other gods in the sack of Pylos and the duel with Kyknos, and finally received him among the Olympians after his death.

952–1090 / 928–1055 *Exodos* A closing scene extraordinary in its use of surprise.

975–77 / 949–51 *You sent a living man down to Hades, / you dispatched him all over the world, made him kill /* Alkmene refers to the twelfth, second, and first labors of Herakles. See the note to **223–24** for the descent to Hades. The

Lernaian hydra, a poisonous watersnake, and the Nemean lion were monsters infesting the environs of Argos. Herakles was assigned to kill them.

982–83 / 957–58 *But here in Athens you found / a free city, free men who weren't afraid of you* Alkmene's praise of Athens has a fateful quality. She follows it with the death sentence upon Eurystheus. The city is "free" to choose vengeance as readily as justice and compassion.

988–1010 / 961–82 The distribution of speakers in this passage is hopelessly confused in the manuscripts, but is critical to the meaning of the play. Possible speakers are the servant-messenger, Alkmene, and the leader of the Chorus. Alkmene must be the speaker who is urging Eurystheus' death throughout the passage. Her interlocutor, at least down to 995 / 967, must be in our view the servant-messenger. He is the only person to whom Alkmene could address the question: "Hyllos agreed to *that?*" The Chorus has never seen Hyllos. The servant has just come from his master's presence. So far our distribution agrees with that of the Budé editor. It is likely that 998 / 970 belongs to the servant; it is quite in character with his earlier plain-spoken attitude. But a new speaker appears to enter the dialogue at 1000 / 972, repeating the servant's prohibition against killing Eurystheus from 988 / 961. Alkmene, too, responds as though to a new speaker at 1001 / 973. Accordingly we assign 1000 / 972 and 1002 / 974 to the leader of the Chorus, departing in this from the Budé editor, who assigns both to the servant. This distribution brings the deep division in the Chorus' mind and the transformation of its role somewhat more plainly into view.

1015 / 987 *you and I are cousins* In fact they were cousins twice over, their mothers being sisters and their fathers brothers. See the genealogy at the note to 213.

1030 / 1002 *I couldn't leave one stone unturned* This appears to be the first occurrence of this durable image in Western literature.

1044–45 / 1014–15 *I'll take my revenge on you— / the noble vengeance of the dead* Eurystheus here establishes the religious titles by which his body and burial place shall be addressed, and which denote the power inherent in his sepulchre, to be explained in his next speech. The Greek *prostropaion* here means the spirit or divinity to whom a murdered victim turns to avenge his death. Eurystheus will avenge his own murder upon the descendants of Alkmene. *Gennaion*, "noble," refers to his future role in protecting Athens.

1061 / 1028 *an ancient oracle of Apollo* The Greek term for the god here is *Loxias*, a title used for Apollo, especially in his role as the god of oracles.

1063–64 / 1030–31 *Bury my body . . . / before Athena's shrine at Pallene* In other versions of the myth, Eurystheus' head was buried at Trikorythos in the Tetrapolis and his body at Gargettos, a town near Pallene. Euripides' version, however, undoubtedly reflects a real cult practice in his time, and is consistent with the theme of the play: Eurystheus as protector of Athens is to be associated with Athena's shrine. See the note to 874.

1080 / 1045–46 *assure your city's safety* The Budé editor preserves the manuscript reading here, which would give the sense: "my city," or "my descendants." This does not seem possible in the context. Even Alkmene could not twist Eurystheus' prophecy into a promise of safety for Argos or the Heraklids. We accept the more usual emendation.

1084–85 / 1050–51 *Kill him! / Throw his body to the dogs* The Budé editor, along with some others, emends the manuscript reading "dogs" (*kysi*) to "funeral pyre" (*pyri*). Alkmene's words are shocking, and the Chorus' agreement with them is revolting. But we do not think that either humane sentiment or consistency is a sufficient reason for altering the reading of the text, especially when it is Alkmene who is speaking.

1085–86 / 1052 *Dead, / you'll never drive me from my father's land again* Alkmene refers to the oracle which Eurystheus has just produced, prophesying his power after death to influence human events. Alkmene's resentment of the divine utterance and her misinterpretation of it would be in keeping with her character. It might also help to explain her command to throw Eurystheus' body to the dogs. So treated, in her mind he could not live again to plague her.

SUPPLIANT WOMEN

Translated by

ROSANNA WARREN

and

STEPHEN SCULLY

INTRODUCTION

I. COMPETING VIEWS

The story behind Euripides' *Suppliant Women* calls to mind global politics: a small and vulnerable country appeals to a major power to defend it against the barbarism of a tyrannical neighboring state. The *Suppliant Women*, which recalls a mythical event in Athenian prehistory, and one which gave the Athenians of the fifth and fourth centuries great pride, is just such a tale of three cities. In it, a helpless Argos, unable to recover her war dead fallen before the gates of Thebes, appeals to Athens for help. Driven by its defense of Greek religious law that all Hellenes, regardless of their sins, deserve burial, Athens agrees to intervene against Thebes on behalf of the dead. These disputed dead occupy the moral center of the play and, far from silent, will by the end of the drama even appear on stage.

While the Athenians of the classical period tended to look upon this benevolent and disinterested gesture as Athens' finest hour,[1] the question remains: Does Euripides echo that sentiment in his *Suppliant Women* (produced between 424 and 419 B.C.)? The Argument accompanying the play's manuscript says yes, calling this play "a praise of Athens." But the many jarring episodes and the unrelieved lament of the Chorus in the last half of the play complicate such an easy interpretation. Responding to these and other episodes, many modern readers simply dismiss the play as flawed, its tone inconsistent, its structure incoherent, its scenes overblown.

The *Suppliant Women* has not benefited from the general modern admiration for Euripides' daring dramaturgy, characterized by contradictory voices and loosely linked, quickly shifting scenes. Euripides

---

1. Cf. Herodotus, I.27; Lysias "Funeral Oration for the Men Who Supported the Corinthians" 7–10 (392 B.C., or later); Isocrates *Panegyricus* 54–58 (about 380 B.C.) and his *Panathenaicus* 168–74 (342 B.C.); Demosthenes "The Funeral Oration" 8 (perhaps 338 B.C.).

creates an energetic but restless surface, fracturing single points of perspective, as in cubist art, offering no point of stability, leaving no position, once established, untested. If such craft in other Euripidean plays is admired, even envied, by modern sensibilities, here it is chastised.

But this general condemnation is, in my opinion, wrong. This is a masterful work, a dramatic poem of formidable power in its uncompromising juxtapositions of conflicting pulls on the human psyche. In the analysis that follows I hope to give some sense of its texture and movement as well as its moral passion.[2]

II. DEMETER AND ATHENA: STRUCTURE AND TONE

Euripides' *Suppliant Women* is usually interpreted as a play of two parts. In the first, Argive supplication leads to war and Athenian recovery of the unburied dead (1–735 / 1–772); in the second part, where the mothers mourn for the dead, the tone shifts abruptly as victory brings lament and brightness gives way to despair (736–1184 / 773–1234). Although one can clearly divide the play in this way, concentration on that structure masks another ordering principle which is, in my opinion, of equal, or greater, weight. Like Euripides' *Hippolytus* of 428 B.C., which begins with a prologue by Aphrodite and draws to a close with Artemis as a *dea ex machina*, this play opens with the worship of one goddess and closes with the appearance of another from the *machina* (or perhaps on the *theologeion*, the roof of the stage building). These goddesses of competing temperaments, Demeter and Athena, frame the play and contain, to some degree, the explosive internal movements.

As in the *Hippolytus*, the two framing deities, though not entirely absent, often seem invisible in the main body of the work and even extraneous to much of the argument about whether or not to support the suppliants. In that regard, we might say that the story is complete without the gods. But the divine "presence" at either end of that drama sets the foreground world of human activity and individual tragedy against a wider background of divine forces, placing the particular and seemingly idiosyncratic in the context of generic and universal forces (or divine beings personifying those universals). Presiding over the human story of

---

2. In recent years a number of critics have begun to reappraise this neglected gem. See Rush Rehm's *Greek Tragic Theatre* (London, 1992), 123–32, and his article "The Staging of Suppliant Plays," *Greek, Roman and Byzantine Studies* 29 (1988), 263–307; Peter Burian, "*Logos* and *Pathos*: The Politics of the *Suppliant Women*," in *Directions in Euripidean Criticism*, ed. P. Burian (Durham, N.C., 1985), 129–55; Wesley Smith, "Expressive Form in Euripides' *Suppliants*," *Harvard Studies in Classical Philology* 71 (1966), 151–70.

supplication and retrieval of the dead, Demeter and Athena represent different and almost irreconcilable aspects of the world: one concerned with fertility, life, death, and renewal; the other with political discourse, military action, and Realpolitik. As seldom as these realms intersect, there is a moment in the play when, in the figure of Aithra, they seem to merge.

Critics of this play rarely mention Demeter, no doubt in part because they are inclined to read rather than to see ancient tragedy. But the opening tableau of sacrifice at the altar to Demeter and Persephone at Eleusis is more than a convenience for the central plot. Aithra is honoring Demeter and her daughter at the annual Panhellenic festival in late October, called the Proerosia, for the first fruits of the year's harvest.

The staging of the opening scene calls attention to the festival. At our temporal and cultural distance from the original, we do not know if tragedy began with the entrance of the participants or at the first spoken words. But evidence in the text of the *Suppliant Women* suggests the following stage directions. Before any words are spoken, Aithra enters with temple attendants from the temple doors. They are robed in ceremonial white, appropriate for the rite they are about to perform. When Aithra moves to the orchestra to take her seat at the altar to Demeter and her daughter, the audience would expect the prologue to begin. But, in a gesture unique among all surviving tragedies, the Chorus (fifteen women), accompanied by its own attendants, enters *in silence* from stage left (Thebes). In its company are Adrastos and the sons of the Dead. Adrastos interrupts Aithra as she is sacrificing—all this without words—and then turns with the sons to the stage near the temple doors. The mothers, dressed in dark "robes not meant for festival" (96 / 97) and with heads shorn in mourning, surround Aithra in a circle of suppliant boughs, in a manner "not reverent...but driven by need" (64–65 / 63). The interruption of Demeter's festival threatens to bring pollution on all of Attica. Only after this tableau does Aithra speak her prologue, explaining the significance of the actions which have just occurred. Like an overture before an opera, this pantomime before the prologue establishes potential tensions between the unfulfilled burial rites and the interrupted fertility rites, each rite making its own demands on the earth and the community.[3]

But in spite of the obvious contrast between worshipers and mourners, the Argive women and Demeter in her festival share points of common experience. Like the mourning women, Demeter is a mother who has

3. For an excellent account of this tableau, see Peter Burian, "The Play before the Prologue: Initial Tableaux on the Greek Stage," in *Ancient and Modern: Essays in Honor of Gerald Else*, ed. J. H. D'Arms and J. W. Eadie (Ann Arbor, Mich., 1977), 79–94.

suffered loss. But unlike her mortal counterparts, Demeter has lived through that grief to experience renewed life and restoration, both in the form of the "death" and rebirth of her daughter Persephone and in the form of nature's annual dying and renewal associated with the Proerosia. There is, then, an implicit harmony, as well as dissonance, between the fore-grounded mortal concern for retrieval of the unburied dead and the body's return to the earth (517–21 / 531–36), and the backgrounded "setting" of nature's renewal and Demeter's mysteries (cf. 174 / 173). Characteristic of Euripidean drama, a pattern ultimately joyous on the divine level will be experienced as grief by mortals.

The earth, invoked over and over in Aithra's opening, reveals how many different ways a single word can be interpreted in this play: earth as the source and nurse of life, as its final resting place, and in political terms as the "homeland of Argos" or the "land of Pittheus." A single concept opens up a whole panorama of oppositions that the play will explore, human and natural, male and female, political and religious. But here we need to concentrate on the first line of the play, "Demeter, hearth [*hestia*]-holder of the Eleusinian land" (in the Greek). Demeter's name not only begins the play but introduces a cluster of values significant throughout: earth and mother, soil and place, and a domestic orientation (*hestia*).

Athena will aggressively reorient such concerns at the play's end. Severely criticized by many readers for her inhumanity and for her demand of blood vengeance, Athena, as Athena Polias, informs Theseus that he must perform sacrifices to cement formal treaties between Athens and Argos and then bury the sacrificial knife in a corner of the earth (1157 / 1206–7) near the burial mounds in Eleusis. If the Argives ever march against Athens, she informs him, this instrument will rise up out of the earth in vengeance. A far cry from Demeter's Proerosia, in Athena's political vision the earth's produce is a "biting knife" (1156 / 1206), its harvest political, military, and bloodthirsty.

III.   MOTHER AND SON: AITHRA AND THESEUS

Aithra, who appears in the first third of *Suppliant Women*, is one of Euripides' greatest visionary characters. Like many women in Greek tragedy, she controls the movement of the scene of which she is a part. While the male figures from Argos (Adrastos and the sons of the Seven) are relegated to the stage in prone mourning positions, she dominates the theater from her seat in the orchestra at the altar, burning cakes of thanks-giving, "bound, but not bound, by (suppliant) boughs" (30–31 / 32). Both Aithra and the Proerosia festival appear to be Euripidean inventions in the story of Argive supplication of Theseus. In other versions of this myth, the Argive women supplicate Theseus directly or are silent as Adrastos speaks to Theseus on their behalf. By adding Aithra to the myth, Euripides is able to set up a contrast between an initial supplication between mothers and a subsequent one between two (male) heads of state, a distinction marked visually as one occurs in the orchestra, the other on stage. Aithra's immediate compassion for the mothers (gray-haired like her) and her reverence for their cause serve as foil for the failed supplication between Adrastos and Theseus. If Aithra responds to the mothers with a sense of religious urgency (she sends for her son, hoping that he will "discharge our obligation through some deed / the gods approve" [**37–38** / 39–40]), Theseus responds to Adrastos with dispassionate, and then antagonistic, reasoned discourse. The juxtaposition of the two supplication scenes can be compared to the point and counterpoint of a fugue, as if the renewed supplication repeats the first exposition in a new key, now of male voices from the stage, expanding and opposing the established themes of female voices in the orchestra.[4]

The new tone is immediately evident when the young Athenian king turns to the aged Argive ruler: "Uncover your head, and stop those groans. / Nothing can be accomplished without speech" (**112–13** / 111–12). For Theseus, speech is a gift from the gods which, making the faculty of understanding possible, sets men (of the polis) apart from beasts. Speech for Theseus will take two forms: a rapid-fire interrogation as he tries to get to the bottom of things (Why did you attack Thebes? Did you have divine backing?), followed by a full-blown rhetorical confrontation wherein each protagonist delivers a speech constructed according to the standard rules of forensic argumentation.

In his debate, Theseus offers a theodicy (much criticized by modern scholars for its supposed irrelevance), in which he pontificates about a divinely benevolent and moral universe. Confident in this model of the cosmos, he lectures the older Adrastos on the realities of political conflict and good forms of government, fully aware that mortals must be on guard against those who (like Adrastos) think they "are wiser than all the gods" (**219** / 218). Prudence requires that Theseus not support Adrastos in an alliance. At no time in his confrontation with Adrastos does Theseus acknowledge the suffering of the Argive mothers or the rights of the unburied dead. If the king's reasoning sounds pompous and irrelevant, as critics complain (but see commentary at **196–219**), it is

---

4. For a fine application of this analogy to Euripidean dramaturgy, see Anne Michelini, *Euripides and the Tragic Tradition* (Madison, Wis., 1987), 119; see also Cedric Whitman, *Euripides and the Full Circle of Myth* (Cambridge, Mass., 1974), 113.

meant to. But only in part. There is something boyish about Theseus—on the verge of manhood, skilled in hunting boar but untried as a king—whose theories about government are still more abstract than tempered by experience.

This play will prove to be Theseus' coming of age, his battle initiation into manhood. In a pattern unique in the stories of extant tragedy, and almost unparalleled in the surviving stories of Greek mythology, his mother will be the one to show him the way. Though Theseus had been unmoved by a direct choral supplication (when the Chorus moved temporarily to the stage [272–83 / 271–85]), he is taken aback by his mother's wails and tears (289–90 / 292). As a woman, Aithra is reluctant to interfere in the affairs of state, as she herself says, but, compelled by her sense of what is good and noble (*kalon*), she can no longer hold back. In one of the great speeches of the play mediating the antitheses of the opening scene—emotional versus rational, personal versus political, female versus male, old versus young—Aithra redefines Theseus' sense of what it means to be a hero, a king, a citizen of Athens, and a member of the whole Panhellenic community.

Her words deserve close scrutiny. Afraid that her son has tripped up (*sphallēi* [300 / 302]), no less than Adrastos did when he helped Polynices (see also 157 / 156), Aithra first speaks of religious matters, correcting and expanding her son's understanding of gods and law: "My son, first and foremost, it's the will of the gods / you have to consider" (298–99 / 301–2). Theseus' theodicy is deficient in at least one respect: honor demands that he stop "those bandits who confound the sacred laws / of all Greece [*nomima pasēs Hellados*]. All civilized order rests / on this; the safekeeping of laws [*nomoi*]" (308–10 / 309–12). This larger appeal is cast within a personal and civic one. Dismissing her own maternal fears, Aithra tells Theseus that it is time for him to move from adolescent, and Heraclean heroics—the hunting of wild boars, "a trifling labor" or sport, as Aithra calls it (*phaulos ponos* [313 / 317])—to manly ones. Aithra's vision of true heroism binds personal identity ("My son, if you are indeed / my son, don't shame yourself" [316–17 / 320]) and personal honor (303 / 306) with civic action and civic glory ("you wouldn't want it said that you hung back, / afraid, when you could have wrested the crown / of fame for the city" [311–13 / 314–16]). Under the pressure of her language, heroic *ponos* is fused with civic *ponos*: "In her labors (*ponoi*)," Aithra exclaims, "[Athens] soars in strength and pride" [320 / 323].

Challenged by his mother, Theseus defends his reasoning and judgment against Adrastos (330–32 / 334–36), but accepts Aithra's larger vision: "I cannot shun this labor [*ponos*]. / What would my enemies say of me if you, / who gave me birth and who still fear for me, / are the first to bid me to take up such labor [*ponos*]? / I'll do it" (**338–42** / 342–46). Personal and state duties formally converge when Theseus announces upon his return from Athens that the people of his city were "more than pleased to accept this labor" (*ponos* [**389** / 397]).

Adrastos, we hear in the prologue, asked Aithra to make the work (of burial) common to Theseus and Athens (**26–27** / 27–28). Like *ponos*, the word *koinon* (common) is important in the play as it joins the communal lament of the grievers, the shared burden of burial, and the equalizing experience of Hades to the laws which are common to all those within a city (**415** / 422, **423** / 430–31) as well as to those linking states (**523** / 538). It is just such a fusion that Aithra achieves through her compassion and understanding of an enlightened heroism, joining people and perspectives that earlier seemed to have little in common. Theseus' move down off the stage into the orchestra to join hands with his mother visually symbolizes Aithra's success in fulfilling Adrastos' wish. The "soprano" and "tenor" voices, as it were, competing contrapuntally from the orchestra and the stage, appear at this point to have achieved unexpected harmony. The force of this tragedy, however, will be that, despite Aithra's character and Theseus' personal maturation (still to be seen in full), the discovery of "common ground" will fail.

IV. THESEUS: WORD AND SPEAR

After Aithra's speech and Theseus' change of heart, we witness a new harmony of views, as Chorus and actors, orchestra and stage appear to share a common language and common goals (**361–735** / 365–772). So the mothers sing of *eusebēs ponos* (holy labor), "[which] brings an honored prize / to our cities, and gratitude [*kharis*] / "forever" (**369–71** / 373–74), and they adjure Theseus to "Take care: don't stain the laws / of mortals" (**374–75** / 378). One mark of this harmony is the greatly reduced role of the Chorus over these four hundred lines. There are only two odes in this section, and the first is among the shortest in all Greek tragedy (**361–76** / 365–80). Both serve to provide space between related events: the first allows Theseus to leave for Athens to consult with the people (*dēmos*) and muster an army; the second acts as a bridge between Theseus setting out for war against Thebes and the news of his victory (**578–607** / 598–633). The "bridge" effect of these songs conveys the sense of a seamless flow of events as the mothers and the city work toward a common end.

Echoing his earlier debate with Adrastos, Theseus in the second episode enters into a struggle of words (**421** / 428) with an older herald from Thebes. Euripides surely pokes fun at the young king's compulsive need to argue with his seniors, even when as here his elder is a "clever herald" from the enemy camp. But behind that fun is a more serious note, revealed in part by the reverse order of the new argument as compared to the first debate. Whereas the first "contest" proceeded from cross-examination to sustained set pieces and eventual successful persuasion, this confrontation begins with formal debate and degenerates into one-line exchanges, anger, and insult. The self-conscious repetition and reversal are deliberate, designed to reveal the inability of words to settle certain hostilities. Euripides makes the point yet again when Athens, with its army before the Cadmean Gates, tries a second time to persuade by diplomacy rather than by war. Creon responds in silence, perhaps the most articulate marker of language's impotence to settle disputes between states. Athena's impatience with verbal promises at the end of the play, though much criticized by later readers, surely derives from a superior wisdom about the power of language to control military passion.

Theseus' debate with the Theban Herald about the relative merits of democracy and tyranny (394–452 / 399–462), has also been criticized as dramatically irrelevant. Far from irrelevant, the debate displays before our eyes that in a democracy small men enjoy equal footing with the rich and powerful. In Theseus' words: "when a wealthy citizen does wrong, / a weaker one can criticize, and prevail, / with justice on his side. *That's* liberty" (427–29 / 435–38). This characteristic of an idealized Athens is crucial for the city and to the play itself as we have witnessed a woman, not even a citizen, unable to keep silent, change the course of Athenian history and the narrow view of its leading figure. When the Theban Herald echoes Theseus' earlier sentiment that it would be impious to help those who are themselves impious (483–93 / 494–505; cf. 158 / 157, 229–31 / 229–31), the Athenian ruler answers by repeating the lesson he has learned from Aithra. But in so doing he expands upon the reasons his mother had so succinctly given (cf. 504–45 / 517–63 to 298–327 / 301–31, esp. 512–26 / 526–41 to 308–10 / 309–12) and reveals in that "repetition" a new and broader awareness of his own humanity: "Now, let the corpses be hidden in the earth / from which each came to light; let soul release / to air, body to earth. We do not own / our bodies, but are mere tenants there for life, / and earth that nursed them takes them back again" (517–21 / 531–36). Not only has Theseus learned from Aithra, but he seems to have gained an insight into the rhythms implicit in Demeter's festival itself. Far from being irrelevant, Theseus' theorizing sets the Demeter themes into a new political context and shows in the *agōn* of debate how the ideal city balances the claims of the living and the dead.

But it is equally crucial to realize that this debate is not an unabashed praise of Athens. The Herald's questions about democracy's vulnerability are never fully refuted. At the time of this play, demagogues in Athens did, as the Herald says literally in the Greek, "puff up the citizens by words" (405 / 412). With new self-made leaders like the leather merchant Cleon, the rope seller Eucrates, and the lamp maker Hyperbolus, the Herald's words have bite: "it's a disease, when, fresh / from his ditch, some dirt farmer bridles the mob / and drives it with the witchery of his tongue" (416–18 / 423–25). Theseus' quip, "Well, what a clever herald!" (419 / 426) is funny but feeble. His taunt that the Thebans have little to fear from the buried dead ("Can children in earth's womb / beget revenge?" [529–30 / 545–46]) is equally insufficient and will be refuted by the play's end.

The Herald's fear that all Greece is mad for war (474 / 485) is even more significant. If he as an emissary from unjust Thebes is easy to dismiss, his words are not. When, later in the play, Adrastos grieves at the sight of the retrieved corpses and cries out for peace, we cannot but be deeply moved (904–9 / 949–54):

> Tormented race of man,
> why do you take up spears, and bring down death
> upon each other? Stop! Leave off those labors,
> guard your city in peace. The needs of life
> are small. You should provide for them
> gently, without such gruesome labor.

The heroic labors (*ponoi*) which Aithra encouraged, Adrastos here denounces. Civic action is suddenly less glorious when seen in the face of personal anguish; positions once thought noble are rephrased in a different key. Such juxtaposition vibrates at the heart of Euripides' contrapuntal art and it is to his credit that he does not try to soften, or resolve, the strain of competing values.

Tested in war, Theseus has proven himself every bit the hero in a civic cause and with civic moderation. Not only does he win the day but, just as impressively, he exhibits self-restraint in victory. But if Adrastos responds to war with a new pacifism, the experience of battle has transformed Theseus in a different way—the sententious and neophyte king has been humanly touched by war and by death "common" to all (760 / 797). Far from the figure who said to Aithra "You shouldn't suffer their grief" (289 / 291), Theseus, washed like the other combatants in "rivers of blood" (658 / 690), feels an affection (*ēgapa* [728 / 764]) for the war dead whose bodies he washes with his own hands and prepares for cremation. The verb (*agapaō*), found only in Euripides among the tragic poets and only in the context of loved ones caring for the corpses of nearest kin (a father for a son's body, a wife for a husband's), testifies to the bond of kinship Theseus feels for the dead.

When not performed by family members, the washing of the wounds and cremation of the body are normally associated with slaves, as Adrastos says in the Greek a "bitter" labor even for them (724 / 762). Few critics seem to have appreciated the full force of this passage. Adrastos says such work would be "a terrible burden and shame" (730 / 767) for Theseus. But for the young man the experience of battle appears to have obliterated class distinctions, so king and slave are one and the same, and the common lot makes us all a "family." By calling these tasks that Theseus undertakes for the dead a labor (*ponos* [725 / 763, 893 / 939]), Euripides continues to examine and redefine the meaning of this word. Confined neither to the trifling *ponos* of boar hunts nor to the civic labor of this war, in this new usage *ponos* joins, or makes common, hero and slave. That grounding of the heroic in the necessities of mortality is not unlike war itself with its "dust storming up to heaven" (656 / 687–88).

V. VICTORY AND LAMENT

Even this unique form of "heroism" proves unstable and short-lived. In the last third of the drama, where the rituals of mourning are reenacted step by step, changes in mood are sudden and sharp and the meanings of words shift abruptly. Exposing the contradictory emotions associated with public funerals, the *Suppliant Women* juxtaposes savage grief with civic eulogy, old with young, personal pain with forms of "heroism." In response to the Athenian recovery of their sons, the Argive women lament: "My joys woven with sorrow" (741 / 778). If glorious for Athens (742–44 / 779–81), for the mothers to look upon "my sons' corpse" is a "horror and beauty— / longed-for, unhoped-for day, / seen at last, greatest in tears" (745–48 / 782–85) (the use of the first-person singular intensifies the sense of pain felt individually). Demeter-like in her despair at the loss of a child, each mother grieves over the "children torn from my arms" (756 / 793).

The outpouring of grief intensifies when Adrastos brings out the bodies. Though most commentators argue that he leaves the bodies in the orchestra, the pathos of the scene is increased, as we shall see, if they are carried to the stage in sight of the mothers but beyond their reach. The *kommos*, or lyric exchange, between an actor and the Chorus (and between orchestra and stage [757–96 / 794–837]) expresses the pain that binds the two areas of the theater together. In this scene, tragedy verges toward opera and discourse toward song as sounds frequently break beyond the boundaries of coherent speech. Fifteen choral members with seven children of the dead in the orchestra and Adrastos on stage with ten (or fourteen) Athenian pallbearers carrying five biers, close to forty people in all, make up this spectacle in one of Euripides' most elaborate theatrical displays. A cry that Adrastos begins (on stage), the Chorus ends (in the orchestra) (e.g., ADRASTOS: *iō, iō* CHORUS: *tōn g'emōn egō* [768 / 805]; ADRASTOS: *epathomen, ō*...CHORUS: *ta kuntat'algē kakōn* [770 / 807]). The call and response between king and Chorus allow for a harmony in grief, but it is one which will be shattered by a new dissonance.

The tone of the mourning changes with Theseus' reentry as the king transforms remembrance of the dead from dirge to eulogy. Though patient while the Argive mothers and Adrastos grieve, he wants Adrastos to use the moment for civic objectives, seeing in the funeral an opportunity for teaching young citizens lessons in the meaning of virtue and (military) excellence. Delivering an encomium, Adrastos concludes this oration with the following maxim: "Noble upbringing begets nobility / ...high courage [*euandria*] / can be taught, just as a babe is taught / to speak and listen to things he doesn't know" (865–69 / 911–15). How can we understand these long periodic sentences, in their measured cadences and praise of reasoned speech, coming from a man who moments before was unable even to utter articulate sounds? How are we to reconcile this Adrastos with the man who recently concluded from Athens' victory that man lacks even the power of thought (700–701 / 735–36)? Both before and after the funeral oration Adrastos laments that a wiser race would use reason, not the sword, to resolve differences (710–13 / 748–51, 905–9 / 950–54). Does Euripides mean for us to read the teachability of courage ironically? The irony seems most apparent when the Argive dead are expressly praised for the qualities they expressly lacked. In particular, Capaneus, hubristic and justly avenged by Zeus as the Herald (484–89 / 496–501) and the Chorus (499–500 / 511–12) have already said earlier in the play, is now praised for moderation: "He set his sights / no higher than a poor man" (821–22 / 862–63). How do we reconcile such obvious contradictions within the play? Poor craftsmanship or deliberate strategy? The praise seems stereotypic, as if the occasion of public remembrance, rather than fact, determines language. The obvious discrepancy between truth and funerary rhetoric in the case of the Argive heroes shows vividly how public praise absorbs the dead to civic need, and, as in the earlier, discordant versions of democracy, reveals discrepancy between the ideal and the actual as part of the play's structure.

The surprising transition from *kommos* to public funeral oration may again be understood as a fuguelike interplay of voice and counter voice, showing paradoxical perspectives of the living toward the war dead. Rather than being disingenuous, Adrastos' change of mood from lyric grief to public praise reveals how one in mourning tries "not unwillingly" (817 / 857, literal translation) to find something uplifting, ennobling, inspirational in pain. While we sense irony in the gulf between the actual deeds of the dead and the clichés designed to instruct the living, there is an even greater irony in the clash between public need and personal grief. That tension Euripides explores for the remainder of the play.

As soon as Adrastos finishes his oration with the maxim quoted above, the mothers sing a short, but powerful, iambic strophe of seven lines (872–78 / 918–24). Oblivious to the words of public praise, they force us to see the dead again in terms of personal and maternal loss. Echoing their earlier invocations of the labors of birth and loss (86 / 83–85), they refer to the pains of childbirth as labors (*ponoi*) and hardship (*mokhthon athlias*) (876–77 / 920–22), and further force us to see a woman's world as an alternative heroism centered around an identity with the house and procreation rather than with military courage and city glory. Medea, in Euripides' play of the same name (431 B.C.), similarly suggests that the labors of childbirth—and the female role in the house—greatly exceed the dangers (and values) of conventional Greek views of heroism: "Men say of us that we have a peaceful time living at home, while they go to war. How wrong they are! I would much rather stand three times in the front of battle than bear one child" (248–51).

Theseus speaks next, picking up where Adrastos left off, as if the choral interlude had not occurred. The beginning of his recitation, "and furthermore" (*kai mēn* [879 / 925]), makes a smooth transition from Adrastos' praise of the five whose bodies have been recovered and Theseus' remembrance of Amphiaraos and Polynices. This is orchestration at its best: the male voices from the stage in measured iambic trimeters, the mothers' voices from the orchestra in quickened, often abbreviated iambic dimeters.

Before the funeral oration, the mothers had asked to embrace their sons, a request that Adrastos appeared to have granted (777–79 / 815–17). Apparently they never reached, or touched, the corpses on stage as is evident when Adrastos over a hundred lines later says to the Chorus: "Go, bereaved mothers, approach your children" (895 / 941). Without warning or compromise, Theseus prevents this long-awaited contact. Shocked, Adrastos asks: "What do you mean? Shouldn't mothers touch their children?" (897 / 943). But he then backs down: to Theseus, "you win" (literally translated); to the Chorus, "Be brave, and stay there. / Theseus is right. When they've burned on the pyre, / you can embrace their bones" (901–3 / 947–49). Theseus has appropriated the women's cultural right for himself and for the city, personally washing the bodies of the dead and requesting that the mourning of the dead serve a civic purpose.[5] Are we to understand his rationale ("[The mothers] would die, seeing the mutilation" [898 / 944]) as a civic desire to curtail the impassioned and disorderly laments of women and the house (*oikos*)? I think so. In concert with his other actions, Theseus' prohibition appears as an attempt to define kinship civically and to suppress personal cries of pain with a more verbally self-controlled, pedagogic mourning ritual. The competition between voices is becoming more focused, exposing a deep-seated cultural struggle between the competing claims of city and house, male and female. If I am right, that polyphony is visually accentuated when the mothers about to mount the stairs to the stage are abruptly stopped by Theseus. Aithra's union of reason and emotion, city and family is a thing of the past as public and private grief pull in different directions.

The next episode—among the most daring and experimental in the entire Euripidean repertoire for its complete liberty from legendary material, its raw emotionality, its unannounced introduction of new characters, its fresh development ("inadequately motivated," critics moan)—is linked to the preceding ode by meter and theme. Bride of the hubristic Capaneus and the daughter of Iphis, Evadne enters from a cliff overhanging Eleusis high above the stage. Dressed in wedding clothes, she reveals in an arialike monody (in Aeolics, like the previous ode) that she intends to leap from the cliff into her husband's pyre. As the song draws to a close, Iphis rushes in from Argos, searching for his daughter. In front of her father's eyes, indifferent to his pleas, Evadne leaps to her death (into Capaneus' pyre), making this and Ajax's suicide in Sophocles' play the only deaths "seen" by an audience in Greek tragedy.

But how successful is the experiment? Thematic concerns motivate the scene. By exclusively focusing on the family and introducing a fresh death, the scene clearly revives and expands the theme of parental anguish. The collective pain of the mothers is concentrated on a single person; parental grief, conventionally expressed by women, finds a male voice. Like the mothers, Iphis claims that if he had it to do over again, he would have neither a son (Eteoklos, killed at Thebes) nor a daughter. Now in this play both mothers and a father look forward only to death.

Seeing her suicide as a marriage, Evadne asserts that she is going to join her husband in Persephone's marriage chambers (translated literally) (973 / 1022), a union she imagines with erotic anticipation: "melting

5. Nicole Loraux sees a further appropriation, in the Athenian State Theater taking over the song-making traditions of lamentation; see *Les Mères en deuil* (Paris, 1990).

in radiant flame, / my body will mingle with yours,...loved husband, flesh to flesh" (970–72 / 1019–21; cf. 960–61 / 1007–8, 1023 / 1071). The word translated as marriage chamber (*thalamos*) can equally well mean funeral chamber, as it does elsewhere in Euripides, easily joining themes of marriage and death in Evadne's mind. Evadne's reference to Persephone's marriage further evokes, rather parodies, the Demeter/Persephone story: the daughter desires marriage and actual death rather than life with her parent, and the daughter is oblivious to parental pain.

The Evadne story also reverses the family pattern in the opening scenes in which a mother, appealing to reason and an enlightened sense of human suffering, was able to prevent a son from wrongheaded action. Evadne, probably played by the Theseus actor (while Iphis is most likely played by the Adrastos actor), subverts, or perverts, and parodies much that Theseus has come to symbolize: contrary to the king's contest of words, Evadne engages in a prolonged, self-absorbed monologue; she speaks in a "riddle" (1016 / 1064) rather than in language (translated literally) "that makes the faculty of reason possible" (204 / 203–4); contrary to Theseus, she has little desire to understand or to be understood by Iphis ("My plans would anger you if you heard them, / so I can't tell you, Father" [1002–3 / 1050–51]). Most perverted is Evadne's sense of heroism. Life, rather than action, is laborious for her (*ponos* [957 / 1005]). Her death leap is "for glory" (*eukleia* [967 / 1015]); she claims a glorious triumph in coming to Eleusis (*kallinikos* [1011 / 1059]; the word echoes Adrastos' invocation of Theseus at 114 / 114); dying with her husband is an act of excellence (*aretē* [1015 / 1063]). Such language more properly evokes memory of Homeric heroes on the battlefield or Theseus' courage at Thebes. If the Chorus moves toward a heroism contrary to that of male values, this female imitation of a male heroism is narcissistic rather than ennobling, self-absorbed rather than altruistic in its self-sacrifice. As with the funeral oration, the disparity between true heroism and the rhetoric of heroism is deeply unsettling.

Evadne's position high above the stage visually testifies to her detachment from human sensibilities; the distance between her and Iphis down below (probably in the orchestra) accents the gulf between them. Contrary to the union of Theseus and Aithra, symbolized by the touching of hands, Evadne in farewell to her father says: "It's useless. You...can't take my hand" (1021 / 1069). While her manic wrenching of the heroic ideal cannot undo the significance of Theseus' achievements and nobility of soul, her actions do force us to question the cost in human terms of all acts of glory. We cannot help but ask whether Adrastos was not right that humankind should strive for a life—short as it is—of peace, free from strife (905–10 / 950–54).

Sustaining the intensity from the last episode, the ashes of the dead, cremated during the Evadne/Iphis scene, are carried into the theater and onto the stage. Imitating the first *kommos* between Adrastos and the mothers, the sons of the Seven (silent throughout the play until this moment) and the mothers lament over their loved ones (in the play's final *kommos* [1065–1116 / 1114–64], where iambics are used again); once more, the male voices come from the stage, the female from the orchestra, but the repetition is designed to point up difference. When the corpses first appeared, the aged Adrastos and the gray-haired mothers joined in a common grief; but the ashes stimulate extreme responses, diametrically opposed. Though the text here is quite corrupt in places, the general shape of the scene is reasonably clear.

Worn down by grief, the mothers praise pacifism (1099–1101 / 1148–49). By the play's end they abandon their earlier interest in civic *ponos* and *kharis* (369–71 / 373–74), now imagining alternative and specifically female meanings for these words of war and heroism. Remembering their breast-feeding and maternal sleepless nights, they ask (translated literally): "Where is my burden [*ponos*] of children? where is the reward [*kharis*] of childbirth?" (1086–87 / 1135–36). The sons of the Seven, on the other hand, oblivious to this female language, aspire to an ancient, even ancestral, form of virtue: "Father, do you hear your children mourn? / Will I ever avenge your death with my own shield? / May that day come for your child" (1094–96 / 1143–45). The sons' prolonged silence so dramatically broken after a thousand lines is Aeschylean in technique, and chilling. At the end of the play, the young speak for the first time only to clarify and deepen the tragic themes of the play as Adrastos' foolhardy war leads to further senseless war. The new voices confirm that the living have every cause to fear the power of the dead. As the Herald feared, a madness for war, not reason, is in the Greek blood. The sons, unquestionably, show that for Euripides the legend exposes the permanent impulse toward aggression and revenge and the fragility of calls for peace and renewal. The sons, and not the weary mothers, will "hold their noble fathers' bodies / in both hands" (1118–19 / 1166–67; cf. 1075 / 1124). The language of orchestra and stage could not be further apart.

VI.   COMPETING CLOSURES

This is a play of apparent resolutions and deep irresolution. In a short farewell between Theseus and Adrastos, harmony again appears to be restored as the play seems to conclude. The Athenian king ends by saying that the Argives "must *remember* these acts of kindness [*kharis*]," passing on "from son to son...these same words...to honor our city, enjoining them to remember what you have obtained from me. Zeus and the gods above are witness" (translated literally) (**1121–27** / 1169–75; emphasis added). Acknowledging Athenian beneficence and nobility, the Argive leader in return promises "undying thanks" (*kharis* again [**1130** / 1178]). *Kharis* has been restored to its political sense. Everlasting memory has been requested and promised. Words have been trusted to seal the bond. Zeus has been invoked as witness. Assuming the play is over—bodies recovered, cremations performed, gratitude expressed—the principals, Chorus, and many mutes start to move toward the two exits.

But any sense of resolution is lost when Athena, appearing abruptly from high above the stage, halts the exodus. Her intervention is swift and impatient: "Listen, Theseus, to Athena's words" (**1135** / 1183). Although this epiphany is criticized by many as harsh and unnecessary, it is crucial to the play both formally and thematically. In a world where words have shifting meanings and in which emotions for revenge are no less strong than cries for peaceful coexistence, Athena has little tolerance for verbal promises of gratitude. She demands an alliance with Argos which is anchored by sworn oaths, sacrificial blood, and sacred relics, not verbal avowals of *kharis*. A tripod, not words, will serve as physical *reminder* (**1155** / 1204). She further demands a written record, not verbal memory; a tripod in Apollo's shrine at Delphi, not an invocation of Zeus, as divine witness. Remote and indifferent to human suffering (not unlike Evadne), Athena reminds us of the stern laws of a political reality. In her world, civic order demands that mutable words be made fast in bronze and infused with divinity (Apollo's shrine and sacrifical blood).

For the second time in the play, Theseus has been rebuked by a woman. In both instances, he acquiesces, but here the goddess is criticized by many as being "repulsive" for vindicating vengeance, or as being reprehensible for debasing Theseus' generous altruism and enlightened humanism, or as being "morally inferior to men" showing that the gods are neither "just" nor "kindly." But when were the ancient gods ever (simply) just or kindly? If less sensitive than humans to suffering, Athena bestows a divine form upon the grim and uncompromising realities of war and civic order. She is the necessary complement to Demeter and the pacific spirit that takes shape in *Suppliant Women*. As in *Hippolytus*, human beings are torn by competing goddesses who impose conflicting necessities on the human psyche.

Not a play of sublime language, and neither Aeschylean nor Sophoclean in lyric density, Euripides' *Suppliant Women* is a play of uncompromising force; in a sense its very refusal of poetic embellishment constitutes its peculiar power. Euripides' refusal to resolve competing claims upon the human psyche makes this a particularly painful work.

Neither Athena nor Demeter prevails as the play tests the shifting weights of words and contradictory pulls upon our public and private selves. The *Suppliant Women* may rightly be criticized for its endless twists and reversals which could prove difficult to present on the modern stage. The multiple arenas of the Greek theater (orchestra, stage, and elevated "roof"), all used in the play, could, however, define spatially and render visually the drama's themes and variations. And at the heart of the play, magnetizing all language and gesture, lie the dead, whose speechless eloquence still makes claims on the living.

VII.   THE DATING OF EURIPIDES' *SUPPLIANT WOMEN*

In lieu of external evidence, the dating of the play depends on the discovery of possible historical allusions within the play and comparative stylistic analysis with other Euripidean dramas. Both pieces of evidence suggest a date between 424 and 419 B.C.

Possible historical allusions: in victory after the battle of Delium in November 424 B.C., Thebes refused to return the bodies of Athenian war dead for burial. In July 420 B.C., Athens and Argos formed a hundred-year alliance (cf. Thucy. 5.47, 5.82). Critics have argued that one, or both, of these events are alluded to in this play. We need to be leery, however, about making simple equivalences between the play and current events. The one-sided Argive indebtedness to Athens in the play hardly corresponds to the treaty agreements of 420 B.C. Similarities in the language of the historical treaty and Athena's demands for a formal alliance at the end of the play may suggest nothing more than Euripides' careful imitation of the conventions of diplomatic terminology. So it would be wrong to conclude that Euripides must be copying from the treaty or that he is arguing for the creation of such a treaty, although both theories have been proposed. It has also been argued that Euripides echoes dissenting political slogans circa 424–21 B.C. When considering the date of the play, the Athenian reorganization and revitalization of the Proerosia festival a Eleusis circa 420 B.C. should not be ignored,[6] and it is with this revival in mind that we prefer a production date circa 420. (For the Proerosia, see commentary *ad* **27–30**.)

Comparative stylistic analysis of Euripidean metrical practices suggests that *Suppliant Women* comes from roughly the same period as his *Hecuba*, which can be dated no later than 423 B.C.

---

6. See *Inscriptiones Graccae* I, 2nd ed., 76. Proposed dates for this inscription range from 423/22–419/18 B.C. For a translation of its key passages, see W. Burkert, *Greek Religion*, trans. J. Raffan (Cambridge, Mass., 1985), 67–68. See also H. W. Parke, *Festivals of the Athenians* (Ithaca, N.Y., 1977), 73–75.

VIII.   THE TEXT

Euripides' *Suppliant Women* has benefited greatly from recent textual criticism and commentary, in particular from a fine edition of the play by Christopher Collard, *Euripides, Supplices* (Leipzig, 1984), itself improved by the careful work of James Diggle in his *Euripidis, Fabulae II* (Oxford, 1981) and its compendium, *Studies on the Text of Euripides* (Oxford, 1981). Collard also produced a commentary (and text) of very high quality: *Euripides, Supplices*, 2 vols. (Groningen, Neth., 1975). We are indebted to all these works; unless otherwise noted in the commentary, our translation is based on Collard's text of 1984.

STEPHEN SCULLY

We are grateful to Derek Walcott's Poets' Theatre in Boston and to Qwirk Productions, directed by Peter Dalto in New York City, for dramatized workshop readings of this play. We are also indebted to Rush Rehm for his two 1993 productions of the play, one at Stanford University, Stanford, California, and the other at The Folger Library in Washington, D.C.

ROSANNA WARREN AND STEPHEN SCULLY

SUPPLIANT WOMEN

Translated by

ROSANNA WARREN

and

STEPHEN SCULLY

CHARACTERS

AITHRA   mother of Theseus

CHORUS   mothers of the Seven "Argive" Dead who fought against
Thebes

THESEUS   king of Athens

ADRASTOS   king of Argos, leader of the Seven against Thebes

HERALD   a Theban

MESSENGER   an Argive, reporting from Thebes

EVADNE   an Argive; widow of Capaneus, one of the Seven; daughter of
one of the mothers in the Chorus; sister of Eteoklos, also of
the Seven

IPHIS   Evadne's father, an Argive

CHILDREN   sons of the Seven

ATHENA   protecting deity of Athens

Argive handmaidens; Temple priests; Athenian herald; Athenian
pallbearers

Line numbers in the right-hand margin of the text refer to the
English translation only, and references to the text in the Notes
beginning at page 239 are keyed to these lines unless otherwise
specified. The bracketed line numbers in the running heads
refer to the Greek text.

The scene is Demeter's temple at Eleusis, where Aithra has come to celebrate the Proerosia, an annual ritual held in late October where preliminary sacrifices are offered up for the land's tillage. In the orchestra, wearing ceremonial white, Aithra sits at an altar to Demeter and Kore and burns cake offerings. Demeter's priests stand in the background; the whole ensemble is surrounded by a chorus of women in black mourning clothes, holding suppliant boughs. On the stage, the sons of the Dead surround Adrastos, who lies prostrate in front of the temple doors.

AITHRA Demeter, hearth goddess, guarding here
this land Eleusis, and you, her priests, now bless
me, bless Theseus my son, our city
Athens, and the land of Pittheus,
where my father raised me in a noble house
and married me to Aigeus, Pandion's son,
as Apollo willed.
              Even while I prayed
I looked on these old women here. They left
their homeland, Argos, and stunned by grief on grief
traveled with suppliant boughs to fall   10
at my knee. They have lost their children:
seven princely sons lie dead
by the gates of Thebes. Adrastos, King
of Argos, led them there, eager to win
a share of Oedipus' power for Polynices,
his exiled son-in-law.
              These mothers wish
to lay in the earth the corpses of their sons,
but the rulers of Thebes, spiting the gods' laws,
refuse to let them gather up their dead.
Sharing the heaviness of their need for me   20
Adrastos lies, right here, eyes wet with tears
for the war and that doomed troop
he led from home. He urges me
to beg Theseus to rescue the dead
for sacred burial, by persuasion or by the spear.
He entrusts this task in common to my son
and to our city, Athens.
              I was just now
burning gifts for the fresh-plowed land: I came

from home to this shrine where the wheat
first pushes its bristling shoots above the earth.   30
Bound, but not bound, by boughs, I wait
here by the altars of the goddesses
Kore and Demeter. I am touched by these graying
mothers, cut from their sons: I honor their wreaths.

My herald has gone to Athens, calling Theseus
to free our land of their laments, or else
discharge our obligation through some deed
the gods approve. A wise woman
works most wisely through a man.

CHORUS

Old woman, I beg your help,   *strophe*
   falling at your knee,   41
   my voice harsh now with age.
Set my children free
   from lawless men who leave
   bodies, sodden in death, flung
as food for mountain beasts.

Look, you see my eyes   *antistrophe*
   swollen, sluiced with tears,
   my gray and wrinkled flesh
shredded by my own hands. Why?   50
   Because I did not lay out
   my own dead son at home,
cannot see his grave in our Earth.

You gave birth yourself, once, Queen,   *strophe*
   to a boy who made your husband
   rejoice in the marriage bed. Join
your thought with mine, and share
   this grief I bear
   for the dead I brought from my womb.
I ask you, have your son   60
   go to Ismenus, bring back
   to my arms my son's strong body
   shamed, unburied, defiled.

Not reverent, I come, but driven   *antistrophe*
    by need, falling forward, entreating,
    I intrude on these altars.
My claims are righteous, and you,
    blessed with child, have power
    to heal my sorrow. I beg,
let your living son place in my hands   70
    a corpse, let me cradle
    my poor dead child.

                    Addresses female attendants.

Now wail struggles with wail,   *strophe*
    servant girls clap hands and call.
Come, beat breasts in time,
    come, share in our hymn,
    dance the dance Death loves.
Furrow nails in white
    cheek, bring blood: cry out!
    Grief is the debt of grace we pay the dead.   80

Joy of weeping, insatiable, thrusts me on   *antistrophe*
    in pain, as spring-water frets
down the cliff face, high,
    unendingly, ever in tears.
    For woman, the child's death begets
labor pains of lament:
    let me bury
my sorrow, and die.

        Enter THESEUS, *into the orchestra, from the right.*

THESEUS What's all this groaning, breast-beating, cries
    mourning the dead? The temples ring with echoes.   90
    I've rushed here, fearing: what if
    Mother, who left the house long back,
    has met some danger?
                    What in God's name?—Why is my mother
    sitting at the altar, an old woman surrounded by women,

strangers, with disorderly signs
of grief: old eyes driving tears
to Earth, butchered hair, black robes?
            Mother, what
is going on here? Speak up—
What in the world does this mean?   100

AITHRA Child, these are the women whose sons—
            the seven generals—died at the gates of Thebes.
            See, my son: they guard me here
            in their circle of suppliant boughs.

THESEUS And this man, groaning at the door?

AITHRA Adrastos, they call him, King of Argos.

THESEUS And these boys around him? The women's sons?

AITHRA No. The sons of the men who died.

THESEUS What are they doing *here* with suppliant boughs?

AITHRA Let them speak for themselves, my child.   110

                              THESEUS *moves to the stage.*

THESEUS You there, draped in that shawl.
            Uncover your head, and stop those groans.
            Nothing can be accomplished without speech.

ADRASTOS Theseus, glorious in victory,
            Lord of Athens, I come to you and your city,
            a suppliant.

THESEUS   What is it? What do you ask?

ADRASTOS You've heard of that army I led and lost?

THESEUS You hardly marched through Greece in silence.

200

ADRASTOS I destroyed my men, the finest of Argos.

THESEUS Those are the wages of war.   120

ADRASTOS I went to Thebes, asking for our dead.

THESEUS So you could bury them properly?

ADRASTOS Yes, but the Theban killers wouldn't allow it.

THESEUS What did they say? Your request was sacred.

ADRASTOS Since when has victory made men wise?

THESEUS You want my advice? Or something more?

ADRASTOS More, Theseus. To rescue the lost sons of Argos.

THESEUS What about Argos? Were her boasts so empty?

ADRASTOS We've fallen. We've come to you.

THESEUS Is this your idea, or the whole city's?   130

ADRASTOS All Argives beg you to bury the dead.

THESEUS Why did you lead your seven troops against Thebes?

ADRASTOS To help my two sons-in-law.

THESEUS Which men of Argos did you choose for your daughters?

ADRASTOS No Argive joined our house.

THESEUS You married your girls to foreigners?

ADRASTOS To Tydeus, and to Polynices the Theban.

THESEUS What made you do that?

ADRASTOS Apollo's riddles lured me.

THESEUS What did Apollo advise for their marriages? 140

ADRASTOS To give my girls to a boar and a lion.

THESEUS How did you unravel that?

ADRASTOS One night two exiles appeared at my door—

THESEUS Who? Speak. There were two, you say?

ADRASTOS Tydeus and Polynices. Fighting.

THESEUS So you gave your daughters to those beasts?

ADRASTOS Because they fought like animals.

THESEUS Why had they left their fatherlands?

ADRASTOS Tydeus spilled a kinsman's blood, and fled.

THESEUS And Oedipus' son, why did he leave Thebes? 150

ADRASTOS His father's curse, that he would kill his brother.

THESEUS He was wise, then, to leave of his own free will.

ADRASTOS Yes, but those at home robbed those who left.

THESEUS His brother robbed him? In his absence?

ADRASTOS I went to Thebes to right those wrongs. And lost.

THESEUS Did you consult prophets and sacrificial fires?

ADRASTOS That's just it, you've seen where I fell short.

THESEUS So you went without the gods' favor, it seems.

ADRASTOS Worse. I went against Amphiaraos' will.

THESEUS You defied the gods so casually?   160

ADRASTOS The younger men confused me with their uproar.

THESEUS You were all courage, no second thought.

ADRASTOS Yes. That has ruined many generals.
But, most stout-hearted leader in all Greece,
Lord of Athens, I fall in shame at your door,
touching your knee with my hand,
I, a gray-haired man, once a glorious king.
But now misfortune sets its heel on my neck.
Rescue our dead, take pity on my grief;
pity these mothers whose children have died.   170
Old and barren, they dared to travel here
to a foreign land, on legs too weak for walking.
They dared to come here, not
for Demeter's sacred mysteries, but to bury
their dead, those sons by whose hands
they should have received their own funeral rites.
Listen: it's as wise for a wealthy man to look on the poor,
as for the poor man to study the rich, and imitate,
to plant the love of money deep in his heart
Fortunate men should pity the sorrow of others.   180
You'd be wise to learn from me, though my story's grim.
Take the poet: if he gives birth to a song
he joys in the birth. But if, like me, he grieves
from trouble at home, he can't please others:
that wouldn't be decent. You'll ask, no doubt
why we ignore Sparta and burden Athens
with such labor. It's only right that I answer.
Sparta is harsh, dishonest in her dealings;
Other cities are small and weak. Only yours
has the strength to take up such labor.   190
Athens takes notice of pain, and in you has
a noble, youthful shepherd: without such men
for generals, many cities have been destroyed.

CHORUS   Theseus, I join my plea
          to his: take up our cause.

THESEUS   I've wrestled with others in this argument:
          I've heard that life provides more pain than good.
          I beg to differ. Indeed, it seems to me
          that life abounds in goods for humankind.
          If it weren't the case we wouldn't still be here   200
          in the light of day. And I praise the god
          who brought our human life from savagery
          and delivered us from the condition of beasts.
          First he granted us reason, and then the tongue
          as messenger of words, to enable speech.
          He taught us to raise food, and down from heaven
          sent rain to nourish crops and quench our thirst.
          And that's not all: he taught us how to endure
          winter, and how to ward off the sun god's glare
          in summer, and gave us navigation so we can trade   210
          with neighbors whatever our own land lacks.
          As for mysteries and things we don't clearly know,
          our priests read them in fire and pry in the folds
          of entrails, and decipher birds in flight.
          Now, don't we seem pampered weaklings, demanding more
          when a god has given us such preparation for life?
          But we in our arrogance lust to know
          more than the god, and preening in pride of mind
          we think we're wiser than all the gods together.
          I'm afraid you're in that crowd, my friend, a fool   220
          binding your daughters up in prophecies
          and packing them off with strangers as if the gods
          had given them. You mixed the bright with the muddy,
          wounded your house. A wise man, now,
          never joins pure to impure bodies the way you've done:
          he brings only fine, prosperous friends into his house.
          For the god gives common fortunes to those who live
          in common, and destroys the blameless and healthy
          if they've touched infected ones.
                                   So, you led all the men
          of Argos into war, insulting your seers,   230

snubbing the gods; you wrecked your city.
You lost your wits to the youths, you say,
hoodlums roaring for glory no matter what
the cost, no matter how foolish the cause,
or how many citizens die, just so one boy
can play general, another grab hold of the state,
another get rich, with no regard at all
for the people, and how they will suffer.
                                        There are three
classes of citizens. The wealthy are useless, leeches
always sucking for more. As for the poor,   240
they're monsters, bums and beggars inflamed
with envy, itching to raid the rich,
at the mercy of party bosses. Of the three,
only the moderate class can save the city,
keep law and order, and guard the constitution.
And after your idiocy, you are expecting me
to be your ally? You think I can recommend
such plans to my people? Good day to you.
You've made your bed, now lie in it.

CHORUS He made a mistake. It's common in the young.   250
        You ought to pardon this man here as well.
        We came in the hope, my lord, that you would heal us.

ADRASTOS Theseus, I didn't come here looking for a judge.
          I don't need punishment and scolding
          for my errors. I came to ask your help.
          If you're not willing to give it, I accept
          your verdict, as I must. What else can I do?
          Come, old women, rouse yourselves. Leave your
          silvery suppliant branches on the ground
          and let the gods and Earth and Light of Sun   260
          and Demeter who carries fire be witnesses:
          we prayed to the gods, and nothing came of it.

CHORUS Theseus, you're Aithra's son. She was born
        of Pittheus, son of Pelops. We of the land
        of Pelops share paternal blood with you.

What will you do? Will you betray your blood
and drive from your land old women who cannot obtain
what is rightfully theirs? Never! A beast has a cave
for shelter, a slave has altars, a city in storm
turns to another city. For nothing mortal remains   270
blessed straight through to the end.

> *The* CHORUS *divides into two groups as it moves from
> orchestra to stage and breaks into song.*

A   Go, poor women, leave Persephone's
     holy floor, go stretch your hands around his knees:
     hold him, have him bring back those bodies tossed
     beside the walls of Thebes where they were lost.

B   By your cheeks, I implore, oh noble king, our friend:
     kneeling, I clutch your knee, your gracious hand.
     Pity my lost sons, pity the surge
     of my lament far from home, a mother's dirge.

A   Child, in your youth, don't scorn men the wolves will
                                              ravage   280
     in Cadmus' land. They died: they were your age.

B   Look on my weeping: at your knees I crawl
     and beg you—give my son a burial.

THESEUS   Mother, are you sobbing? Do you hide your face
          in your delicate veil? Have these women's cries
          affected you? They've pierced me as well.
          Come, raise your white head. You mustn't weep
          at Demeter's holy altar.

  AITHRA (*wails*)

THESEUS   You shouldn't suffer their grief.

  AITHRA Poor women, poor women.

THESEUS   You're not related to them.   290

AITHRA My child, may I speak, for your own good, and for the city's?

THESEUS Of course. Even women can talk good sense.

AITHRA I'm afraid you'll disapprove what I have to say.

THESEUS I'll disapprove if you hide good advice from us.

AITHRA I'd rather speak, than later blame myself
for wrong-headed silence. Nor should fear
make me veil what I know to be right.

My son, first and foremost, it's the will of the gods
you have to consider, so you won't make some fatal mistake.
In this matter alone, my child, you've lost your way.   300
What's more, if we didn't have to be brave
for the sake of the innocent, I would hold my peace.
But you ought to know that this action will honor you,
and I enjoin you solemnly: you *must*
punish those violent men who keep
corpses from due burial and holy rites;
with your own hand you must strike
those bandits who confound the sacred laws
of all Greece. All civilized order rests
on this: the safekeeping of laws.
                        And another thing: 310
you wouldn't want it said that you hung back,
afraid, when you could have wrested the crown
of fame for the city; that you battled a boar in sport
but faced with helmets and spearpoints, when you had
a real battle, man to man, you were found to be
a coward.
            Never! My son, if you are indeed
my son, don't shame yourself. Do you not see
how your fatherland, rebuked for meddling,
stares back at accusers with wild Gorgon eyes?
In her labors she soars in strength and pride.   320

207

But peaceful cities, in shady diplomacy,
haggle behind the scenes for hidden ends.
So, child, won't you help the dead and their sorrowing
mothers, since they're in need? This is just cause
for war. And even though the Thebans have won
for now, I think they'll find a different throw
of the dice next time. The gods reverse everything.

CHORUS Beloved Queen, you have spoken well to him,
and to me. We are twice rewarded.

THESEUS The words I spoke, Mother, fit him perfectly   330
and I stand by my judgment
of those plans which ruined him. But I see
and accept the point of your correction.
I would not be Theseus if I fled
danger; with many heroic deeds
I have spread my reputation throughout all Greece:
Theseus, always the avenger of wrong.
So you are right. I cannot shun this labor.
What would my enemies say of me if you,
who gave me birth and who still fear for me,   340
are the first to bid me to take up such labor?
        I'll do it. I will go and free the dead
by words, if possible. If not, by spear.
The gods will not begrudge this. But I must have
the agreement of all Athens for such an act.
Athens will back me, since I wish it. But if I explain
I'll have the people more inclined to consent.
For I set them up as monarchs of themselves
and freed the city, giving them equal votes.
Taking Adrastos, then, to confirm my words,   350
I'll go to the citizens. When they're persuaded
I'll rouse the best youths of Athens and return
here. Prepared for battle, I'll send word
to Creon, demanding the bodies of the dead.
        But, old women, set my mother free
from your garlands so I can lead her home
by her dear hand. A child who will not serve

his parents degrades his life. Such service is
our noblest gift. A man's care for his parents
is given him by his children in their turn.   360

Exeunt THESEUS, AITHRA, ADRASTOS (*the sons of the Dead
move off the stage into the orchestra, where they will sit in
silence until the end of the fourth episode,* [954]).

CHORUS

Argos rippling with horses, my father's field,   *strophe*
hear the king speak, hear
matters sacred to the gods,
glory for Argos and the Peloponnese.

Let him press till all my sorrow is repealed,   *antistrophe*
let him carry here
my prize soiled in blood,
let his help to the land of Argos bind him to us.

This holy labor brings an honored prize   *strophe*
to our cities, and gratitude   370
forever. What will Athens do?
Befriend us? Bury the sons we bore?

Protect her, protect the mother, city of Pallas.   *antistrophe*
Take care: don't stain the laws
of mortals. You honor justice, it's true,
cut back the wicked, rescue the injured and poor.

        THESEUS *returns, from right, with* ADRASTOS *and an*
                            Athenian herald onto the stage.

THESEUS   Herald, you know your trade, serving
          the city, and me, with your proclamations. Now,
          cross the rivers to Thebes and report
          to their proud ruler: 380
          "Theseus bids you, as a favor, bury the dead.
          He speaks as your neighbor, worthy of courtesy,

and wants to ensure Athenian friendship with all."
If the Thebans agree, praise them and march
straight home. If not, make this other speech:
"Attend our party, and our sharpened spears."
The army is camped and ready for war, nearby,
in ranks by Demeter's holy spring.
And the Athenians were more than pleased to accept this labor
since they knew I wished it.

                      Who is this   390
interrupting us? I'd say a Theban herald
by his dress. See what he wants. He may relieve
you of your labor: his visit is well timed.

      Enter Theban HERALD, *from left, onto the stage.*

HERALD Who is the sovereign here? To whom should I report
Creon's words? He rules now in Thebes
since Eteokles died at the seven-mouthed gates
killed by his brother, Polynices.

THESEUS You've already begun badly, stranger,
when you seek one master here. Our city is free,
not run by a single man. The people rule   400
by turns in yearly succession. So our poor
have equal voting power with the rich.

HERALD You've given me the advantage in this game.
Our city is ruled by one man, not a mob.
No one there buffets the city this way and that
with windy boasts, all for private profit,
quick with the soft touch and backroom favors,
then milking the city dry, concealing old graft
with new, ducking all prosecution. And, besides,
if the people can't distinguish true from false,   410
how can they keep the city safe on course?
Knowledge comes with experience, not in a flash.
Even if a peasant were not an ignorant clod,
with all his labors, he would not have time
to look to the common good. Indeed,

for the upper class, it's a disease, when, fresh
from his ditch, some dirt farmer bridles the mob
and drives it with the witchery of his tongue.

THESEUS Well, what a clever herald! Moonlighting
as an orator. Since you started this argument,   420
now listen. You began the debate.
There is nothing worse for a city than a sovereign,
when first no laws are common, and he rules
alone, taking himself for law. That way
nothing is equal. But when the laws are written,
the poor man and the rich have equal rights.
Then, when a wealthy citizen does wrong,
a weaker one can criticize, and prevail,
with justice on his side. *That's* liberty.
Anyone with sound advice for the city's good   430
can make it public and shine among his peers.
The reticent keep quiet. What could be
more equal or beneficial for the city?
What's more, when the people rule their land
they delight in the young men growing up.
But a single lord finds that intolerable
and those whom he judges noble or smart
he kills, to preserve his reign. How then
can a city thrive, when someone hacks the spears
of wheat from the spring field, and harvests our young?   440
Why should we gather a living for our children
if it's just a tyrant's livelihood we swell?
Why keep our daughters virtuously at home,
sweetmeats for the tyrant's passing urge,
tears for their parents? Let him die
if he marries my child by force.
                                    Now, all these points
I pit against yours. What do you want from our land?
If this weren't official business, you'd return
in tears, for all your cant. A messenger
should state his errand and leave in double time.   450
Next time Creon sends a man to Athens
let it be someone more tight-lipped than you.

CHORUS   Whenever a god lets the corrupt prosper
         they gorge on pride, thinking their luck will last.

HERALD   A word, if you permit? On these sore points
         let's agree to disagree. Creon proclaims:
         "I and the people of Thebes refuse
         Adrastos entry into Athenian land.
         If he is there, drive him out, I say
         before the god's light sinks; scatter the suppliants'   460
         sacred boughs. Do not take up
         his dead by force: you have no business with Argos.
         If you obey me, you'll steer your city safe
         across calm water. But if you refuse
         a wave of spears will crash upon us all."
         Consider well, and since you claim your city's free,
         don't let my message goad you to reply
         in rash rage when you stand on weaker ground.
         Don't trust in hope: it's sent many cities to war
         whipping them into frenzy. Whenever war   470
         comes up for the people's vote, no one counts on
         his own death; each thinks the other man
         will suffer. But if death rose before your eyes
         when you cast your vote, Greece in its craze for spears
         would not be destroyed in battle. All men know
         which of two words is better: between peace and war,
         which is evil and which good, and how much more
         peace benefits humankind. She is most dear
         to the Muses, hated by Vengeance. She loves
         strong children, she rejoices in wealth. But we   480
         choose war, in our evil, and enslave the weak,
         man lording it over man, town over town.
              But will you still help those despised dead, burying
         those killed by criminal pride? Surely Capaneus'
         thundered body should still smoke—
         he who hurled the very ladders at the gates,
         swearing to smash the city, whatever god willed?
         And didn't a whirlwind snatch the fortune-teller,
         flinging his four-horse chariot into a chasm?
         Don't the other captains lie at the gates of Thebes,   490

212

skulls shattered by rocks? Either you boast
you now know better than Zeus, or you'll confess
the gods were right to kill those hell-bent men.
　　　To sum it up: A wise man loves, first, his children,
then parents and country, which he should protect,
not ruin. A hothead leader, a young captain,
spells danger. A man calm in crisis is wise.
In fact, courage truly defined is foresight.

CHORUS Zeus punished them enough. There was no need
for you to be so proud, beating down their pride.　　　　500

ADRASTOS You vicious—

THESEUS　　　　　　　Silence, Adrastos. Hold your tongue.
Don't thrust in your speeches before mine.
He came heralding to me, not you, this fellow,
and I must answer him.

　　　　　　　　　THESEUS *turns to the* HERALD.

　　　　　　　Now, point by point
I'll answer you. First, I am not aware
That Creon has the right to order me,
or is the stronger, so Athens must obey.
The world would be upside down if we let ourselves
be bullied so. And another point: I didn't start the war,
I didn't march with them onto Theban soil.　　　　510
But burying the corpses, I bring no harm
to Thebes, I threaten no war. I'm in the right
preserving the holy law of all the Greeks.
What's wrong in this?
　　　　　　　Granted the Argives hurt you,
they are dead. You beat back the enemy
honorably, and shamed them. Justice was done.
Now, let the corpses be hidden in the earth
from which each came to light; let soul release
to air, body to earth. We do not own
our bodies, but are mere tenants there for life,　　　　520

213

and earth that nursed them takes them back again.
Do you think you punish Argos, not burying the dead?
Far from it. This is the common creed of Greece
to ensure that no one keeps the dead from burial
and proper rites. Brave men would turn cowardly
if your deeds became the law.
                      So you came threatening me
with frightful words, yet you fear the dead
if they're buried? Why? Can they destroy your land
when buried? Can children in earth's womb
beget revenge? This is nonsense, to fear   530
such phantoms.
                You fools, think of life's
real struggle. Some mortals thrive
now, some will in the future, others did in the past.
The god prospers, anyway. A man in trouble
placates the god in hope of better days;
a rich man, fearing for his life, reveres
the god as well. Knowing these struggles,
you shouldn't rage at such small injury,
or harm your city with injustices.
    What do we ask? Give back the dead   540
and let us bury them with reverence.
Or else it's clear: I'll bury them
by force. It will never be said in Greece
that the gods' ancient law, coming to me
and to Athens was despised.

CHORUS Take heart. Most men will praise
you if you save the light of justice.

HERALD Shall I oblige you with a brief reply?

THESEUS Speak, if you wish. You're not the silent type.

HERALD You'll never take the Argive children from our land.   550

THESEUS Now listen, if you'll be so kind.

HERALD Of course. I wouldn't keep you from your turn.

THESEUS I shall carry the dead from Thebes, and bury them.

HERALD You'll have to test the case with shields.

THESEUS I've survived many other labors.

HERALD Your father raised you to conquer everything?

THESEUS Only the proud. We do not punish the good.

HERALD You're truly enterprising, you and your city.

THESEUS Yes. Athens' great labor wins great reward.

HERALD Come! Our dragon spears will hurl you in the dust.   560

THESEUS What god of war is born from a dragon's tooth?

HERALD Suffering will teach you that. You're still a whelp.

THESEUS You won't enrage me with your boasts. Get out,
          leave our land, pack up your empty words.
          It's pointless, talking.

                              Exit HERALD, *to the left.*

                              Now, we must marshall
          every foot soldier and charioteer,
          and horseman, foam flecking the bit, to charge
          to Thebes. I'll march to their seven gates,
          myself the captain with iron in my hand,
          myself the herald. As for you, Adrastos,   570
          wait. Don't mix your fortunes with mine.
          With my own guardian spirit I'll command
          the army, a fresh man with a fresh spear.
          I need only one thing: the support of all those gods
          who honor justice. If I can count on them,

victory is mine. A man can never win
glory without a god at his side.

Exit to the left all actors except ADRASTOS, *who remains
onstage.*

CHORUS (*in two groups*)

—Useless mothers of useless generals—   *strophe*
What green terror lodges in my entrails?

Enter MESSENGER, *from the left, onto stage.*

—What news do you bring? What word is this?   580

—How will Athena's army stand the test?

—Did you speak with spears, or word to word?

—May victory come! But if Ares preferred
death, if the city fills with groans,
with gashes, blood, and beaten breasts,
what word, what accusation, will be heard?

—Thebes' luck may turn this time, and quench her fire: *antistrophe*
this hope binds courage all around my fear.

—You speak of the spirits of justice.

—What others give fortune to us?   590

—The gods give many things for man to bear.

—You are undone by an old fear.
Justice called to justice, death to death.
The gods, who know how everything on earth
will end, grant ease to mortal care.

216

—How can we leave the Demeter's flashing stream   *strophe*
   and reach the mighty towers of the plain?

—If some god winged your feet, you'd fly
   to Thebes' two rivers: you would see
   your friends, and you would know their fate firsthand.   600

—What lot, what fortune crouches for the brave king of this land?

—We call on gods we have called before: *antistrophe*
   they are our first defense against fear.

—Zeus, who begot the heifer, ancient mother of Inachos,
   be a faithful ally to Athens, protecting us.

—Bring the prize, the city's guardians, in their shame:
   Carry them here to the funeral flame.

MESSENGER Women, I come with happy news, both my own escape
              and Theseus' victory. I was captured
              in that war the seven captains waged   610
              against Thebes, by the River Dirke.
              But I'll spare you a long account.
              I served Capaneus, whom Zeus killed,
              thundered to cinders with his lightning bolt.

   CHORUS What joy, to hear of your return,
              and Theseus' success. But if the whole army
              of Athens is safe, that will be blessed news.

MESSENGER Safe. And it achieved what Adrastos ought
              to have done, with the Argives, when he marched from home
              by the River Inachos to take Thebes.

   CHORUS   How did Theseus,   620
              grandson of Aigeus, and his troops claim victory?
              Speak! You were there: tell us: we were far away.

217

MESSENGER A dazzling blade of sunlight, a clear rod,
            struck the earth. There, on a tower, I stood
            at Elektra's gate, I could watch everything.
            I saw Athenians, three divisions, come:
            on the right flank, infantry stretched
            up the hill of Ismene, as they call it there;
            Theseus, famous heir of Aigeus, led:
            his men were of old Athenian blood.   630
            On the left came Paralos holding high his spear
            as far as the spring of Ares. Flanking the foot soldiers
            rode the cavalry in detachments
            of equal number. Chariots massed below
            Amphion's sacred tomb. The Theban troops
            waited by the walls, keeping the dead
            behind them—the dead for whom all fought. Horsemen stood
            poised against horsemen, chariots against chariots.
            Then Theseus' herald made this speech:
            "Silence, troops. Silence there, in the Theban ranks.   640
            Listen. We come to retrieve the dead
            and bury them. We wish to protect the law
            of all the Greeks, not to threaten death."
            Creon said nothing, but stood among his men
            without a word. Then chariots launched the war,
            hurtling through each other's ranks to place
            their fighters in formation. Swordsmen clashed,
            the chariots drove back into the melee
            charging the infantry. When the captains saw
            the turmoil, they joined the fight: Phorbas, leader   650
            of the Athenian cavalry, and the Theban marshalls
            surged and staggered back in waves.
            I saw it all, I didn't just hear of it—
            I stood where the chariots and the horsemen fought.
            How can I tell it? I saw such agonies:
            dust storming up to heaven, choking-thick;
            men flailing up and down, yanked by reins;
            rivers of blood from foot soldiers, and riders
            catapulted from chariots, pitched headlong
            to the ground alongside splintered cars.   660
            When he saw our horsemen conquering, Creon snatched

a shield, and stalked into the battle swarm to keep
his allies from despair. Theseus' men
would have been routed then and there, but the young king
seized shining arms, and plunged into the fight.
Core against core, the armies slammed together;
they butchered and were butchered, and with great cries
roared out commands to one another:
"Smash Thebes!" "Slash Athens with your spear!"
That army of men born from dragon's teeth   670
was a deadly force: it splintered our left flank.
But their right wing collapsed. The fight was even.
And this is where Theseus truly must be praised.
He didn't just ride on the crest of his success,
but rushed to the spot where his men were faltering.
He let out his battle cry, and shook the earth:
"Boys, if you don't beat back those Dragon Men,
we're lost!" He rallied courage throughout his ranks;
he himself snatched up the Epidaurian mace,
that terrifying club, and whirled it round: 680
he mowed down heads and helmets, snapping off
neck stalks with his wood. They could hardly stumble
over their feet fast enough to flee.
I howled for joy and danced deliriously,
clapping my hands. They poured up to the gates.
Throughout the city rose wails from young and old:
in terror, they jammed the temples. The Athenians could
have roared in through the gates, but Theseus
checked his men. "We didn't come to destroy
the city," he cried, "but to rescue the dead."   690
That's the kind of general to choose, one brave
against all odds, who hates the arrogant mob—
that mob which, though prosperous, tries to climb
the ladder's highest rung, and wrecks that fortune
that required better care.

CHORUS   Unhoped-for day! I see it, true at last,
        and now I believe in the gods. The horror subsides
        since Thebes has been brought to justice.

ADRASTOS Zeus, why do we mortals
boast of intellect? We depend on you,   700
we obey your slightest wish. Argos was not,
as we thought, invincible, though we were young,
strong of arm, and many. When Eteokles
offered to compromise on moderate terms,
we refused, and were destroyed. But the Thebans then,
reveling in good luck like an upstart beggar
newly come into money, swelled with pride
and in that pride they, also, were destroyed.
Foolish mortals: you don't obey your friends
but circumstance. And cities, which could resolve   710
their differences through words, conclude affairs
with butchery instead. But enough of this:
I want to hear your escape, and then the rest.

MESSENGER While the confusion of battle rocked the city,
I slipped through the gates where the Thebans came
streaming in.

ADRASTOS And did you bring the dead they were fighting for?

MESSENGER No. Only the seven famous captains.

ADRASTOS What happened to the common soldiers who died?

MESSENGER They were buried by Cithaeron's folds.

ADRASTOS On which side of the mountain? Who buried them?   720

MESSENGER Theseus did, on this side, by Eleutherae's shady ridge.

ADRASTOS Where have you left the dead he did not bury?

MESSENGER Nearby. A short distance, for swift desire.

ADRASTOS Did it trouble the servants to carry them from the field?

MESSENGER No slave took part in that labor.

ADRASTOS Theseus carried the corpses?

MESSENGER So you'd say, if you'd seen how he cared for the dead.

ADRASTOS He himself washed the poor men's wounds?

MESSENGER Exactly. He laid out the beds, and covered their limbs.

ADRASTOS What a terrible burden and shame to take on himself!   730

MESSENGER Why should we think of our common griefs as shame?

ADRASTOS Oh gods—I wish I had died with them.

MESSENGER Your laments are useless. You're making the women weep.

ADRASTOS Yes. They are my teachers now.
          But I'll go raise my hands to greet the dead
          and pour out the hymns of Death for my friends
          who have left me in my misery to weep
          alone. This is the only mortal loss
          whose expense can't be recovered: the mortal soul.
          Lost money can be restored, not human life.   740

                   Exeunt MESSENGER *and* ADRASTOS *to the left.*

CHORUS
          My joy is woven with sorrow.   *strophe*
              Glory crowns the city
              and double glory crowns
              the generals and their spears.
          But for me to look on my son's
              corpse, is horror and beauty—
              longed-for, unhoped-for day,
              seen at last, greatest in tears.

          Time, the ancient father   *antistrophe*
              of days, should have let me stay   750
              unmarried forever here.

221

Why did I need sons?
I shouldn't have had to bear
      this pain if I'd been free
      of marriage, but now I see
the worst: loved children torn from my arms.

Enter, from the left, ADRASTOS *and ten Athenian pallbearers, who carry the Argive corpses to the stage.*

CHORUS (*chant*)
But here are the bodies now
      of my lost children. How
      can I die with my children,
      going down to Hades in common?   760

(*lyric exchange between* ADRASTOS *and* CHORUS)   *strophe*

ADRASTOS Shout, oh mothers, cry
            for the dead going under the ground:
            wail responses to my
            groans for their burial mound.

CHORUS Children, bitter target
            of your loving mother's moan:
            I call to you, though you are dead.

ADRASTOS Ai ai—

  CHORUS   Of all my sorrows, I . . .

ADRASTOS Ai ai—

  CHORUS   —Ai ai

ADRASTOS We have suffered—

  CHORUS   —obscene grief.   770

ADRASTOS City of Argos, do you see what has happened to me?

222

CHORUS And you see me ripped from my sons.

ADRASTOS Bring in the bodies, soaked in blood,   *antistrophe*
                of those unlucky dead,
              Shamefully slain by the shameful
                on whose battleground they fell.

  CHORUS Give him here, let me hold my boy
                folded in my embrace,
                let my hands caress his face.

ADRASTOS You hold, you hold—

   CHORUS   —the weight of the world.   780

ADRASTOS Ai ai—

   CHORUS   Why don't you speak to the parents?

ADRASTOS Hear me.

   CHORUS   You groan for both of us.

ADRASTOS I wish the Thebans had struck me down in the dust.

  CHORUS I wish my body had never been yoked
                to a husband's bed.

ADRASTOS A gulf stretches before you, mothers   *epode*
                torn from your sons.

  CHORUS I've raked my face with my fingernails, I've poured
                ashes on my head.

                Enter THESEUS, *with some young Athenian soldiers,*
                                        onto the stage.

223

ADRASTOS (*wails*) Let earth gape and swallow me, let a storm   790
rip through me, let the flame
of Zeus crash my skull.

CHORUS You see those bitter marriages
and Apollo's bitter tale.
The Fury, slinking from Oedipus' house,
drags his groans to us.

THESEUS I wanted to ask, but couldn't interrupt
the lament you poured out for the army. Since I let it pass,
let me question you now, Adrastos.
How did these men attain such heights of courage   800
among mortals? Since you are wiser, speak
to the young men of the city. You know the facts.
All they know is that the heroes' deeds,
besieging the city, were greater than words can tell.
But I won't make a joke of it by demanding
a blow by blow account, who stood against whom
in battle, and the spear wounds each received.
That's idle chatter, for listener and teller both,
and nonsense to think a man plunged in fighting
with a hail of spears before his eyes, could see   810
clearly enough to tell who's been heroic.
I couldn't bring myself to ask such things,
or believe them, if someone tried to trot them out.
A man meeting the enemy head on
can hardly see what he really has to see.

ADRASTOS Hear me, then. I am happy to take up
this charge of yours, eager to praise
my friends with truth and justice.
Do you see that man, shattered by the lightning bolt?
That is Capaneus. He had massive wealth   820
but took no pride in it. He set his sights
no higher than a poor man, fleeing those
who heap their tables up with luxuries
and spurn what will suffice. He took delight
not in stuffing his stomach, but in moderation.

He was a true friend to friends, both near and far:
there are not many like that: honest to a fault,
courteous, and as dutiful at home
as to his fellow citizens.
                              The second
I praise is Eteoklos. His honesty   830
was of a different kind. A poor youth,
he later rose to eminence in Argos.
And though friends often offered him gold, he shied
from it, and would not bind himself
by taking slavish gifts. He loathed
guilty persons, not the whole city of Thebes,
since a city should not be blamed
if its captain steers it wrong.
                                    The third I praise
is Hippomedon. As a child, he dared
already to spurn the arts and the cushioned life,   840
but roamed the fields, with a taste for the roughest tasks.
He delighted in feats of courage, loved the hunt
and horses and the bow taut in his hand.
He trained his body as a useful gift to Argos.
        And I praise the child of the huntress Atalanta,
Parthenopaios, that handsome boy.
He was Arcadian, but came to our River
Inachos, and was trained in Argos.
There he reached manhood. He took great care—
as is right for a resident alien in the town—   850
not to make trouble or envy the city's wealth
or stir up quarrels, which weigh upon us,
whether from citizen or foreigner.
He joined the army just like a native Argive,
defended the land, cheered at the city's success,
and grieved if the city were harmed
        Great praise of Tydeus may be brief.
Not in speeches, he shone, but in his shield;
terribly expert, butcher of the untrained.
In mind his brother Meleager far outstripped him,   860
but Tydeus won equal fame in the art of the spear,
and drew his own music from his ringing shield.

Do not be amazed, Theseus, hearing all this,
that these men dared to die at the towers of Thebes.
Noble upbringing begets nobility.
Any man trained in virtue is ashamed
to do a wrong. And this high courage
can be taught, just as a babe is taught
to speak and listen to things he doesn't know.
Lessons learned early stay with us till old age.   870
So train your children well.

CHORUS (*breaking into song*)
Child, it was for doom
    I carried you in my womb:
    and labored in Herculean pain.
Now Death takes as his spoil
    the fruit of my laboring toil:
    I am aged, untended, alone
    though I begot a son.

THESEUS We must also praise Amphiaraos, the noble child
of Oikles. The gods clearly singled him out   880
for honor by dragging him and his horses, still alive,
into the folds of the earth. And Oedipus' son,
Polynices, we can truthfully praise.
He was my guest when he first fled from Thebes,
before, by his own choice, he went on to Argos.
But do you know what I plan to do with these men?

ADRASTOS I know only one thing: to obey your every word.

THESEUS Capaneus, struck by Zeus' fire—

ADRASTOS —You'll bury him apart, as a holy corpse?

THESEUS Yes. But the others will all go in a single pyre.   890

ADRASTOS Where will you set Capaneus' tomb?

THESEUS By the temple: I'll build it in stone.

ADRASTOS The slaves should see to that labor.

THESEUS No, we'll take care of these.
                                              (*to attendants*) Carry off the dead.

ADRASTOS Go, bereaved mothers, approach your children.

> *The* CHORUS *moves toward the biers at the edge of the
> stage.*

THESEUS That is the worst thing you could advise, Adrastos.

ADRASTOS What do you mean? Shouldn't mothers touch their
children?

THESEUS They would die, seeing the mutilation.

ADRASTOS It's a bitter sight, the blood and wounds of the dead.

THESEUS Then why do you want to inflict such pain?   900

ADRASTOS I give in. (*to* CHORUS) Be brave, and stay there.

> *The* CHORUS *abruptly comes to a halt, having never
> reached the stage.*

Theseus is right. When they've burned on the pyre,
you can embrace their bones.

> *Attendants begin to carry Argive corpses behind the skēnē.*

                    Tormented race of man,
why do you take up spears, and bring down death
upon each other? Stop! Leave off those labors,
guard your city in peace. The needs of life
are small. You should provide for them
gently, without such gruesome labor.

Exeunt THESEUS *and* ADRASTOS *behind the skēnē; the stage is now empty. The secondary chorus of the sons of the Dead leave their position in the orchestra, move across the stage, and exeunt behind the skēnē. The theater is now empty except for the* CHORUS *of mothers.*

CHORUS

No longer blessed with child, not blessed   *strophe*
    with son, I am cursed   911
    among full-wombed Argive women.
And Artemis, goddess of birth,
    won't visit those who are barren.
Life without life, I roam,
    a cloud darting high over earth,
    in winter's storm.

Seven mothers, we brought to the world   *antistrophe*
    seven sons whom Argos called
    glorious: but we endure in pain.   920
Now, without son, without child,
    I grow old, grieving alone;
neither dead nor alive, but set
    apart from all, compelled
    by my estranging fate.

Tears only remain   *epode*
and useless mementos of my son
in empty rooms, and my own cropped hair
without a wreath, and libations poured
over the dead, and songs which the golden Lord   930
Apollo will not accept. I'll rise
each morning weeping, and drench my eyes
and every fold of my gown
on my breast with tears for my son.

And now I see Capaneus' funeral chamber,
    his sacred tomb, and just outside
    the temple door, Theseus' funeral gifts
    for the rescued dead.

           EVADNE *appears on a cliff overhanging Demeter's*
                                         temple.

Look! Here comes Evadne, the peerless wife
    of Capaneus, struck by Zeus' bolt,   940
    Evadne, daughter of Iphis. Why is she climbing
    the path? Why does she take her stand
    high on the airy rock
    which towers over the shrine?

EVADNE *(solo aria)*
    What torchlight, what brilliant glare   *strophe*
did sun and moon drive through the air
    with nymphs swiftly banishing shade
when the city of Argos, proud,
    towering, ringing with song
    exulted the whole day long   950
    at my marriage to glorious
    bronze-armored Capaneus?
I've rushed here from my house
    like a Maenad running loose
to see the pyre's light and the holy tomb,
    and to lead my soul
    from life's long toil
into Death's great room.
Death is voluptuous,
    to die with our lovers   960
    if the god lets it come to pass.

CHORUS And you can see, from where you stand, just under you,
    the pyre, Zeus' treasure-chest, where
    your husband lies, mastered by the brilliant bolt.

EVADNE
    Yes, I see my deliverance.   *antistrophe*
    Fate keeps step with my dance.
      For glory I'll cast myself

from this jut of cliff
   and leap to the funeral pyre:
melting in radiant flame   970
   my body will mingle with yours,
   loved husband, flesh to flesh,
   down in Persephone's house—
   I'll never betray your death
by clinging to life on earth.
   Sunlight, goodbye. Goodbye,
marriage. Not for me those
beds of virtuous
   weddings which bring
forth children to Argos.   980
My true wedded husband
   melts in a pure wind
   with his wife in a single fire.

CHORUS Look: here comes Iphis himself, your father:
he will grieve at your strange words.

Enter IPHIS, *from the left, onto the stage.*

IPHIS Women of sorrow, I come, a most sorrowful
old man, with a double grief. I must bring home
by ship Eteoklos, my son, killed
by a Theban spear. And I must find my daughter,
Capaneus' wife, who fled from home in frenzy   990
and yearns to die with him. Till now, I've kept
her guarded in the house. But in this new
turmoil, I released the guards, and now
she's fled. But she must have come here.
Have you seen her?

EVADNE   Why ask those women?
Here I am on the rock, perched like a bird
over Capaneus' pyre, hovering
in sorrow, Father.

IPHIS   Child, what wind, what voyage, what reason 1000
made you steal away from home and find this land?

EVADNE My plans would anger you if you heard them,
so I can't tell you, Father.

IPHIS What? It's not right for your father to know?

EVADNE You wouldn't know how to judge what I have in mind.

IPHIS Why have you dressed yourself up so gorgeously?

EVADNE A special glory requires it, Father.

IPHIS You don't look like a wife in mourning.

EVADNE I have dressed myself for quite another purpose.

IPHIS Then why come here, to the tomb and the pyre?   1010

EVADNE Because here I'll win glory in victory.

IPHIS What victory? What are you talking about?

EVADNE Victory over all women under the sun.

IPHIS By handicrafts, or by some work of the mind?

EVADNE By heroic action. I shall lie with my husband in death.

IPHIS What are you saying? What is this rotten riddle?

EVADNE I shall leap right here into Capaneus' pyre.

IPHIS Daughter—you haven't told this to anyone?

EVADNE On the contrary: I want all Argos to know.

IPHIS I'll never permit such a thing.   1020

EVADNE It's useless. You can't reach me, can't take my hand.
My body falls: whatever you suffer
my husband and I burn together.

231

EVADNE *leaps into flames, behind skēnē.* CHORUS *and*
IPHIS *break into song.*

CHORUS   Woman, what horror!

IPHIS   I am finished, daughters of Argos.

CHORUS   To have lived through such savagery—
            can you bear to see what she dared?

IPHIS   You couldn't find a more broken man on earth.

CHORUS   Poor wounded man:
            Oedipus' fate has touched you,   1030
            you, and my whole city.

IPHIS   Oh gods, why can't mortals have a second youth
        and then grow old again? In daily life
        at home, if something fails, we patch it up
        and make it better second time around.
        But a whole life-course never comes again.
        If we were young and old twice over
        we could correct all mistakes on the second try.
        I used to envy others who had children
        and thought I would die with desire for my own.   1040
        But if I had known the suffering that comes
        from losing children, I wouldn't be here now
        in this nightmare, having a noble son
        born to me, then suddenly snatched away.
              So be it. Now what can I do?
        Go home? And see that echoing void
        in room after room, my whole life out of place?
        Or should I stay by Capaneus' tomb?
        Life was sweetest then, when I had my girl.
        But she is gone, who used to kiss my cheeks   1050
        and hold my head in her hands. For an aging father,
        nothing is gentler than a girl.
        Sons are nobler of soul, but daughters give
        softest caresses.

> Won't you lead me away, quickly,
> lead me away and shut me in the dark,
> and let my old body melt away without food
> and die? What good would it do me
> to touch my daughter's bones?
>   Old age, I despise this wrestle with you.
> I despise those fools who coax out life's last days   1060
> with fancy diets and potions and witchery,
> diverting life's course, trying to bypass death.
> They ought, rather, when they're useless with old age,
> to clear out of the way and leave room for the young.

> *Exit* IPHIS, *to the left; from behind the skēnē enter sons of
> the Dead and servants, who carry the ashes and bones of
> the Dead in jars onto the stage.*

CHORUS   (*turning to personal attendants and chanting*)
> The bones—they're bearing the bones
>   of my dead children. No,
>   hold me, I can't stand alone—
>   I'm too weak from sorrow—
> I've dragged out too long a life,
>   melting in grief after grief: 1070
>   what greater grief can there be
>   for mortals, than to see
>   our own children, ash and bone.

> *The sons of the Dead advance and receive the funerary
> jars. Lyric exchange between sons and mothers of the
> Dead.*

CHILDREN   I bear them, I bear them—   *strophe*
> Sad mother, I bear my father's bones from the flame.
> So heavy they are, so weighted with grief, my whole
>   life in a jar so small.

CHORUS   (*wails*)
> Child, bring your beloved
>   mother these tears for the dead,

this small heap of ash, not the great   1080
  bodies that once paced Mycenae's street.

CHILDREN You are childless, childless,   *antistrophe*
  and I am torn from my father in distress,
  in lonely hallways, orphaned,
   wrenched from my father's hand.

CHORUS (*wails*)
  Where are the pangs of labor? The nights beguiled
   by long watches over the sleeping child?
  Where are the suckling, the rocking, the tenderness
   of kissing his sweet face?

CHILDREN They are gone. Forever. My father—   *strophe*
  They are gone—   1091

CHORUS   —into air.
  Their bodies have melted into ash and fire,
   to the Underworld they have flown.

CHILDREN Father, do you hear your children mourn?
  Will I ever avenge your death with my own shield?
  May that day come for your child.

  With god willing, we may win   *antistrophe*
  justice for our fathers.

  Movement of CHORUS *and sons toward each other stops.*

CHORUS   Enough pain!
  Enough sorrow, enough   1100
   fruitless grief.

CHILDREN One day the River Asopus at Thebes will shine
  and receive me as I march, leading the men of Argos
  in bronze armor to avenge my father's loss.

234

Father, you seem to hover before my eyes—   *strophe*

CHORUS Leaning close to clasp and kiss—

CHILDREN But your heartening message flies
        into thin air and disappears.

CHORUS He left a double grief: one for the mother,
        one for the son who will grieve forever.   1110

CHILDREN The burden crushes out my life.   *antistrophe*

CHORUS Let me smear my breast with ash.

CHILDREN I hate these words of grief:
        My heart extinguishes.

CHORUS Child, you are gone. My prize, my joy:
        I'll never rock you to sleep, my lovely boy.

Enter THESEUS *and* ADRASTOS *onto the stage.*

THESEUS Adrastos and women of Argos, look on these
        children. They hold their noble fathers' bodies
        in both hands, bodies which I won.
        The City of Athens and I entrust them to these boys.   1120
        But we count on you to commemorate our kindness,
        to preserve the memory of those whom we restored,
        by recounting it to the children, and passing it on
        from father to son, into posterity.
        Thus you will remember always to honor Athens.
        May Zeus and the gods in heaven witness what
        a debt to us you take away with you.

ADRASTOS Theseus, we witness all those noble deeds
        you performed for the Land of Argos, in our need.
        You have our undying thanks. I am forever   1130
        in debt to the grandeur of your help to us.

THESEUS What further service may I render you?

ADRASTOS Fare well, and prosper. You and your city deserve it.

THESEUS We shall indeed fare well. May you also thrive.

> *Enter* ATHENA, *in full armor with helmet, aegis, and*
> *spear, on a concealed platform on the roof of the skēnē.*

ATHENA Listen, Theseus, to Athena's words.
I tell you what you must do to ensure this pact.
Do not give up the bones so easily,
letting the Argive children carry them off.
In return for the pains you and your city have taken
an oath must be sworn. Adrastos, here, must swear it.   1140
He is king, and can make a treaty for all Argos.
The treaty shall be: "Argos will never come
as a hostile force invading Athenian soil.
And if others invade, Argos will fend them off."
If they violate the oath, and attack Athens,
pray that the Land of Argos be destroyed.
Now listen to the method of the sacrifice.
You have a bronze-footed tripod in the house;
Herakles left it when he had just sacked Troy
and was rushing off to perform some other feat: 1150
he pledged you to set it up at the shrine at Delphi.
Cut the throats of three lambs in it, and inscribe the oaths
in the tripod's hollow basin. Then offer it
to Apollo at his shrine in Delphi, to preserve
as a memorial of the oaths, and a witness to Greece.
As for the biting knife with which you slit
the lambs' throats, bury it in the earth
there by the seven heroes' pyres. If Argos
ever marches on Athens, the knife, revealed,
will strike them with terror and bring them evil luck.   1160
Accomplish these rites, and then release the bones.
Then build a shrine where the sacred pyres burned
at the triple crossroads by the road to Argos.
This I declare. But to the Argive children

I proclaim: reach manhood, and destroy Thebes.
Avenge your fathers' deaths. You, Aigialeus,
instead of your father, Adrastos, will lead the assault,
along with Tydeus' son, Diomedes.
Hold back for now: wait till your beards have grown
to rush as the bronze army of Argos against   1170
the seven-mouthed gates of Thebes.
You will be bitter for them: you have been nursed
as lion cubs, destroyers, doom of Thebes.
It shall be so. Epigoni, you will be called,
Avenging Sons. Your fame will resound in song,
so mighty an army you'll form, as you march with the god.

THESEUS Queen Athena, I shall obey your words.
You straighten my path, you keep me from all error.
I shall bind this man to an oath. For only you
guide me in justice. If you look kindly on us   1180
we will flourish safely for all time to come.

CHORUS Come, Adrastos, let us swear a vow
to Theseus and his city. It is just
to honor those who have given us their best.

NOTES

ORCHESTRA AND STAGE

Greek (really Athenian) tragedy is organized by alternating rhythms of speaking roles (episodes) and choral song/dance (*odes*). Formal distinctions in dialect, meter, and movement set these two voices of the drama clearly apart. The Theater of Dionysus, with its twin spaces of orchestra and stage, may well have helped to accent those formal structures of tragedy which distinquish choral from actors' parts. While our knowledge of the fifth-century theater is unfortunately meager, most scholars believe that by 420 B.C. the Theater of Dionysus consisted of a circular orchestra joined to a slightly raised, narrow rectangular stage (called the *logeion*) behind. Stairs, of no more than three or four steps, made communication between the two spaces possible.

Behind the stage, there was a building called a *skēnē*. As well as appearing in the orchestra and stage, actors could also appear above this building, either by being suspended from a crane known now as *deus ex machina* or by standing on a platform, called a *theologoeion* (the place for divine address), near the roof of the *skēnē* hidden from the audience's view, though in point of fact neither the *machina* or the *theologeion* was used exclusively for divine personages. The theater thus offered a tripartite order (orchestra, stage, and area above the *skēnē*) which, like the Globe Theater of Shakespearean London, suggested the structure of the *kosmos*. That is, in the shape of the theater we witness the interaction between the Chorus, who in some fashion represents our common humanity, in the orchestra; the actors (usually heroes), who shape the welfare of the human community, on a raised platform; and the gods, or extra-ordinary human figures, who oversee all from their imperious remove, above the *skēnē*. All three acting areas are used in this play.

Contrary to most commentators on this play, we believe that the altar must be placed in the orchestra. If it were on the stage as is usually claimed, that narrow space would have to hold at least thirty people in the opening scene and the Chorus would have to rise to the stage before the beginning of the prologue, leave for the orchestra for its first dance (the parodos, **40–88** / 42–86), then return to the stage after the song to supplicate Theseus (**272–83** / 271–85), before moving down into the orchestra a final time for the first stasimon once it has released Theseus' mother (**361–76** / 365–80). The latest full study of the play describes its "exceptionally fluid movement," (C. Collard, *Euripides, Supplices*, vol. 1 [Groningen, Neth., 1975], p. 17), but it isn't that. Such movement is dramatically incoherent and unnecessary. The only study to offer an alternative staging does away with the stage altogether (see R. Rehm, "The Staging of Suppliant Plays," *Greek, Roman, and Byzantine Studies* 29 [1988], 283–90). On the other hand, if the altar is in the orchestra, as a number of recent studies have shown is certainly possible for the fifth-century B.C. theater, (see J. P. Poe, "The Altar in the 5th Century Theater," *Classical Antiquity* 8 [1989], 116–39), interaction between Chorus and actors is smooth and theatrically powerful.

When does the play begin? The opening of *Suppliant Women* reveals the nature of this problem in a most dramatic way as more than thirty people, some going to the stage, others remaining in the orchestra, arrive before the first words are spoken. Without a curtain it is hard to know when the Athenians thought that the drama "began." Does the audience consider all preliminary motion to be invisible or, as we prefer, is the pantomime before the prologue like an overture before the first words?

1–39 / 1–42 *Prologue* A narrative prologue is a Euripidean trademark which he uses in almost a naive or primitive manner to introduce the story. Hardly a sign of poor craftsmanship, however, it serves, along with the *deus ex machina*, which closes so many Euripidean dramas, as a framing device to contain the complex twists and reversals of the Euripidean plot.

Masks and Clothing: Both Aithra and the Chorus have masks and clothing which reveal that they are old women (geraiai, **54–56** / 54–56 and **34** / 35, respectively), with gray hair and of noble birth. But in other respects, their costumes show marked contrast: Aithra's bright ceremonial dress clashes with the choral mourning clothes ("not meant for festivals," **97** / 97) and masks of shorn hair. Adrastos' mask (sallow to indicate misfortune and perhaps with matted hair to suggest extreme grief), as his clothing, reveals "a gray-haired man, once a glorious king" (**167** / 166). He must be younger in appearance than the mothers but is bound to them in the mask's expression of grief and advanced years. The sons of the Seven wear masks of prepubescent boys which signify both royal birth and mourning. The simple outlines of a tragic mask depicting a character's age, gender, social station, and pervasive mood invite us to interpret a stage figure in generic terms, defined less as an individual person subject to psychological study than as a type perceived in broad social and religious terms.

1 / 1 The opening line introduces important words in the play: hearth-holder (in contrast with the more common epithet of city-holder for Athena) establishes Demeter's connection with house, family, and renewal. The word *chthōn* (earth) is given particular weight by its place-ment at the end of the line here and in five other instances in Aithra's prologue (4 / 4, 9 / 9, 17 / 17, 28 / 28, 36 / 38). In its repetition, a single concept (land) used to represent different orien-tations opens up a whole range of concerns that the play will explore.

20–24 / 20–24 Adrastos lies prostrate *on the stage* in front of the doors (literally "at the gate" [105 / 104]) to Demeter's temple. The emphatic "this one here" (*hode* at 21 / 21 and 105 / 104) may be read as a stage direction, signifying a shift of attention from Chorus to Adrastos and from orchestra to stage.

26 / 27 Both James Diggle (*Euripidis, Fabulae II*, Oxford, 1981) and Christopher Collard (*Euripides, Supplices*, Leipzig, 1984) now accept *koinon* (in common), instead of the manuscript *monon* (this task above all).

27–31 / 28–31 The choral lament and interruption of a fertility festival in progress threatens to pollute the entire ritual, bringing divine retribution on Attica. Far from feeling threatened by her captivity, however, Aithra responds to the women with sympathy (9–11 / 9–12), pity (33–34 / 34–36), tears and wailing of her own (284–89 / 286–91) and, most important, religious awe (37–38 / 39–40).

Aithra's sacrificing of first fruits at Eleusis is an unmistakeable allusion to the Proerosia, literally "the preliminary to the ploughing." The annual ritual at Eleusis was held on the fifth or sixth day of Pyanopsion (the latter part of October). Athens' motive for reviving and enlarging the festival circa 420 B.C. appears to be anything but reverent: citing Delphi and ancient custom, it required the cities of her empire, and invited all other Greek cities, to contribute a six-hundreth of their barley crop and a twelve-hundreth of their wheat as a first-fruit offering to the earth goddess.

SUPPLIANT WOMEN

40–88 / 42–86 *Parodos* (choral entry song) This is a *parodos* in name only as the Chorus has already entered the theater. (For a parallel, see Aeschylus' *Eumenides*.) Aithra is in the orchestra; Adrastos and the sons of the Seven are on stage during this ode. When not entering or exiting the theater, the chorus of Greek tragedies dance in rectangular movements.

73–88 / 71–86 Reference to attendants here signifies most probably a semichorus, not an extra chorus (cf. 1074 / 1123). Some have argued from this passage that the Chorus (fifteen in number in Euripides' day) consists of seven mothers, seven attendants, and the coryphaeus (or leader). Such precise division of roles is hardly necessary. Although the number of mothers is often listed as seven (cf. 12 / 12, 919 / 963), surely Jocasta is already dead and Amphiaraos' mother is absent. One might consider it odd if Eteoklos' mother (wife of Iphis and mother of Evadne) kept silent while her husband came on stage and her daughter committed suicide. Though all are called Argive women, Polynices' mother (Jocasta) is Theban, Tydeus' mother is Calydonian, and Parthenopaios' mother, Atalanta, is Arcadian. Nor, the audience would know, could Amphiaraos and Polynices be counted among the seven as they were already "buried" (also evident, e.g., in Adrastos' funeral praise of the five recovered corpses [819–62 / 860–908]). As one commentator noted, adherence to "realistic" presentation for the Chorus "would be an unnecessary touch of pedantry" (N. C. Hourmouziades, *Production and Imagination in Euripides* [Athens, 1965], 81). The handmaidens must be seen as mute stage extras.

89–360 / 87–364 *First episode*

89 / 87 Theseus, Aithra's son, enters near the end of the song. How are we to visualize Theseus? He is a young man, much the junior of Adrastos, but is he beardless? Aithra speaks of him frequently as "son" or "child" (*teknon*) (cf. 101 / 100, 110 / 109, 291 / 293, 300 / 307, 316 / 320, 323 / 327) and once as "my son" (*pais*, 298 / 301). Theseus, in turn, calls Aithra "Mother," both in address (284 / 286 and 330 / 334) and when referring to her (92 / 90, 93 / 93 and 355 / 360), but he also calls her "an old woman" (94 / 93). Terms of intimacy like "mother" and "son" must be considered timeless. But the Chorus also calls Theseus *teknon* (280 / 282), which, when used, must be translated "child." Earlier, however, the Chorus spoke of supplicating Theseus by touching his "cheek" (a convention often for beard) (276 / 278) and say that he is the same age as the fallen sons (282/ 283) who, we remember, also have sons who are old enough to

242

speak and to desire revenge. Later, Theseus says that he is old enough
to have survived many toils (335–36 / 339–40, 555 / 573; Aithra clarifies: a
boar hunt, 313 ff. / 316 ff.), but the Herald counters that Theseus is "still a
whelp" (veanias, 562 / 580). In his young manhood, he stands between
the aged Adrastos and the boys of the fallen heroes. The action of this
play will be his coming of age.

How regal was his appearance? Although Theseus was a legendary
king of Athens and Adrastos calls him "most stout-hearted leader in all
Greece, / Lord of Athens" (164–65 / 163–64; see 115 / 113), Theseus
himself speaks of Athens as if, contemporary with the democracy of
Euripides' day, it were a free polis where "the people rule" (399–401 /
404–6). It would thus seem inappropriate for him to wear a crown.

89–100 / 87–99 Theseus enters through the eisodos to the spectator's right (i.e., the
road from Athens). Theseus' opening words follow a typical Euripidean
pattern: they begin with comments made in isolation, addressed to no
one in particular (89–93 / 87–91), followed by visual contact, in this
instance of his mother at the altar surrounded by mourners (signified at
first by an extra metrum cry, "ea," then 93–98 / 92–97). Only then comes
the question which initiates dialogue (98–100 / 98–99).

103–4 / 102–3 It is repeatedly emphasized that the Chorus encircles the altar (see 31 /
33, 94 / 93, 355–56 / 359–60). The area surrounding the altar must also be
large enough to accommodate Aithra and temple attendants.

105 / 104 Theseus for the first time notices, or rather hears, Adrastos who is lying face
down on the stage. When Aithra says, "Let them speak for themselves,
my child" (110 / 109), the play takes a sudden turn as female entreaty
gives way to male debate. We cannot, of course, know how the staging
was managed but, with this shift in focus, it seems reasonable to imagine
a corresponding shift in the place of action from orchestra to stage (at
111–12 / 110–11) where the new themes of rational and political deliber-
ation will be introduced.

111–262 / 110–270 This is the first of the play's two debates or agōnes, popular in
Euripidean tragedy. A fast-paced stichomythia (dialogue of alternating
lines of verse, 116–63 / 115–62) is followed by formal argument (164–249 /
163–249). Theseus' severe interrogation indicates that he, unlike his
mother, will not be swayed by pity or compassion. A scholion to Sophocles' Oedipus at Colonus (at 220) comments (it will amuse some to know)
that Euripides introduced this scene "to lengthen the drama."

132–55 / 131–54 In this version of the myth, Polynices leaves Thebes voluntarily to avoid fulfilling his father's curse. Tydeus was exiled from Calydon for killing his brother Melanippus in a hunting expedition. Though Tydeus claimed the death was an accident, the Calydonians suspected foul play owing to an oracle which had prophesized that Melanippus would kill him. The emblem of Thebes is a lion and that of Calydon a boar. When the two fugitives Polynices and Tydeus were dining in Argos at Adrastos' palace, they began a dispute about the glories of their respective cities. Remembering the prophecy, Adrastos married Aigeia to Polynices and Deipyla to Tydeus and promised to aid each in regaining their lost cities. At Thebes, Tydeus dies from a wound inflicted by a Theban who happened to be named Melanippus.

196–219 / 195–218 Theseus' theodicy. Hardly irrelevant as some have argued, critics have shown how Theseus' speech carefully rebukes Adrastos' plea point by point. Like other fifth-century B.C. theories of evolution, Theseus' view that civilization arises from a primitive, bestial state redresses the older, pessimistic view found in Hesiod's *Works and Days* (109 ff.) that civilization is characterized by a fall from piety. But this argument, which attributes the birth of civilization to the teachings of "some god," also differs from the fifth-century theories represented in Sophocles' "Ode to Man" (*Antigone* 332–71) where man is said to have taught *himself* the arts of language, agriculture, and commerce, or in Aeschylus' *Prometheus Bound* where the rebellious Prometheus, in defiance of the Olympian gods, *taught* man the above-mentioned arts and that of seeing as well.

263–71 / 263–70 Choral use of dialogue trimeters for more than one or two lines "marks its formal engagement in the main action" (Collard, *Euripides, Supplices*, vol. 2 [Groningen, Neth., 1975], 178).

272–83 / 271–85 The Chorus moves from orchestra to stage. These astrophic dactyls do not constitute a regular *stasimon* (i.e., they do not signify a dance), but mark extreme tension, exemplified by the fracturing of the Chorus into two half-choruses (see **578–607 / 598–633**). Similar use of lyrics outside the formal *stasima* are found in two other Euripidean "suppliant plays" but are rare in Aeschylus and Sophocles. Fluctuation in choral voice between first person singular and plural is common throughout the play and suggests that the mothers experience the agonies of despair and lament both individually and collectively. The wailing o's, e's, and a's in these lines are particularly expressive and almost impossible to capture in English.

295–327 / 297–331 A crucial speech as Aithra mediates between the antitheses
of compassion and reasoned discourse and of female and male. For
the relationship between Theseus and Herakles, see commentary on
1149–53, p. 76.

Theseus' filial devotion is as strong at the end of the first episode as it
was at the beginning. The play will continue to explore parent/child
bonds in the Iphis/Evadne episode and in the second *kommos* when the
sons of the Seven swear devotion to their deceased fathers. Others have
commented well on this aspect of the play; see, for example, Peter
Burian, ed., in *Directions in Euripidean Criticism* (Durham, N.C.,
1985): "as so often in this play, personal emotion spills over into political
signification" (p. 138).

Theseus enters the orchestra and bids the Chorus release his mother
from the grip of its boughs. Mother, son, and Adrastos exit right, through
the *eisodos*. It is at this time that the sons of the Seven probably move down
into the orchestra, though others imagine this to happen at 114 / 113.

313 / 317 What we translate as "in sport," Aithra calls "a trivial labor" (*phaulon ponon*).
Contrary to what she says of the boar hunt here, it was conventionally
regarded as one of Theseus' famous exploits and was, for example,
depicted on the metopes of the Theseion (later called the Hephaesteion)
in the Athenian agora.

348–49 / 352–53 Theseus' claim to have established Athenian democracy is an obvious
anachronism. Words with *iso-* (equal), in them, as here with "equal
votes," are important throughout the play (e.g., 424–33 / 432–41 and 672 /
706, where "the equally-poised *agōn*" before Thebes recalls Theseus'
earlier *agōn* with the Theban herald).

361–76 / 365–80 *First stasimon* The stage is empty for this brief ode; the sons of the
Seven remain in the orchestra. The song gives Theseus time to go to
Athens to win the peoples' (*dēmos*) approval and to return with an army.

377–577 / 381–597 *Second episode*

377 / 381 At the end of the first *stasimon*, Theseus and Adrastos return from Athens
(right *eisodos*). In midconversation with an Athenian herald (nonspeak-
ing part), Theseus *et al.* slowly mount the stairs to the stage where the
play's second agon is about to begin.

394–565 / 399–584 Second agon, framed by the thwarted Athenian embassy (377–93 /
381–98) and Theseus' departure for war (565–77 / 584–97), comprises

most of this episode. Formal argument (**398–545** / 403–563) gives way to stichomythia (**548–62** / 566–80). The mask of the Theban Herald reveals that he is older than Theseus but of lower station. The actor who previously played Aithra now plays the herald. Against earlier, and what appear to be conventional, treatments of this story (i.e., Aeschylus' *Eleusinians*; cf. Plutarch's *Theseus* 29.4 ff.), Euripides chooses to resolve tensions between Athens and Thebes by war. Contrary to most of the "suppliant" plays, the herald here does not attempt to seige the suppliants by force.

It is a mistake to read Theseus as an idealized but poorly disguised portrait of Pericles, Athens' great ruler, recently dead from the plague, who (paraphrasing Thucydides 2.65.9) governed a city democratic in name but monarchical in nature. To see this young Theseus as a mature politician ignores the important lessons he learns about religion, ancient law, and persuasion and fails to acknowledge his initiation into manhood through the experience of war.

430–33 / 438–41 John Milton, who read and annotated Euripides extensively, was particularly struck by these lines, placing them on the title page of his *Areopagitica* (1644).

469–82 / 479–93 No Greek author spoke more passionately than Euripides about the horrors of war, the cause of peace, and the abuse of those defeated in war (see *Hecuba*, *The Trojan Women*), and no one better championed the cause of women and the politically oppressed (see *Medea*). However, Euripides cannot easily be considered a pacifist (see *Heracleidae*) or a staunch defender of women's rights (again the *Medea*; the once-sympathetic Chorus' uncomprehending horror at Medea by play's end; cf. the female Chorus' joy in Dionysus' brutal revenge in *The Bacchae*).

484–85 / 496–97 Euripides puns on Capaneus' name, as if from "Smoke Man," implying his death from Zeus' thunderbolt was fated.

559 / 577 These lines acknowledge Athens' most famous characteristic: its meddling in other's affairs, a quality variously admired or regarded as arrogance leading to the city's ruin.

578–607 / 598–633 *Second stasimon* The predominant meter of this song is iambic trimeter. Adrastos remains on stage; the sons of the Seven in the orchestra. Like the last song, this one "marks time" while Theseus is away at war. It is rare in Greek tragedy for a chorus in a formal *stasimon* to break up, as here, into hemichoruses (see **272–83** / 271–85), and Euripides deviates from conventional form to reveal the mothers' great anxiety over the outcome of war.

608–740 / 634–777 *Third episode* At the end of the last song, a messenger arrives from Thebes and rushes to the stage to announce the news of Athenian victory. Captured earlier in Adrastos' attack against Thebes, but now freed by Theseus, the Argive messenger is able both to criticize Adrastos' conduct in the first war and to praise Theseus' in the second. The mask for this Argive citizen of indeterminate age will reveal, most probably, a male of the middle class (see **243–45** / 244–45). He is played by the actor who played the Theban Herald and Aithra. Euripides was a master of the messenger's report (a tragic convention of reporting offstage events, like battles and violent deaths, which were unsuitable for the theater), and brought the form to new heights. A technique which he used in all but one of his extant plays, the messenger's speech in this play is particularly fine for its relatively unordained style, rapid pace, and epic flavor. The word that we translate as "watch" (**625** / 652) in Greek is *theatēs* (observer or spectator), as if the messenger were recounting a theatrical performance.

623–38 / 650–67 The Athenian army, divided according to infantry (**627** / 654), cavalry (**633** / 660), and chariots (**634** / 662) into three detachments (**626** / 653), surrounds Thebes, as the Argive army did in its attack according to Aeschylus' *Seven against Thebes*. The infantry invests the area south of the walls from the Ismenean hill in the southeast (**628** / 655) to the fountain of Ares in the southwest (**632** / 660); the chariots occupy the area to the north of the walls where Amphion's tomb is found (**635** / 666). The cavalry, in detachments of equal size (**634** / 661), take positions to the east and west of the walls. The messenger, located at the Electran gate in the eastern portion of the city, claims that he was able to *see* the chariots which only seems possible if they moved southward in the course of the battle (**653–54** / 684–85). Theseus commanded the right wing of the Athenian infantry in the southeast, not far from the Electran gate. For the battle reconstruction, see James Diggle, "The *Supplices* of Euripides," *Greek, Roman, and Byzantine Studies* 14 (1973), 252–63.

677 / 712 Claiming descent from the dragon's teeth sown by Cadmus, the Cadmeans (or Thebans) were known as *Spartoi* (Sown Men).

679–82 / 714–17 For the Epidaurian club, see **1149–53** / 1198–1202.

692 ff. / 727 ff. The praise of Theseus here corrects what the Theban Herald had said about brash young leaders and instead identifies Theseus with the wise and brave (cf. **496–98** / 508–10).

699 / 734 Although on stage since **377** / 381, Adrastos has not spoken since **262** / 270, except for the beginning of a speech interrupted by Theseus (**501** / 513). He is likely that he leaves the stage, along with the Messenger, at the end of the episode (**740** / 777). His purpose will be to herald in the corpses.

703 ff. / 739 ff. Eteokles' offer of compromise is not attested elsewhere. Euripides invents the story to illustrate further Argos' aggressive and unwarranted attack against Thebes.

741–56 / 778–93 *Third stasimon* In iambic dimeters and trimeters, this song sets the mood of lamentation that marks choral sentiments for the remainder of the play. The structure of that lament follows closely the pattern of Greek funerary mourning: the carrying out of the corpses with attendant mourners, graveside eulogy, cremation, presentation of the ashes with further choral lamentation (third *stasimon* and first *kommos*, Adrastos' funeral oration, final *kommos*). Although choral lyric comprises less than a seventh of the lines in the first half of the play, it dominates the second half, comprising close to a third of the lines. The sons of the Seven remain in the orchestra for this song.

757–909 / 794–954 *Fourth episode*

757–96 / 794–837 First *kommos* (literally a striking, especially a beating of the breasts, *kommos* in tragedy refers to a song sung alternately by an actor and the Chorus, usually in a mournful dirge) is set off by Adrastos' arrival, with Athenian pall-bearers, of the five recovered bodies. Initial anapests (**757–60** / 794–97) as the corpses arrive give way to a meter similar to that in the last song, though more frequent resolutions and suppressions of iambs mark increased passion. If we are right, Adrastos moves to the stage with the bodies; the mothers and sons remain in the orchestra.

798–800 / 839–41 Textual corruption here requires some guesswork in the translation.

805–15 / 846–56 These lines have been interpreted as a Euripidean sneer at the general convention of messenger speeches. More probably, they serve the needs of the play, pointing out the purpose of Theseus' request.

NOTES

910–34 / 955–79 *Fourth stasimon* This song is in aeolics. For the first time in the play, the Chorus sings in a theater empty of all other characters. The subsequent scene, with its new characters and fresh plot, will be free from all visual associations with the main plot.

935–1064 / 980–1113 *Fifth episode*

935–85 / 980–1033 Anapests (**935–44** / 980–89) for Evadne's arrival lead into her lyric monody (**945–85** / 990–1033), a favorite form in Euripidean dramaturgy to express intense emotion for an actor (in aeolics, linking this song to the ode in front of it). The strophe is separated from the antistrophe by a choral utterance in iambic trimeters (**962–64** / 1009–11). In later experiments with this form, Euripides will abandon the strophic structure altogether, presumably because the formal balance of strophe and antistrophe was felt to inhibit the unbridled emotional outburst characteristic of the monody. Aristophanes in *The Frogs* (1331 ff.) brilliantly parodies these scenes.

Evadne is played, most likely, by the same actor who plays Theseus. Her mask, like Theseus', shows a young adult of noble standing and, like her attire, conveys joy, not mourning.

939–44 / 984–89 Evadne enters high up on a cliff overlooking the temple precinct. In a personal discussion (December 10, 1991) William Arrowsmith suggested that Evadne's joy speaks of a person unhinged, made mad from grief. As such, she would be another of Euripides' women who are victims of unendurable pain.

How did she enter? Scholars seem agreed that it would be aesthetically unacceptable for both Evadne and Athena to appear as *deae ex machina*. But, as hinted in the introduction, the two may interestingly be compared as both are above the human world and insensitive to it, both display something of a military outlook (see Evadne's language), and both defend violent action whether in the form of suicide or an insistence on revenge. Of course, differences between the two are equally significant: one is mortal and in love with death, the other is divine; one is motivated by eros, the other by political imperative. Perhaps it is best, finally, to see them occupying distinct spaces. Either could arrive on the *machina* or appear on the *theologeion*, and both possibilities have been proposed for each figure, but it is certainly easier to imagine Evadne leaping into the pyre from the stage building than from the *machina*. As Peter Burian has pointed out in personal correspondence (October 1, 1993), late Euripides appears to be fond of human characters appearing from the *theologeion*, as exampled by Antigone in the *Phoenician Women* and the mad tableau at the end of the *Orestes*.

986 / 1034 Iphis is played, most probably, by the same actor who plays Adrastos. His mask, like Adrastos' and those of the Chorus, shows an aged man of noble standing in extreme grief. The visual contrast between the masks of Evadne and Iphis must have been haunting. Feeling a grief analogous to that of the mothers, Iphis most probably remains in the orchestra for the entire scene, where he will also have a better view of Evadne. Iphis' wife, we recall, is also one of the seven mothers of the Chorus.

1011 / 1059 The phrase "glory in victory" (*kallinikos*) recalls Adrastos' "glorious in victory" (*kallinike*) to praise Theseus at 114 / 113.

1021–23 / 1069–71 A fair number of young women in Euripides commit suicide, not so much as Phaedra in the *Hippolytus* to escape shame, but as a female form of heroism (cf. Iphigeneia in the *Iphigeneia at Aulis*, Macaria in *Heracleidae*, Praxithea's daughter in *Erechtheus* [a fragment], and Laodamia in *Protesilaus* [a fragment]). No suicide is more vainglorious and meaningless than Evadne's in the *Suppliant Women*. The most noble of all these self-sacrificers, who dies for honor and to escape shame, is Polyxena in *Hecuba*. In *Heracles Mad*, suicide is seen as a less heroic path than that of facing one's shame. Almost certainly, Evadne jumps to a pyre offstage.

1024–31 / 1072–79 The short second *kommos*. As Evadne leaps, the Chorus and Iphis break into agitated dochmii, formally joining them in their shared feelings of horror and loss.

1065–1116 / 1114–64 The third (and final) *kommos*, replaceing a final stasimon. The Chorus announces in anapests (1065–73 / 1114–22) the return of the sons of the Seven with the ashes. At 1074 / 1123, the sons, a secondary chorus, first on stage (1–360 / 1–364) and then in the orchestra (361–900 / 365–946) before they leave to cremate the remains of their fathers, moves back to the stage and speaks for the first time. Rather than regard this long silence "as one of the many weaknesses in Euripides' *Suppliants*, a play with none of the intensity or scenic and dramatic economy of Aeschylus' *Suppliants*," as Oliver Taplin says in *The Stagecraft of Aeschylus* (Oxford, 1977), 236–37, we believe it is a masterful stroke. Economical in its clear imitation of, and divergence from, the first *kommos*, intense in its testimony that the buried dead are still very much alive and to be feared (see 526–31 /

542–48), scenic and visual in its portrayal of the unbridgeable gulf between orchestra and stage, expressed here as the gulf between the desire for peace and the blood urge for revenge.

A number of plays in Greek tragedy have a secondary chorus, but Euripides is the only tragedian to give speaking parts to children. As here, all instances occur in lyrics.

1074–1112 / 1123–60 There are many textual difficulties in these lines, but the most serious problem concerns the designation of parts for primary and secondary chorus. In this, we deviate from Collard (1984) and follow Diggle (*Euripidis, Fabulae II*, 1981).

1117–84 / 1165–1234 *Exodos* This term refers to the remainder of the drama after the final choral song. It is a signature of Euripidean dramaturgy to conclude with a divine epiphany or an epilogue (in nine of his seventeen extant plays), but no divine appearance is more abrupt than this one. Athena is played by the same actor who played Aithra (and the Theban Herald and Argive Messenger). For her entrance, see **939–44** / 984–89. Her mask, perhaps imitating the ivory and gold cult statue of *Athena Parthenos* in the Parthenon completed by Phidias in 438 B.C., signifies her divinity.

1149–53 / 1198–1202 Herakles' tripod. As often in Attic mythology, Theseus is a double of Herakles, here suggested by reference to Theseus' boar hunt, his Epidaurian club like Herakles' telltale weapon, and the tripod which Herakles won at Troy and gave to Theseus to dedicate at Delphi. Has Theseus been remiss in his obligations? The story appears to be another Euripidean invention. As the tripod in the past marked Theseus' debt to, and bond with, Herakles, so now it testifies to Adrastos' debt and obligation to Theseus.

1163 / 1212 For the reading "by the road to Argos" we follow an emendation suggested by B. Heath in 1762, accepted by Collard (1984), but not by Diggle (1981). There are several manuscript difficulties with the line, not the least of which is the reading *theou* (of the god), in place of Heath's *hodou* (road.) But it is not at all certain what deity is meant; suggestions range from Hecate to Poseidon to Metaneira to Leucothea. Others read *theōi* (to the god), referring to Apollo. Road makes good sense: the exact location of the *temenos* marking the pyres of the dead (except for Capaneus who is buried in Demeter's sacred precinct, **942–44** / 987–89) and the placement of the buried sacrificial knife is unspecified, but as Collard remarks no place would be more suitable than the fork where the road from the Isthmus divides, one leading to Thebes, the other along the coast to Athens (Collard, *Euripides, Supplices*, vol. 2 [Groningen, Neth., 1975], 417–18).

1173 / 1223 The image of the Epigoni as lion cubs recalls the oracle in which Apollo instructed Adrastos to wed his daughters to a boar and a lion (see 141 / 140). Calling humans *skumnoi*, used of young animals (whelp, puppy, etc.), is common in Euripides and deliberate, as it suggests a bestial ferocity and emnity, as well as courage, in man when the young mature.

1182–84 / 1232–34 It is the convention in Greek tragedy that the Chorus marches out of the theater to mark the close.

ION

Translated by

W. S. DI PIERO

With Introduction and Notes by

PETER BURIAN

INTRODUCTION

I

The *Ion* is one of those plays of Euripides that refuses to stay put. Is it a
savage attack on Apollo and traditional Greek religion? a celebration of
Athens' divine origins and imperial destiny? or a sophisticated and
disenchanted comedy of ideas? It has been claimed as all these things
and more. Although the various readings seem fundamentally incom-
patible, none can simply be dismissed as without textual foundation. But
attempts to fix the play's meaning by reference to a religious or political
thesis or even to escapism dictated by the hard times in Athens around
410 B.C.[1] are inevitably reductive. Even a cursory glance at the action is
enough to suggest what disturbing riptides of thought and feeling run
just below the shimmering surface of Euripidean melodrama.

Kreousa, queen of Athens, and Xouthos, her foreign husband, arrive at
Delphi to ask Apollo's help in ending their childlessness. The god,
however, had long ago raped Kreousa and left her with a son whom
she bore in secret and abandoned. Unbeknownst to her, Apollo had the
baby brought to Delphi and raised to become a temple servant. Now,
when the boy is already entering young manhood, Apollo bestows him
on Xouthos as the latter's child. Kreousa, who does not know the truth
about the child's identity, reacts to her husband's good fortune by trying
to kill—as an interloper—the very son she has despaired of finding. The
attempt providentially fails, but it is only after the boy in turn threatens
Kreousa with death that the Pythia at last reveals the birth tokens that
permit the mother to recognize and embrace her son. The child of
Kreousa and Apollo will now shoulder his Athenian destiny, and

---

1. The date of the *Ion* is not certain, but metrical and other considerations suggest the period
412–410 B.C.

Xouthos will be left content in the belief that the boy, whom he has named Ion, is really his own.

We, as audience, are let in from the very start on what otherwise only the gods know—who Ion is—and thus the sort of irony that has come to be called tragic from countless discussions of Sophocles' *Oedipus* (a play that shares the *Ion's* underlying myth of the foundling's return) pervades the entire work. Only here, because the prologue also assures us that the ending will be "happy," the effect is more like that of comedy. In fact, the plot is quite similar to that of a comedy by a fourth-century playwright, Menander's *Arbitration (Epitrepontes)*.[2] This helps to explain the unease many have felt about the play's genre, for it seems to oscillate between tragedy and something else, not comedy as fifth-century Athens understood it, but what was to become the comic tradition from Menander to Molière and beyond. This is not, of course, to say that the nature of the *Ion* is fully revealed by claiming it for comedy. Its plot, after all, is also reminiscent of innumerable accounts of heroic births and childhoods, for example, that of Persian king Cyrus in Herodotus' account.[3] And for all that it ends in resolution, the *Ion* again and again arouses a *frisson* through its near misses, intentions, and actions that almost end in disastrous overturns of fortune.

Later theories of genre notwithstanding, Greek tragedy in the later fifth century, especially that of Euripides, clearly welcomes such mixtures with open arms. In that respect, the *Ion* belongs squarely with Euripides' *Iphigeneia in Tauris* and *Helen* (two plays close in date) that also show features of romantic melodrama and depend on recognitions that lead to happy endings; but they also deal in serious ways with ignorance, violence, cruelty, and the threat of death as well as with the possibility of hope and of healing. It is precisely in the mixture of opposites, in an irreducible doubleness, that the particular genius of this play finds its expression.

The play itself provides a fitting emblem of its own doubleness at the midpoint, when Kreousa, queen of Athens, decides that the interloper Ion must be destroyed. To accomplish this, she produces a bracelet containing two drops of Gorgon's blood given by Athena to her ancestor Erichthonios: "One kills, the other cures" (**979 / 1005**). Kreousa wants to

---

2. We possess something like two-thirds of *Arbitration* in fragmentary papyri. The plot is clear: A young woman has been raped by a rich young man, the baby is exposed but saved, and a recognition restores order by establishing that the father is none other than the man the mother subsequently married.

3. Herodotus *Histories* 1. 108–24. Cyrus, like Ion, is adorned in burial clothes, placed in a basket, and left in a remote place; brought up in a slave's family, he is eventually recognized, is reintegrated into his royal family, and fulfills his destined role as king.

use only the lethal drop, and the healing drop is never mentioned again, but its presence here can hardly be a mere nod in the direction of the conventional etiology of Athena's aegis, which Euripides otherwise sets aside.[4] It represents a possibility that the play will realize at last (and in the nick of time) when Kreousa and Ion stand revealed to each other as long-lost mother and son. Kreousa keeps the drops apart, for she believes that "good and evil do not mix" (991 / 1017). The play shows that she is wrong; that in the world the two are always and inextricably linked, indeed, are often the same thing differently experienced, differently understood. As the elaborate plot unfolds, any claim to final certainty about good and evil is undercut. Kreousa's drops of blood—"a double gift from the goddess" (984 / 1010)—function as a symbol of a deep double-ness in life that the play painfully encodes and that becomes, as much as anything, what it is about.[5]

II

A characteristic form of doubling in the *Ion* is the repetition of the past in the present.[6] The story of Apollo's rape of Kreousa and the secret birth and exposure of their child in the cave is told no less than five times; different contexts and tonalities mark the successive stages of its progress toward fulfillment in the drama. Hermes, who saved Ion without Kreousa's knowledge after she had exposed her son, now introduces the action that will reunite mother and child. Ion's survival replicates that of his mother, lone survivor among Erechtheus' daughters, sacrificed by their father (266–69 / 277–80). His birth is symbolically repeated, with naming and birthday feast, and when at last he is united with his mother, he comes to feel that he has been born again: "Dear mother, I was dead once, now in your arms I'm alive again" (1397 / 1443–44). Kreousa, who set him out to die in her despair, again attempts to kill him; Apollo, who spared him once, saves him again. Similarly, the plot itself shows several crucial doublets: two consultations of the oracle, Kreousa's hindered by Ion and Xouthos' successfully concluded with Apollo's gift of Ion; two recognition scenes, the deceptive one between Ion and Xouthos, the genuine one between Ion and Kreousa; two attempted killings,

4. See further section III of this Introduction.
5. It is worth noticing how this doubleness is encoded for Greek culture specifically in the representation of gender. The monstrous Gorgon, whose look turns men to stone; the goddess Athena, virgin and warrior; and Kreousa, mother and (potential) murderer—all suggest the equivocal status of female subjectivity in the Greek (male) imagination.
6. For repetition as "the principal means of the play's construction," see Christian Wolff, "The Design and Myth in Euripides' *Ion*," *Harvard Studies in Classical Philology* 69 (1965): 169–94. Wolff's article remains one of the best general introductions to the play.

Kreousa's of Ion and Ion's of Kreousa. Finally, the Pythia's appearance at the end of the drama to return Ion's birth tokens and send him on his way to Athens replicates—on the spot where she found him—her divinely guided decision to take him in as foster child on the god's behalf. Through the tokens, unwittingly—but once more inspired by Apollo— she restores him to his true mother.

As the *Ion* recounts a story of origins, familial and dynastic, its most obvious and persistent doubling—indeed, multiplication—is that of parents, real and imagined. Ion, of course, is one of the Greek heroes (Herakles is the most famous) for whom the tradition claimed dual paternity, human and divine. Yet Ion can say as the play begins, "No mother, no father / watches over me" (99–100 / 109). For him, Apollo is only *like* a father, the Pythia takes the place of a mother, but his real origins remain hidden. Prompted by Apollo, Kreousa's husband, Xouthos, will claim Ion as his son and on Apollo's orders will be left with this illusion even as Ion comes to know that he is truly the god's own child. As regards his mother, Ion speculates that she was "a woman treated wrongly" (314 / 324), and Xouthos, happily bemused to find he has a son at Delphi, recalls an earlier visit "for the torchlight mysteries of Dionysos" (528 / 550) when he slept with a local girl. Kreousa's old retainer goes so far as to imagine that Xouthos deliberately "takes to bed some slave girl" (788 / 819) after he sees that his wife will bear him no children and that he thus stages the trip to Delphi to find Ion by seeming accident. Only later, after Kreousa's attempted murder and Ion's threatened revenge, do hated stepson and stepmother find in each other the parent and child each has longed for. At that point, however, when Ion learns that Xouthos is not his father, he supposes that he must be the fruit of some secret, shameful love affair, and he refuses to accept Kreousa's word for Apollo's paternity. Only Athena's appearance *ex machina* stops him from confronting the god to "ask point-blank" (1516 / 1547).

The imagined doubling of parents implies, of course, a corresponding duplication of children. Ion becomes through Apollo's gift the son Xouthos never knew he had. Kreousa, who assumes that Apollo has abandoned their child to die, invents a fictitious double through whom she tells of the loss of a son just Ion's age. And only after attempting to kill the son she believes to be Xouthos' does she discover that he is the very one she lost.

Corresponding to this doubling of parents and children is a pair of opposing models of generation and birth that seem to vie for primacy within the play. A specifically Athenian tale of autochthony, birth directly from earth, defies the usual sexual model of generation, and this tension persists throughout the play.[7] Athenians in Euripides' day apparently still believed that they were an indigenous people, subject neither to invasions nor migrations; their early history, prominently featuring kings born from the soil itself, confirmed this and reinforced their pride in their racial purity. Tension initially arises in the *Ion* because only Kreousa—emphatically connected to the tradition of autochthony as the sole surviving descendant of earthborn Erichthonios— can perpetuate the royal line, through sexual union, of course, and the motherhood she so deeply desires. Xouthos, on the other hand, is an outsider, a Euboean whose military aid to Athens has won him Kreousa as a "war prize" (**287** / 298). Thus, when Ion appears to be his son but not hers, she attempts to kill one who might, as the king's son, wrest Athens from its indigenous ruling house.

The fact that autochthonous nobility in this story is invested in the female exposes the central political issues of racial purity and exclusivity to a particular kind of irony. Autochthony, although in itself suggesting the motherhood of Earth, functions in Greek myth largely to exclude the female element in the ideology of birth and birthright. An autochthonous Athens is first of all a city of male warriors sprung from earth, needing no human mothers and therefore not subject to the uncertainty of sexual generation. Yet the future of autochthonous Athens depends on Kreousa's bearing a child who will perpetuate the royal line.[8] With appropriate irony, the Chorus of Kreousa's attendants invokes the virginal, motherless goddess Athena, "Delivered from the summit / From the head of Zeus / By Titan Prometheus" (**435–37** / 455–57), in its prayer that Kreousa be granted a child.

A further irony in Kreousa's role as preserver of the autochthonous Athenian line is that by giving birth to a male heir who survives, she definitively removes reproduction from the sphere of woman to that of man. The motherless Erechtheus gave birth only to women, then returned to a chasm of the earth from which he sprang (**266–71** / 277–82). Kreousa alone of his daughters survived and conceived a child by Apollo, but the baby was adorned for death and returned to a hollow in the earth

7. Autochthony has been much discussed in recent years in relation to the *Ion*. See George Walsh, "The Rhetoric of Birthright and Race in Euripides' *Ion*," *Hermes* 106 (1978): 302–15; Arlene W. Saxonhouse, *Fear of Diversity* (Chicago 1992), 76–89; and Saxonhouse, "Myths and the Origins of Cities: Reflections on the Autochthony Theme in Euripides' *Ion*," in J. Peter Euben, ed., *Greek Tragedy and Political Theory* (Berkeley and Los Angeles 1986). Of particular interest is Nicole Loraux, "Kreousa the Autochthon: A Study of Euripides' *Ion*," in John J. Winkler and Froma I. Zeitlin, eds., *Nothing to Do with Dionysos?* (Princeton 1990): 168–206.

8. Loraux (see n. 7 above) 191–92 points out that ensuring a lineage to autochthonous beings, whose origin is not held to lie in sexual reproduction, is highly problematic. Kreousa's childlessness is thus a reflex of the larger problem of ensuring descent in an autochthonous line.

(**1458–61** / 1494–96). The discovery that Ion was rescued will change the pattern; the boy is to become a man, beget children, and bring the Athenian line into the orbit of male procreation. Autochthony henceforth will conform to the model of patriarchy.

Beyond these ironies, the mixture of Apollonian and chthonian in Ion's blood that confers upon him his destiny as founder of cities and ruler of men also marks him out as radically impure, as a compound of beast and god—in short, as quintessentially human, as the hero he is to become. Ion, immersed in a dream of pure service of a god whose whole essence is purity, must come to accept himself as the product of that same god's violent lust and as destined for future greatness. And he learns his origins only after he feels the murderous violence of which his own soul is capable.[9] Indeed, Ion's very existence belies the idyll of purity and simplicity that is his Delphic life, calls into question the Apollo of his devotions, the Apollo he dreams of as ideal father (**126–31** / 136–43).

One further, equally crucial point about birth and birthright must be made here. The Chorus, as it prays on behalf of its mistress, wishes for the same boon: "children of my own blood" (**466** / 487)—and the play presents this desire as universal. (For Ion, of course, it takes the form of wanting to know his true parents.) But the inverse proposition seems also to be universal: No one will want what is *not* his or hers. Apollo concerns himself with Ion's well-being solely because of his paternity. There is no suggestion at all that a more general (or less selfish) providence is at work shaping Ion's fate. Not surprisingly, Apollo understands the need to trick Xouthos into accepting Ion as his own. Although Apollo is god of prophecy, he fails to read Kreousa's heart or divine that she will feel the same way. The astonishing fact that Apollo's plans go awry is due to nothing more or less than Kreousa's unwillingness to accept into her home (and Athens' ruling line) an alien child while she herself still suffers from the loss of her own son and the pains of her subsequent barrenness. This is what brings her, with the old tutor egging her on, to the point of murdering Ion.

Only the Pythia, priestess of the oracle at Delphi, seems capable of loving what is not her own: the baby Ion whom she is horrified to find at the door of the temple, but then accepts "with Apollo's help" (**39** / 47–48) and raises as if she were his mother. The Pythia, after all, has sacrificed private life and family, and she is to that extent exempt from the interests and jealousies that move both gods and men. Her rescue of Ion is an act of loving kindness, the sort of pure caring, apart from ties of blood or hopes of gain, that in Euripides can illuminate even the most bleakly tragic scene

9. I owe this suggestion to Professor Herbert Golder.

(one thinks particularly of Theseus in the *Herakles* gently leading the hero back to life after he has slaughtered his own children). Ion has come to call the Pythia mother (**310** / **321**), a name she gladly accepts "though it's only a name" (**1277** / **1325**). But the relationship cannot be understood simply in terms of human solidarity, for just as Hermes connects the Pythia's pity with Apollo's plans for his son, so she herself emphatically associates her nurture of the baby Ion and her saving of his birth tokens with Apollo's inspiration (**1298–1301** / 1346–49, **1309–12** / 1357–60). Thus, the Pythia, without knowing how or why, salvages the god's secretive and nearly botched bestowal of Ion's birthright, cuts him loose from the imaginary idyll of her maternity, and sends him out into the dangers and promise of a life that befits a man, the life of the *polis*.

III

The fact that the play is set before Apollo's temple at Delphi is no doubt in the first instance a way of emphasizing the role of the god in the story,[10] but place functions in the *Ion* in typically multivalent and ironic fashion. The extraordinary *parodos* (**164–225** / 184–236) casts the Chorus members as awed and delighted tourists seeing the famous sanctuary for the first time, with Ion as their local guide. There is nothing like it in extant tragedy; the closest parallel comes from a fragmentary satyr play of Aeschylus, the *Theoroi* or *Isthmiastai*, in which a chorus of satyrs describe images of themselves that they carry as votive offerings to hang on the temple of Poseidon at the Isthmus. If the origins of the scene are thus comic rather than tragic, that is entirely in keeping with Euripides' technique in this play.[11] What Euripides has the Chorus see and inter-pret, and thus conjure up in our mind's eye, is a series of mythological scenes that show victory over monstrous creatures born of earth: Herakles killing the Hydra with the help of his companion Iolaos; Bellerophon mounted on Pegasos slaying the Chimaera; and finally the Gigantoma-chy, the great battle of gods and giants, with Athena brandishing her shield, Zeus his lightning, and Dionysos his thyrsus against the rebels. The theme and its treatment, not dictated by the actual temple decor-ations at Delphi,[12] suggest Apollo's triumph over Kreousa, whose descent

10. We know that Sophocles wrote a *Kreousa*, and it is likely, although impossible to prove, that this play dealt with the same subject as the *Ion*, preceded it, and was set in Athens.
11. For a discussion of the Aeschylean fragment in relation to the drama of Euripides, see Froma I. Zeitlin, "The Artful Eye: Vision, Ecphrasis and Spectacle in Euripidean Theatre," in Simon Gold-hill and Robin Osborne, eds., *Art and Text in Ancient Greek Culture* (Cambridge 1994): 138–96, esp. 138–39. This article contains an illuminating analysis of the *parodos* and other ecphrastic elements in the *Ion*, 147–56.
12. On this subject see Vincent J. Rosivach, "Earthborns and Olympians: The Parodos of the *Ion*," *Classical Quarterly* 27 (1977): 284–94.

from the offspring of Earth is emphasized in her subsequent dialogue with Ion. Kreousa is associated throughout the play with chthonian serpents such as the Hydra and Chimaera; like the giants, she finds herself in increasingly open rebellion against the Olympian Apollo. But the images bespeak not only violence, for the heroic defeat of monsters and the gods' suppression of the giants are for the Greeks—from the time of Hesiod onward—above all, emblems of the imposition of order and civilization on a chaotic and anarchic world. A similar constellation of ideas informs the loving description of another Delphic space shaped by art, the tent set up to celebrate Ion's "finding" by Xouthos, only to become the scene of Kreousa's attempt to kill Ion.[13] The decoration consists of elaborate tapestries seized by Herakles when he subdued the Amazons: hangings that depict the harmonious order of the heavens but are filled also with equivocal images of monsters, of Athenian king Kekrops and his ill-fated daughters, and of a Greek fleet facing barbarian ships (1108–31 / 1141–65).

Such depictions and remembrances of violence subduing violence underline the fact that Delphi in this play is ironically the scene of a rebellion against Apollo's power. Kreousa comes to Apollo's shrine ready to denounce him to his face for his violence, much to Ion's horror (351–67 / 362–80). The old tutor, when he learns that Apollo has given Xouthos a child and (as it seems) denied one to Kreousa, first suggests the mad revenge of burning down Apollo's temple (948 / 974). The saner plan that Kreousa settles on will still, if it succeeds, produce pollution beyond all imagining by killing Apollo's servant (and, as we know, his son) in the sacred tent during his feast of thanksgiving. The Delphians condemn her to death by stoning for "conspiring to pollute / the precinct with blood" (1176–77 / 1224–25). Ion, whose cult of purity is given charming embodiment in his shooing of the birds that soil the sacred offerings, threatens them with his bow, but does not shoot out of reverence for "message-bringers / from the gods" (160–61 / 179–80). And, indeed, it is a bird, a dove wandering free in Apollo's sanctuary, that the god prompts to drink the wine poured on the ground, thus exposing Kreousa's plot. Ironically, however, Ion threatens to cause pollution in turn by seizing Kreousa at the altar where she has taken refuge, thus giving herself "into the god's keeping" (1236 / 1285). The ironies of this scene are the culmination of all that came before. Kreousa, who denounced Apollo's violence and lack of care, now stakes

13. For a detailed analysis and interpretation of the tent's representations, see Froma I. Zeitlin, "Mysteries of Identity and Designs of the Self in Euripides' *Ion*," *Proceedings of the Cambridge Philological Society* 35 (1989): 144–97, esp. 166–69.

her life on his protection. Ion, whose life has until now been dedicated to Apollo's service, doubts the justice of his dispensation. Despite Kreousa's claim of divine protection, Ion feels no pity for her, though he pities his absent mother (**1225–26** / 1276–77). But in answer to the reproach that she "tried to poison Apollo's child," Kreousa reminds Ion that he now belongs to Xouthos, whereas she is Apollo's (**1237–40** / 1286–89). Ion chastises Apollo for allowing a criminal to be his suppliant ("No stained hands / touch this holy shrine" [**1267–68** / 1315–16]) and is moving to seize Kreousa when the Pythia suddenly appears. The revelation she sets in motion of Ion's parentage is one that Athena later tells them Apollo would have preferred to postpone but permits to prevent them from killing each other (**1533–39** / 1563–68).

Athens, of course, as the origin and destination of virtually all the characters of the play, is its other crucial place, equally mixed in its meanings. The emphasis on Athenian purity that, as we have seen, is focused around the autochthonous racial exclusivity of the Erechtheid line, has often been thought to appeal to local pride, but the *Ion* is notable for its absence of praise of the city and her institutions. Ion mentions Athens' democratic politics only to reflect on how as an immigrant he will be barred from taking part (**565–78** / 589–606). Unlike earlier Euripidean dramas (such as the *Children of Herakles* and the *Suppliant Women*) that celebrate Athens as a refuge for foreigners, the *Ion* makes outsiders a source of undefined but powerful fears. Very likely this reflects the "enormous fear and consternation" (Thucydides 8.1.2) that followed on the disastrous Athenian defeat in Sicily (413 B.C.) and the subsequent Spartan occupation of Decelea, only about fifteen miles north of Athens and in a key position for controlling much of the Attic countryside. Athens had shown herself vulnerable, and waves of anti-Athenian feelings swelled within and without her empire. In this light, the treatment of "purity" in the *Ion* is deeply ironic: Fears of the foreigner almost lead to the death of the true native-born king. At the end of the play, Athens' patron goddess appears *ex machina* to establish beyond doubt Ion's paternity and set him on his future course. From Athena we learn that Ion's children will found the four Ionian tribes and that his half brothers, to be born to Kreousa and Xouthos, will be the eponymous ancestors of Achaeans and Dorians. Thus, the seeming vindication of autochthony itself argues against exclusivity and for a Panhellenic perspective. Athens' enemies and allies alike all share a story of mixed beginnings. Athenian racial purity is also associated with violence from the very beginning. As a race sprung from earth, the Erechtheids are naturally drawn into the orbit of the monsters figured on the temple and tent at Delphi. Euripides stresses the connection by associating Kreousa's magical drops of Gorgon's blood with the Gigan-tomachy (961–77 / 987–1003). To do this he must ignore the usual and well-known version in which the Argive prince Perseus slays the Gorgon and bestow the honor instead on Athena in battle with the giants. Athena in turn gives the drops to Erichthonios, whom she pulls from the Attic soil and protects by twining serpents about him (commemorated in Ion's own birth tokens [1374–84 / 1422–31; cf. 18–22 / 21–26]). The Athenian site most often evoked in the play and most central to the action—the cave below the Acropolis where Apollo assaulted Kreousa and where their baby was born—epitomizes both by its nature as a crevice in the earth and by its association with legends and rites of the Kekropid past the mixture of splendor and violence that characterizes the *Ion*'s treatment of myth.

IV

Myth is the matrix of Greek tragedy, but few plays *use* myth as richly or as problematically as the *Ion*. The foundling's divine paternity is never put in doubt, even though none of the characters suspects it until the end, but its meaning certainly is. The claims of Apollo and of Athens are reconciled at last, but by a process that denies the possibility of simple, satisfying closure. Cognitive and emotional strains remain as the price of trying to live the myth and still be true to one's own needs and desires. Human knowledge is shown to be limited and unreliable, but in the interaction of divine and human wills the gods are also revealed to be ignorant, for they do not know the depth and intensity of human feelings. Although in the end Apollo reveals that he has saved his son, restored Kreousa's fortunes, and left Xouthos happy in his illusion of paternity, the plot itself is woven from the resistence of humans to the capriciousness even of divine benevolence. Divine power, fully manifest in the play's denouement, goes only so far in enforcing the standards of truth and justice that humans ascribe to their gods. The gods Ion longs for correspond to something we might recognize as a divine impulse in ourselves and to nothing else in the world. But just as the passions and weaknesses of humankind infect the gods, so the violent dissonances of the myths trickle into every corner of human life. Euripides seems not to challenge the authority of myth (as an earlier generation of rationalist critics argued) but rather to assume it for the sake of argument and then to tease out the deeply disturbing consequences of that assumption.

The issues raised by the treatment of myth in this play can perhaps best be traced in the outcomes and understandings that the various characters achieve. At one extreme is the old tutor, whose loyalty to the house of Erechtheus is such that he has neither questions nor doubts.

Learning of Xouthos' newfound son, he leaps to the conclusion that the foreigner is trying to foist his bastard on the Athenian royal house (778–801 / 808–31). It is a fine specimen of sophistic argument from probability, it embodies precisely the charges that Ion feared from the Athenians (567–69 / 593–97), and it is disastrously wrong. And, although the tutor's concern is to defend Athenian purity as he conceives it, he first suggests burning down Apollo's temple and murdering Kreousa's husband before finally settling on killing Ion as the best available revenge (948–56 / 974–82). In spite of his decrepitude, when next we hear of him he is zealously carrying out the attempted murder (1136–48 / 1170–85). Convinced by his own diatribe, sure of his own righteousness, utterly unscrupulous in pursuing his ends, the tutor leads Kreousa to plan the death of the same child she accuses Apollo of failing to save, the very offspring of the royal house for whose integrity she is fighting.

Xouthos, more temperate in judgment and certainly kindlier in intent, is equally bound by his certainties, equally remote from the mysterious possibilities of myth. He is treated as something of a comic character, becoming as it were the cuckolded husband who alone does not know that the child in question is not his. The decision to keep Xouthos in ignorance is Athena's (1566–69 / 1601–4), no doubt in accord with Apollo's wishes, but the scene in which Xouthos appears suggests that his ignorance is also self-chosen. Although he has no knowledge of having fathered a child, when the Delphic oracle tells him that he already has the son he seeks, it would surely be unreasonable not to accept his good luck joyfully. Xouthos inquires no further, forgetting in his happiness even to ask who the mother was, as he tells Ion (519 / 541). He will continue in the untroubled belief that Ion is his son, and we have no reason to think that he will give the matter of the mother another moment's thought. This lack of interest, signifying as it does that maternity matters less than paternity, in some sense validates the ideology of motherless autochthony, but when Ion naively suggests that the earth might have given him birth, Xouthos' wry reply, "Son, the earth doesn't have children" (520 / 542), sounds at once like a critique of the myths that form the heritage of Kreousa's house and like common sense. The improbable world of myth is a reality in the play to which Xouthos, for all his being a son of Zeus, seems to have no access. That is suggested, too, by the tone of comic realism struck at the beginning of the scene when Ion repels what he apparently takes to be Xouthos' pederastic advances (495–503 / 517–25). The contrast with the sympathy, the half-conscious recognition of kindred fates, that characterizes Ion's meeting with Kreousa could not be more pronounced.

For Kreousa, of course, the world of myth is very close, dangerously so. Indeed, she is a figure overdetermined in relation to myth, both a Persephone—the maiden, her flower yet unplucked, raped while gathering flowers in the meadow—and a Demeter—the mourning mother wandering in search of her child.[14] Apollo's rape and the child she bore him are at the very center of her being, first as suffering and loss to be endured in reproachful silence, then as attempted revenge, and at last as recognition. Having experienced his violence, Kreousa awaited his grace, so she believes, in vain. But she has not yet abandoned all hope. Although apparently convinced that the infant she exposed is dead, she still has come to Delphi to learn whether he may be alive or whether Apollo will at least grant her a new child by Xouthos. Even after Ion prevents her from consulting the oracle, Kreousa explicitly allows the possibility of reconciliation to Apollo's past deeds if only he will grant her the child she craves: "But if he heals this wound, / I will accept it, because he is a god" (**409–10** / 425–28). It is only when it seems that Xouthos has been given Apollo's favor and she denied it that Kreousa despairs of a miraculous change in her fortunes and turns to violence. Reasons of state dictate the death of Xouthos' son, but Euripides has arranged the dialogue between Kreousa and the old tutor to lay bare her more intimate motive: revenge. If she cannot attack Apollo directly, she can at least kill the child he has given Xouthos (**945–53** / 971–79). Her weapon will be blood of the Gorgon that Earth bore long ago to fight the gods. In her anger she herself becomes something like a chthonian monster: "Fireblooded dragon snake spawned / by the bull-shaped river god" (**1211–12** / 1261–63), as Ion calls her. Kreousa's overwhelming emotion, her feelings of pain, loss, abandonment pent up for years and, now that hope is gone, unleashed, surprise Apollo and topple the plan Hermes revealed (**61–63** / 71–73). Yet, in the end, Kreousa is not implacable, nor did she ever demand more of Apollo than he would give her. By giving him her child, he has finally healed her and won her praise (**1576–78** / 1609–10).

Kreousa's acquiescence does not, however, constitute a complete vindication of Apollo. About the god's role the most divergent views have been expressed, and in truth it would be hard to find a simple, satisfying answer to the questions: what does he represent? who *is* he? We must obviously keep in mind that Apollo is not strictly a character in the drama—though his nonappearance is in effect an event. His fathering of Ion fits a well-known pattern in which the (usually violent) satisfaction of divine desire engenders the founder of a city or clan.

14. This point is developed by Loraux (see n. 7 above) 199–203.

Stories of rape, even divine rape, have divergent and conflicting meanings in Greek culture,[15] but if Apollo raped Kreousa, that is, as Ion points out with sardonic emphasis, simply the gods' way (418–24 / 437–43). The Greeks regularly treated divine lust as honorific for its mortal objects and the offspring of these unions as heroes. Apollo may seem to have forgotten his son, but he has not. Hermes, who did his brother the favor of rescuing the child from the cave where Kreousa left him, assures us in the prologue of Apollo's continuing concern and announces the plan by which all will be made right. At the conclusion of the action, Ion has found father and mother with the god's help, and Kreousa her child. Even Xouthos is apparently content in the belief that Apollo has given him a son. Athena concludes the prophecies of glory for Athens that end the play with the suave comment, "Apollo has worked it all out perfectly" (1560 / 1595), and so, up to a certain point, he has. But whether the neatness with which all the threads are sewn up really cancels all the violence and fear that permeates the play remains open to doubt.

The doubt runs through the play at several levels. We have already spoken of the way in which Apollo's saving care for Ion, far from being attributed to some generalized divine providence or benevolence, fits a pattern of attachment to what is one's own, reversible at least potentially into hatred of what is not. We have seen, too, that Apollo's plan almost fails because the god who "chants forever what is to be" (7 / 7) misreads the future out of an inability to fathom the intensity of human feelings, the rawness of human needs. It remains to turn our attention to Apollo's child, Ion himself, whose "life has been / one song of purity" (47–48 / 56), and whose innocent piety makes demands that the god cannot meet and calls into question the meaning of the myth whose protagonist he was born to be.

V

We first see Ion as he sets joyfully about his task of cleansing the courtyard of Apollo's temple. His every word and gesture breathe the innocence and purity of a devotee who lives apart from the world. If it seems incongruous for a tragic figure to wield a broom, Ion dignifies the gesture by his rapturous dedication. The broom itself is made from Apollo's laurel, gathered "where everflowing streams / burst from sacred myrtle leaves" (107–8 / 118–20); the lustral water is drawn "from the Kastalian spring, chaste / as these hands that serve the god" (136–37 / 148–50). If there is something faintly comic about Ion's brandishing of

---

15. See Froma Zeitlin, "Configurations of Rape in Greek Myth," in S. Tomaselli and R. Porter, eds., *Rape* (Oxford 1986): 122–51.

the bow and arrow (Apollo's arms) to shoo birds from the sacred offerings, Ion's earnest effort to maintain the precinct undefiled also ennobles the threatened violence. Above all, his lyrical monologue expresses a deeply felt kinship with the god he repeatedly refers to as father.

Ion's devotion is deeply unworldly, and it soon emerges that to the extent that he does not know the outside world, he cannot fully know Apollo or himself. Apollo is not merely the god of pure light, the singer, and prophet; and Ion is not his son only. Kreousa's arrival begins his necessary education. In the mutual sympathy of queen and temple servant before they know each other are the makings of the recognition scene that will take another thousand lines to come. But Ion is distressed by the woman's tears, ill omened and (in his view) wholly out of place in Apollo's shrine (230–34 / 241–44). And when he learns the reason for Kreousa's misery, he is at first reluctant even to admit that Apollo slept with a mortal woman, but eventually concludes that in his treatment of their child. And, although he advises Kreousa that she cannot confront Apollo with his shame in his own temple, he is deeply enough disturbed by what Kreousa has said to consider doing so himself (417 / 436–37).

It is worth noting that Ion's shock is not a matter of ignorance of the many tales of divine adultery; on the contrary, the fact that the gods so often violate the very "rape laws" (427 / 445) that they enforce against men is precisely what distresses him. "Don't. Not you," he tells Apollo. "You have such power, / your power ought to serve what's right" (420–21 / 439–40). The fact of divine seduction, simply taken for granted in so many myths (including his own) is unacceptable to Ion because the gods' conduct contradicts the moral law they themselves have forged (423–24 / 442–43). Ion does not yet know that he is the fruit of such divine violence, and thus his words reflect the limitation of his knowledge. Yet he points to a fundamental incompatibility between myth and the world it describes, on the one hand, and the notion of justice that the gods enforce among men, on the other hand. It is the same incompatibility that led Plato, a generation after Euripides' death, to ban the old tales from his ideal state, and neither Ion nor the play can resolve it.

When Xouthos claims Ion as his son, the boy is reluctant to accept the seeming good fortune Apollo has bestowed on him because it will mean the loss of his unworldly happiness, of the "simple, painless, balanced" (601 / 632) life at Delphi. That Ion is drawn to public life the whole speech (561–617 / 585–647) makes clear, but at the same time his sensitivity to origins tells him that the son of an immigrant king and some foreign woman can claim no political rights in Athens, that his very presence there will provoke envy and hatred. The loss of Ion's innocence is enacted here in reflections that are surprisingly contemporary in tone. Ironically, however, they are based on the false genealogy provided by Apollo. Ion is not, as he believes (and as Kreousa will also), extraneous to Athenian power. And as the true son of Apollo and Kreousa, he cannot withdraw from the violence that is part of his story since the moment of his conception or from the power that is his destiny. The fear Ion here expresses of his presumed stepmother (580–83 / 608–11) is followed almost immediately by her plot to kill him. Indeed, the loss of innocence culminates in the play with Ion's willingness to use violence in the very sanctuary that he here describes as an oasis of tranquility.

In the end, then, Ion's acceptance of his dynastic and political role brings with it, of necessity, the loss of Delphic isolation and peace, just as the acknowledgment of his true parentage brings with it the end of the idyllic illusion of Apolline purity. Ion's passage from the innocence of childhood to the responsibility of manhood is both a return to true origins and an abandonment of beautiful dreams. Ion's picture of his life as Apollo's servant makes clear what he must sacrifice when he shoulders his adult responsibilities: the simple contentment "all men want, / but lose in the asking" (610–11 / 642). Ion's unwillingness simply to accept, as Kreousa does, the conjunction of tales that reveal him as Apollo's physical son shows the depth of his longing for the pure god who was his (imagined) spiritual father. Could Apollo, Ion's Apollo, really have fathered him or does Kreousa merely "blame me / on a god, to save me from shame" (1491–92 / 1525–26)? How could Apollo deceive Xouthos by telling him that Ion was his? In the end, Ion, who earlier told Kreousa that she could not force the god to speak, tries to do so himself to learn what Apollo has kept hidden, only to be stopped on the threshold of the temple by the appearance *ex machina* of Athena.

Athena's appearance is logical enough:[16] she is the right deity to reveal to Ion his Athenian future, to escort him as it were from childhood to maturity, from private ideal to public reality, from holy servitude in Delphi to heroic kingship in Athens. Yet she herself says that she comes in Apollo's stead. This has often been taken as a sign of cowardice on his part, but what did he have to fear from these mortals? What Athena says about Apollo's desire to avoid open blame (1525–28 / 1555–58) reminds one of what Ion himself tells Kreousa when they first meet: do not try to make the god denounce himself in his own temple (358–67 / 369–80). Apollo's intolerance of blasphemy is well illustrated in his horrifying

---

16. But it is characteristic of this play, and a chief feature of what one might call the formal exasperation of its ending, that the *dea ex machina* is in effect a doublet of the Pythia, once again (and now definitively) stopping the action at a moment when it seems about to go badly wrong.

treatment of Achilles' son Neoptolemos in Euripides' earlier *Andromache*. In that play, Neoptolemos has actually returned to Delphi to make amends for having once demanded reparations of Apollo on account of his father's death. Orestes sows suspicion among the Delphians, and it is they who kill Neoptolemos, but a mysterious voice from the depths of the temple clearly marks the deed as Apollo's, and the messenger concludes his account by commenting that the god who is "judge of what is right for all mankind" has himself behaved "like a base man remembering an old quarrel" (*Andromache* 1161–65). As in the *Ion*, the god is shown to enforce one code and live by another.

Surely Apollo's absence has another meaning, though, like his absence from the prologue. Apollo is central to the drama, but is at pains to keep his distance from its characters and their emotions. He is unprepared for the intensity of the human feelings that his plan unleashes, and to prevent Ion and Kreousa from killing each other, he must reveal the whole truth to them in Delphi rather than wait until they arrive in Athens (1533–39 / 1563–68). Humans act as reason and their passions dictate, but inevitably they are ignorant, and so their actions may have dangerous consequences. Gods, for all their knowledge and power, cannot always understand or respond to human needs precisely because they are not human. They intervene when and how they choose and for their own reasons. Is it any wonder that life as it is lived is so full of uncertainties, seems so subject to chance?

VI

The contrasts of this play, with its mixture of violence and beauty, passion and irony, emerge most fully perhaps in Kreousa's extraordinary *monody* (826–95 / 859–922). The Chorus, in open defiance of Xouthos, has revealed the (false) oracle that grants Ion to him, and to her nothing. After some initial outbursts of desolation, Kreousa stands silent as the old tutor indignantly caricatures Xouthos as a man who, like some Jason, has betrayed his wife and now conspires to smuggle his bastard into the palace under her very eyes. (The charge, repeated by the Chorus at the end of the third *stasimon*, is particularly ironic in view of the fact that the child is really Kreousa's, not his.) He urges vengeance, a suggestion Kreousa will later make her own, but for now it is not Xouthos or even Ion but Apollo against whom she cries out. With hope of children gone, her thoughts return to that other wept-for child (835–37 / 868–69), and the tale she earlier told to Ion on behalf of a fictitious friend she now claims as her own story, filling it out in a rush of emotion with intimate details of lived experience. Most extraordinarily, the denunciation of Apollo, a veritable explosion of outrage and loathing, takes the form of a hymn of praise.[17] Apollo is invoked as god of music, and the rape itself is tinged with a golden sunburst and the gold of the flowers Kreousa was plucking (846–58 / 881–90). Even the hatred of Apollo she ascribes to Delos, where Leto gave birth to the god, seems somehow tempered by the beauty of the feathery palm and laurel that she pictures there (889–95 / 919–22). Violent emotion and the detached contemplation of beauty are mixed here as they are in the descriptions of the Delphic temple reliefs and the tapestries that cover the tent where the attempt is made on Ion's life or in the evocation of the great torchlight procession of initiates from Athens to Eleusis, which the Chorus prays that Ion will never live to see (1045–60 / 1074–86).

Beauty and violence are mixed in the gods and in the world, despite Ion's dreams of unmixed purity. In the end, for Ion, the mixture produces recognition and power, but successful initiation into a new phase of life also implies the loss of what went before. Discovering his real link to Apollo, Ion must give up the feeling of kinship to the god of intense purity and radiant truth he had always harbored within himself. And he must recognize his bonds to the earthborn monsters that rage violently against gods and men, for he discovers that their violence is also part of his inheritance. But Apollo has shown him that his future belongs to the city and to action. For Kreousa, Apollo offers the means of transforming shame and apparent abandonment into glory and continuing divine favor. For Athens, Apollo offers in his son the promise of patronage and the means for future dominance. But what all this shows is just that gods, like humans, love their own and care for them as they think best. Can it be said to constitute a theodicy?

Gods and humans differ in knowledge and in power. Gods may do whatever they wish with impunity. Humans are far more restricted, and the consequences of limits may be disastrous. In the *Ion*, Apollo prevents a disaster, the mutual destruction of mother and son, but the crisis results in the first instance from his withholding of knowledge from Ion and Kreousa and from his outright lying to Xouthos. He averts catastrophe only by abandoning the convenient compromise he had planned and revealing the whole truth before he intended. Such is the force of human feeling, even against that other, divine order of knowledge and power. But the efficacy of this force depends entirely on Apollo's favor for his son, on bonds of kinship, and it does not allow us to draw any easy conclusions about divine benevolence at large. As shapely as the *Ion* is in its patterning of melodramatic intrigue and

17. See Anne P. Burnett, "Human Resistance and Divine Persuasion in Euripides' *Ion*," *Classical Philology* 57 (1962): 95–96.

recognition, it unsparingly withholds the moral satisfaction that, for Euripides, can no longer be made to attach to the enactment of myth. The special distinction of this play is precisely the way in which it brings the myth to its necessary "happy ending" without ever letting us lose sight of how complex, contingent, and confusing it is to live in, to live through myth itself. Within it, as without, mortals manage as best they know how, and for the rest must trust to chance, or the chance of a god's smile.

PETER BURIAN

TRANSLATOR'S ACKNOWLEDGMENTS

I studied ancient Greek as an adult for only two years, so I have never had the skills or learning to translate Euripidean drama on my own. I have relied heavily on what others have been willing to offer me, and they have contributed a lot, directly or indirectly, to this translation. The late William Arrowsmith helped to shape my sense of the meaning of the *Ion* and of Euripidean drama. Herbert Golder offered detailed criticism of several passages in earlier versions. Rush Rehm generously and patiently led me line by line through the Greek and along the way shared with me his impressive knowledge of Greek theatrical conventions. I'm grateful for all his help. At a late stage in the evolution of the translation, I benefited very much from Peter Burian's corrections, instigations, and suggestions.

W. S. DI PIERO

ION

Translated by

W. S. DI PIERO

With Introduction and Notes by

PETER BURIAN

CHARACTERS

HERMES messenger of the gods

ION servant of Apollo's shrine at Delphi, son of Apollo and
Kreousa

CHORUS of Kreousa's female attendants

KREOUSA Ion's mother, Xouthos' wife, daughter of Erechtheus

XOUTHOS Kreousa's husband

TUTOR to Kreousa, retainer of Erechtheus' household

MESSENGER

PYTHIA priestess of the oracle at Delphi

ATHENA patron goddess of Athens

A crowd of people of Delphi

Line numbers in the right-hand margin of the text refer to the
English translation only, and the Notes beginning at page 337
are keyed to these lines. The bracketed line numbers in the
running heads refer to the Greek text.

Dawn. Before the temple of Apollo at Delphi. The temple is decorated with images. To one side is a grove of laurel.

Enter HERMES.

HERMES Atlas! Bronze-backed Titan stooped forever
              under the grinding weight of the house of the gods—
              Atlas slept with a goddess and fathered Maia,
              who slept with almighty Zeus and gave birth to me,
              Hermes, the gods' lackey. I've come here to Delphi,
              the world's core where Bright Apollo sings to men
              what is, and chants forever what is to be.
              There is a city—it has had its share of glory—
              named for Athena of the golden spear. There shining
                                         Apollo
              took Kreousa, King Erechtheus' daughter, in wedlock,   10
              raped her in a cave, under Athena's sacred hill.
              Athenian lords call that place the Long Rocks.
              Her father didn't know. Apollo wanted her
              to bear the child, but in secret. When her time came,
              she took the newborn to the cave in which Apollo claimed
                                         her,
              exposing it there to die in its cradle's wicker shell.
              And yet, Kreousa honored ancient tradition.
              When Erichthonios was born, pulled from the earth,
              Athena twined two snakes around the infant,
              placing him in the care of the daughters of Aglauros.   20
              To this day, Athenian children wear golden coiled
                                   snakes
              at their throat. Thus, Kreousa,
               swaddling her baby as best she could,
              left him there to die.
                My brother Apollo called for me:
              Brother, go to the earthborn children of Athens,
              the glorious sacred city. Go to that cave,
              get the baby with its swaddling clothes and cradle,

bring him to my shrine at Delphi, and leave him at the
                                                                          door.

He is my son. I will take care of everything.   30
   Apollo Who Speaks Two Ways at Once.
I did what he asked, brought the basket here
and tilted back the lid so the baby could be seen.
When the horses of dawn ran across the sky,
the priestess climbed the steps and found the child
there at the door. Outraged that some town girl
dared to drop her bastard here and pollute the shrine,
she ran to get rid of it, but suddenly,
with Apollo's help, her savagery gave way
to pity. She nursed him, raised him, the temple's child,   40
and doesn't know Apollo is his father,
or who the mother was that gave him birth.
The boy doesn't know who his parents are.
   Growing up, he roamed free as a bird
around the sacred nest. As a young man,
the Delphian lords trusted him as steward
of Apollo's golden wealth. His life has been
one song of purity, serving the temple.
As for Kreousa, the boy's mother, she married Xouthos.
It went like this: War broke out between Athens and
                                                                      Chalkis,   50
Xouthos allied himself with Athens, Athens won,
Kreousa was his reward, though he's not Athenian;
he's Achaean by birth, descendant of Aiolos and Zeus.
Since then, they've planted the garden year after year
and still are childless. So they've come here,
burning for children. Thus Apollo,
never as forgetful as he seems,
controls their fortunes and draws them here.
When Xouthos enters the shrine, the god will give him
his own son, declaring Xouthos the father.   60
His mother will not know he's really hers
until they return to Athens. Thus Apollo's "marriage"
will stay a secret, and the boy will take his rightful
                                                                      place.
The god will name him Ion. Throughout Greece

he'll be famed as the founder of Ionia.
   For now, I'll hide here in the laurel
and learn how things work out. Here he comes,
with his broom, to make the temple shine!
I will be the first of all the gods
to name divine Apollo's son. ION.   70

                           Exit HERMES.
    Enter ION *with temple attendants. He carries a broom*
    made from laurel, a bow, and arrows. On his head he
                                wears a garland.

ION Dawn's gleaming horses raise
    the blazing sun above the earth
    up through air steeped in fire
    where light on light routs
    the faint lingering stars
    into the sacred dark.

    The peaks of Parnassos, untrodden,
    flare, smolder, and take for us
    this day's charge of sun.
    Smoke of desert myrrh   80
    rises to the rooftop,
    shrine of bright Apollo.

    Inside, the priestess sits,
    at the sacred tripod,
    crying to the Greeks
    songs Apollo murmurs in her.

                         (*to temple attendants*)

    Go to the Kastalian spring,
    purify yourselves, bathe
    in its bright blessed dew.
    When you return, to all   90
    who ask about the oracle,
    let your words be pure and kind.

With my broom and sacred garlands
I will purify the entrance,
as I have done so many years,
calm the dust with water drops,
watch for birds that foul
the offerings, flutter them
with my bow. No mother, no father
watches over me. I serve   100
Apollo's shrine that nurtures me.

Radiant work
Day after day
My broom of laurel whisking
Water kissed
Reborn
Where everflowing streams
Burst from sacred myrtle leaves
All day
I toil   110
Sweeping clean the sacred shrine
While the sun's wing soars

O praise and bless
Apollo   Healer   Shining One

No work on earth as sweet
As work I do for you
Leto's son
Where your prophetic voice
Sears the brilliant air
My slavish hand   120
My glory and fame
I serve
Not mortal men
But undying gods
My constant work all easy constant joy
Phoibos   Father   Bright God
I praise
Apollo   Helper

Nurturing lord
I call by name   130
Phoibos   Patron   Father

O praise and bless
Apollo   Healer   Shining One

(He puts down the broom.)

Enough of that. Now, a little water
from the golden jar, to settle the dust.
Water from the Kastalian spring, chaste
as these hands that serve the god.
May I always labor sweetly for him,
or stop only if good fate comes.
No! Get away from there!   140

(He takes up his bow.)

Stay clear of the golden roof.
Fierce, mastering eagle,
messenger of Zeus, your killing talons
rule the sky, but I
will kill you and all the others
that range down from Parnassos
to foul and pollute this holy place.
O red-legged swan
oaring across the air,   150
Apollo tunes his lyre
to your song. Go home to Delos,
or I will drown your song in blood.
My bow sings a different kind of song.
You may not build your nests here.
Go have your babies somewhere else,
by the gentle Alpheios, or the sacred grove
at the Isthmus. I won't let you poison
the sacred offerings with your filth.
I do not want to kill message-bringers   160
from the gods, but that is my work,

my service to Apollo's shrine,
my life's eternal source of food and care.

Enter CHORUS, *admiring the temple images.*

CHORUS So Athens is *not* the only place! Look!
Images of the gods housed here, too!
There's Apollo, Protector.
Fantastic! The light!
It splits, peering
above the face of Apollo's house.
Look at this.   170
Herakles, son of Zeus,
grabbing and killing the Hydra
with his golden sword.
And who is *that*
with the blazing torch?
It must be a story we tell at our
weaving:
Iolaos, sharing
Herakles' toils.
Over here! Can't you see it?
Bellerophon riding Pegasos,   180
killing the fiery Chimaera.
They're all tangled.
How about *this?*
Stone carvings,
dragontailed giants
fighting the gods.
Over there you can see
Athena shaking her shield,
that Gorgon snake-nest,
at the giant Enkelados.   190
Yes! I see Athena.
She is our goddess.
And here is Zeus, poised to strike
from afar, his lightning
blazing at both ends.
I see it!

And Mimas
burnt to ash
by heaven's fire.
            And Dionysos! His wand   200
            wrapped in peaceful ivy
            kills another giant, son of
                              earth.
            Roaring Bacchos!

                    (*to* ION)

          You there, may we enter the temple
          barefoot as we are?

ION It's not allowed.

CHORUS   Will you tell us
          something else?

ION What?

CHORUS   Does it really exist? Is it really here,
          the navel of the earth, inside Apollo's
                              temple?   210

ION Wreathed in garlands, and on each side are Gorgons.

CHORUS   Just as we've heard.

ION If you want an oracle from the god,
     offer grain to the fire. But to go inside,
     you must sacrifice a sheep.

CHORUS   I understand. We won't trespass.
          What we see outside is enough;
          it delights and charms the eye.

ION Look around as much as you like.

CHORUS   Our mistress said   220
                    we could look to our hearts' content.

    ION To what house do you belong?

CHORUS   A royal house, one
                    in Athena's city—
                    here's our mistress now.

                                              Enter KREOUSA.

    ION You must be wellborn, woman, whoever you are,
         as your bearing and manners show.
         Appearances are usually sound evidence
         of a person's birth and standing.
         What's wrong? Why are you weeping?   230
         I'm astonished—everyone else rejoices
         at the sight of Apollo's shrine,
         but you shut your eyes and wet
         those noble cheeks with tears.
         One look at the god's holy cavern,
         and tears flood your eyes.

KREOUSA You're a kind and sensitive child.
         You're a stranger, yet you ask why I'm sad.
         Seeing Apollo's house, I measured back
         an old memory. I feel torn   240
         between two places—my body is here,
         my mind elsewhere.
                             O why are women
         so miserable? And gods so vicious?
         What justice can we ever find on earth
         when the injustice of the mighty destroys us?

    ION Something's hurting you. Does it mean...

KREOUSA Nothing. I've taken my shot.
         I'll be silent. No need to dwell on it.

ION   Who are you? Where are you from?
      What name do I call you?   250

KREOUSA   Kreousa. Daughter of Erechtheus. My home is Athens.

ION   A great city. Noble origins, glorious ancestors. How
                                              lucky you are.

KREOUSA   I'm lucky in this, in nothing else.

ION   There's a story we've all heard . . .

KREOUSA   What do you want to know, stranger?

ION   Your grandfather, Erichthonios, was born from
                                              the earth.

KREOUSA   Yes. His noble blood hasn't helped me much.

ION   Did Athena really pull him from the earth's womb?

KREOUSA   Yes, with virgin hands. She did not give birth to him.

ION   Just like the pictures of it.   260

KREOUSA   She gave him to Kekrops' daughters, to keep him hidden.

ION   But they opened up the cradle, looked inside

KREOUSA   and bloodied the rocks when they jumped to their death.

ION   Yes! And I wonder about another story.

KREOUSA   Ask. I have time.

ION   Did Erechtheus, your father, really sacrifice your sisters?

KREOUSA   For Athens' sake, he had the courage to kill them.

ION You alone were spared?

KREOUSA I was a baby in my mother's arms.

ION And a rift in the earth hides your father?   270

KREOUSA He was killed by Poseidon.

ION And there's a place called the Long Rocks . . .

KREOUSA That! Why do you ask?

ION Apollo honors it. His lightning blazes there.

KREOUSA Honors? It did *me* no good.

ION You hate what the god loves most?

KREOUSA It's nothing. We share a secret, that cave and I.

ION Your husband? Is he Athenian?

KREOUSA No, not a citizen; he's an outlander.

ION Obviously wellborn.   280

KREOUSA Xouthos, born of Aiolos, son of Zeus.

ION Can a foreigner marry an Athenian?

KREOUSA There's a city neighboring Athens—Euboea.

ION The sea marks its boundaries.

KREOUSA My husband helped Athens to sack it.

ION And you were his reward?

KREOUSA His war prize.

ION You're here without him?

KREOUSA With him, but he stopped at the shrine of Trophonios.

ION To look around, or to get an answer?   290

KREOUSA Just one word, from Trophonios and Apollo.

ION About crops? About children?

KREOUSA We're childless, after years of trying.

ION You've never had children? Not even one?

KREOUSA Apollo knows I have no children.

ION Poor woman, lucky in so many ways, unlucky in this.

KREOUSA Who are you? Your mother must be a happy woman.

ION They call me Apollo's servant, and that's what I am.

KREOUSA Were you an offering from some city? Or sold as
                                                    a slave?

ION I know one thing: I am Apollo's.   300

KREOUSA Now I pity you, stranger.

ION Because I don't know who my mother or father is.

KREOUSA And you live here in the temple?

ION No matter where I sleep, this is my home.

KREOUSA How old were you when you came?

ION They say I was a baby.

285

KREOUSA Who gave you milk?

ION No breast fed me. But I was raised . . .

KREOUSA By whom? Your misfortune sounds like mine.

ION I call Apollo's priestess "mother."   310

KREOUSA How have you survived?

ION The altars feed me, and every stranger who visits the
shrine.

KREOUSA The poor woman who had you! Who was she?

ION A woman treated wrongly, and I'm her son.

KREOUSA You're fed, you're well-dressed . . .

ION I'm Apollo's slave, my clothing comes from him.

KREOUSA You mean you've never tried to find your parents?

ION I have no evidence to go on.

KREOUSA I know a woman who suffered like your mother.

ION Who is she? If only she could share my burden.   320

KREOUSA She's the reason I arrived here before my husband.

ION To do what? Maybe I can help.

KREOUSA To put a secret question to the god.

ION You can tell me. I might help arrange it.

KREOUSA Her story . . . No. I'm ashamed.

ION Shame is a lazy goddess; you'll get no help from her.

KREOUSA With Apollo. My friend says she slept with him.

ION Apollo? With a woman? No.

KREOUSA She had his child, too, and didn't tell her father.

ION Impossible. A man did it but she's ashamed to admit it.   330

KREOUSA She says no, and she has suffered terribly.

ION Suffered? She slept with a god!

KREOUSA She had his child, then exposed it.

ION Did it survive? Where *is* this child?

KREOUSA No one knows. That's why I'm here, to ask the oracle.

ION If the baby died . . .

KREOUSA She thinks wild beasts killed him.

ION On what evidence?

KREOUSA She went back to find him—he was gone.

ION Were there traces of blood?   340

KREOUSA She says not, and she combed the ground.

ION How long ago was this?

KREOUSA The child would be about your age.

ION The god was unjust. I pity the woman.

KREOUSA She never had another child.

ION But what if Apollo took him, then raised him in secret?

KREOUSA No right to act alone! He should share that joy.

ION Your story chimes with my own grief.

KREOUSA O stranger, somewhere an unhappy mother yearns
                                                    for you.

ION Don't lead me back to pain I have forgotten.   350

KREOUSA I'll be silent. Will you help me get an answer?

ION If I can. But there's some trouble with your case.

KREOUSA Everything she does brings trouble.

ION How can the god reveal what he wants to hide?

KREOUSA All Greeks share the oracle openly.

ION The god acted shamefully. Don't challenge him now.

KREOUSA But she suffers painfully for what happened.

ION No one will give you this oracle.
Apollo would punish whoever makes him seem,
even justly, wicked in his own temple.   360
Forget what you came for. No one should ask
questions that oppose the god. We can offer
blood of lambs, we can read the flight of birds,
but we beg for trouble if we force gods to say
what they're unwilling to say. Twist truth from them,
their blessings will be twisted,
although we gain from what they freely give.

CHORUS Different men suffer in many different ways.
Who among humankind ever uncovers
one real happiness in life?   370

KREOUSA Apollo, twice unjust to that unseen woman.
Unjust here, unjust there, you failed to save

the one you should have saved, your own child.
You won't use your prophetic gift to say
if that child thrives, or is gone with nothing left
to mark his memory. But that's how it must be,
if the god won't speak and I'm stopped from knowing.
        There's my husband, Xouthos, coming from
                                          the shrine.
Be silent. Not one word of what we've said—
I might be held at fault for keeping secrets.   380
The story wouldn't unfold as we would like.
There would be trouble. Trouble, too often
it's all men seem to think we're good for.
Men mix us all together, evil women
with the good. Misfortune is our birthright.

                                        Enter XOUTHOS.

XOUTHOS   First, I greet Apollo, and offer him
          my blessings. Then you, my wife.
          Did you worry? I know I'm late.

KREOUSA   It's nothing, it's all right, I'm glad you're here.
          Tell me what Trophonius prophesied.   390
          Will we both have children?

XOUTHOS   He refused to guess at Apollo's will.
          But he did say this: I won't go home
          childless. And neither will you.

KREOUSA   O Leto, Queen mother of Phoibos, bless our journey.
          Let the pieces of our past dealings with your son
          soon fall into place.

XOUTHOS   So be it. Does anyone here speak for the god?

     ION Outside, I speak for Apollo. Inside, Delphi's nobles,
          seated by the sacred tripod, will deal with you.   400

XOUTHOS   Good. That's all I need to know. I'm going inside.
          They say the common sacrifice, made for all like me

who came for oracles, has turned out well,
so I want to get my answer now. Kreousa,
spread laurel around the altars. Pray that I bring
good prophecies from Apollo's house.

XOUTHOS *enters the temple.*

KREOUSA So be it. After what he's done,
the love that ties me to Apollo
is changed. But if he heals this wound,
I will accept it, because he is a god.   410

Exit KREOUSA.

ION Why does this strange woman talk so wildly
against Apollo? She must really love her friend,
or else she's covering up something
that begs to stay hidden. Anyway,
what is the daughter of Erechtheus to me?
Not a thing. I'll fetch holy water and pour it
into golden bowls. I really must confront Apollo.
What is he *doing?* Rape a girl, then desert her?
Father children secretly, not caring if they live
or die? Don't. Not you. You have such power,   420
your power ought to serve what's right.
If a man acts badly, the gods punish him.
It's not right for you gods to violate laws
you yourselves have forged. Let's pretend,
for the sake of argument, that you
and Poseidon and great Zeus who rules the heavens
enforced the rape laws against yourselves.
What a price you'd pay! Your temples
would be empty, lifeless, barren.
It's not right to let yourselves go,   430
swamped by a moment's pleasure.
Or to blame us for copying what you
consider good. You are our teachers.

Exit ION.

CHORUS Born without labor
        Delivered from the summit
                From the head of Zeus
                        By Titan Prometheus
        O Athena
        We beg you
        Come to us   440
                Soar down
                Blessed Victory
                        From the golden
                        Halls of Zeus
        To the earth's hearth
                The world's navel stone
        Let the dance go round
        The sacred tripod
                Athena O come
                Tell Apollo what we want   450
                        Artemis untouched girl
                        Apollo's twin
            Virgin goddesses
                Plead our case our cause
                        For the ancient house of Erechtheus
        Let the oracle be straight and clear
                We've waited so long
                        For the great gift   *Children*

        Lush endless happiness
        Belongs to those who see   460
        Shining in their children
        Golden generations yet to come
        Sons protecting a house at war
        And bringing love in peaceful times

        Palace? Wealth? Give me instead
        Children of my own blood
                I hate not having children   I detest
                Those who think that's good
                        Let me have moderate blessings
                        Let me have children   470

O Pan!
Above your knitted caves
Near the Long Rocks
Three spectral daughters
Dance in wet grass
Before Athena's shrine

Flute song rises
From the sunless caves
Where you play your pipes
And where a wretched girl   480
Exposed Apollo's child
As blood-feast for birds

That was a bitter wedding
And I have never heard
In tales or at my weaving
Of any happiness
That ever came to children
Born of gods and men

Enter ION.

ION   Women, still waiting for your mistress?
       The temple is sweet with incense.   490
       Is Xouthos still inside asking about children?

CHORUS   He is. No sign of him yet.
          Wait. I think someone's coming now.
          The door's opening. He's coming out.

           XOUTHOS, *leaving the temple, sees* ION *and approaches*
                            him as if to embrace him.

XOUTHOS   Ah lovely boy! What a nice way to begin.

ION   I beg your pardon? Please watch what you're doing.

XOUTHOS   I want to hold you and kiss you.

ION What? Has some god made you crazy?

XOUTHOS I know what I'm doing. I want to kiss my dearest boy.

> XOUTHOS *tries to hug* ION, *knocking the garland from the*
> *boy's head.*

ION I belong to the god. Keep your hands to yourself!   500

XOUTHOS I claim what's rightfully mine.

ION You'll claim an arrow in your ribs if you don't back off.

XOUTHOS You run from the one who loves you most?

ION I don't negotiate with lunatics.

XOUTHOS Kill me, then. Burn my corpse. Go ahead, kill your
                                                    father.

ION Father? That's outrageous!

XOUTHOS Let me explain. You have to know the whole story.

ION Story?

XOUTHOS I'm your father, you're my son.

ION Who said that?

XOUTHOS   Apollo, who raised you, knowing you were
                                                    mine.

ION *Your* version of the facts.

XOUTHOS   Apollo's! The oracle told me.   510

ION Told a riddle and you got it wrong.

XOUTHOS   Nothing wrong with my
                                                            hearing.

   ION What did Apollo say?

XOUTHOS   The first person I met

   ION Met?

XOUTHOS   Coming from the temple

   ION Was supposed to . . .

XOUTHOS   Be my own son.

   ION Son, or someone's gift?

XOUTHOS   Gift. The gift of my own son.

   ION I'm the one you met?

XOUTHOS   The one and only child.

   ION An odd coincidence.

XOUTHOS   Amazing, for both of us.

   ION My God! Who is my mother?

XOUTHOS   That I can't say.

   ION Apollo didn't tell you?

XOUTHOS   I was so happy I forgot to ask.

   ION Then I was born from the earth—Earth was my mother!

XOUTHOS   Son, the earth doesn't have
                                                    children.   520

ION But how can I be yours?

XOUTHOS   Let the god puzzle it out.

ION Why not work it out ourselves?

XOUTHOS   That's even better!

ION Perhaps you once had an affair?

XOUTHOS   When I was young and
                                              foolish.

ION Before you took Kreousa?

XOUTHOS   Never since.

ION Maybe you got me then.

XOUTHOS   The time fits right.

ION Then how did I *get* here?

XOUTHOS   I have no answer to that.

ION Athens is so far away.

XOUTHOS   It's a real puzzle.

ION Have you been to Delphi before?

XOUTHOS   Once, for the torchlight
                                     mysteries of Dionysos.

ION Where did you stay?

XOUTHOS   With a Delphian, and there
                                  were girls from Delphi.

ION You were initiated, so to speak?

XOUTHOS   The god was in us all.   530

ION So you were drunk?

XOUTHOS   The pleasures of Dionysos can't be
                                               denied.

ION That's when you fathered me.

XOUTHOS   Now, child, fate has found
                                             you out.

ION But how did I get to the temple?

XOUTHOS   The girl must have
                                     exposed you here.

ION At least I'm no slave.

XOUTHOS   And I'm your father. Accept me.

ION I have no right to doubt the god.

XOUTHOS   That's more like it.

ION What else could I want?

XOUTHOS   Now you see what you need
                                           to see.

ION I am son of the son of Zeus.

XOUTHOS   Yes.

ION You're really my father?

XOUTHOS   If we trust Apollo's word.

(They embrace.)

ION Hello, father.

XOUTHOS   That word is all love.

ION This is the day

XOUTHOS   that fills me with joy.   540

ION Mother, whoever you are, I burn to see you
     even more than before, to press you to me.
     But if you're dead, what's left for me to do?

CHORUS We share your happiness but want our mistress
        to have the chance for children,
        to brighten the house of Erechtheus.

XOUTHOS My son, the god spoke straight. He let me find you
         and brought us together. You have the father
         you did not know you had. I feel the same desire
         to find your mother; I, too, need to know   550
         what sort of woman she was. In time,
         maybe together we can find her.
         Leave this place, leave your homeless life
         at Apollo's shrine. Come share my intentions
         in Athens. My wealth and power are yours.
         You will be rich, noble, not sick
         with poverty and namelessness.
         Why so silent? Don't stare at the ground.
         There's something on your mind.
         Don't turn this father's joy to terror.   560

ION Things seen close up are not the same
     seen far away. Things in the distance glow and charm.
     I'm happy to find my father, but now
     I ask myself: What will life be like in Athens?
     They say Athenians are Earth's children,
     all native to their place. I'd be twice afflicted,
     the bastard son of a foreign king. Powerless,
     I'd be a cipher. But if I join political life

try to *be* someone, the weak and poor would
                                                        hate me.
Capable men who, keeping their own counsel,   570
avoid political life, would take me
for a fool who speaks too quickly
in a city filled with fear.
And public men, acting in Athens' interest,
can use the vote to shut me out.
That is how these things tend to be, father.
Men in power are primed to fight
their rivals.
                    Besides,
I'd be foreign goods in your own house.
Your wife is barren, she will feel all alone   580
in her grief, estranged from your good luck.
She will hate me, and with good reason,
and you would have to take her side. If not,
your household will be ripped apart. Women
stab their husbands to death and feed them poison.
And yet, I pity your wife, father. She's so wellborn,
she shouldn't suffer, as she grows old,
the disease of childlessness.
                                    And power—
power enthralls. All order on the outside,
but torment inside. Is it happiness   590
to wear out your life glancing left and right,
vulnerable on every side?
I'd rather live as a man in the crowd
than rule as king. A ruler learns to love
the worst of men, and must protect himself
from the best, since they are the ones he fears.
You say that gold wins out, that wealth is pleasure.
But the rich man, counting his gold, guards it, too;
all he hears is gossip and slander.
Such wealth is a task. I prefer a life   600
that's simple, painless, balanced.
    Please listen, father. What I had here was good,
time to myself, the dearest thing a man can have.
Nobody bullies me. No wild crowds.

It's not a trivial thing, you know,
that people here don't push each other around.
To the gods I offer prayers, and comfort
to my fellow men, serving those who are happy.
People coming or going, I treat them all the same.
My smile is always fresh. What all men want,   610
but lose in the asking, is mine already
by nature and habit together,
in Apollo's service. Father,
when I think it through, I'm sure
I'm better off here. Let me live by my own lights.
The gift is the same. The joy of great things
looms in small things, too.

CHORUS True words, but only if our lady sees,
somewhere in this, joy she can call her own.

XOUTHOS (*to* ION) Enough of such talk. You must learn, my son,   620
to be happy. Now, to start things off,
I want a common feast here where I found you,
and proper sacrifice; we should have done so
when you were born. I'll present you
as my special guest—as an onlooker, though,
not as my son—and we will do the same
in Athens. I don't want to hurt my wife.
She's still childless; she would suffer too much.
When the time is right, I will prevail
on her to let you have the throne.   630
    And I will name you Ion. It fits the way we met.
Ion, the first I set my eye on when I came out.
So, invite your friends to the feast.
Say your goodbyes, then leave this city of Delphi.

(*to* CHORUS)

    And you, not a word. Absolute silence.
One word of this to my wife and I'll have you killed.

Exit XOUTHOS.

ION I'll go. But one thing's missing.
Until I find my mother, my life rings hollow.
O father, if only she were Athenian,
then I could speak out as I want.   640
A foreigner, coming to a pure city,
might call himself a citizen and think
he belongs. But his tongue's a slave.
He doesn't have the right to speak his mind.

Exit ION.

CHORUS   Shrieks, cries, I see more, worse,
to come. Her husband with his own son,
and she barren, left all alone.

Wrecked harmonies break
from your prophetic song,
O Leto's child, Apollo.   650

And what of this boy?
Raised around the temple,
who *is* he?

What womb held him? The oracle
sounds false; I dread to think
where it will lead.

Strange oracle bearing
strange things; the boy
has some cunning and chance.
Why *that* child, an outsider born   660
of other blood? Am I wrong?

Friends, do we tell her?
Stab her with this news?

Her husband—with him
she shared it all, every hope.

Now, as he learns to be happy,
she drowns in all that happens,

fading into old age
while he neglects her.

Did he share? No. He took.   670
Took wife, wealth, palace.

Outlander from the start.
Let him *die*. He robs my queen.

May he suffer worse than she.
        Let the gods turn back his prayers
                and his offerings burn barren, unsavored.

She is the one we love.
The king makes sacrifice and feast—
a new father for a new son.

                Up there! The wine god ramping   680
                on the mountain crag,
                his pine torch blazing both ends
                for his wild ones to follow,
                        their slender feet
                        dancing through the night ...

                Parnassos! Let the boy die here.
                Don't let him come to Athens.
                Our city doesn't need this foreigner.
                To survive, we only need
                        the pure untainted   690
                        bloodline of Erechtheus.

        Enter KREOUSA *with* TUTOR. *She helps him make his*
                                                    way.

KREOUSA Old man, my father Erechtheus chose you long ago
        to be his children's guardian. Now we'll learn

what Apollo Who Speaks Two Ways has prophesied.
Come along, if you can. It's good to share good news
with a friend. If the prophecy turns ugly,
in your kind eyes I'll find sweet consolation.
You served my father well. Though I'm your queen,
I'll show you every kindness in return.

TUTOR   Daughter, your father would be proud.   700
You're noble, just as he was,
truly one of Earth's children.
But don't let go. Help me up a bit.
We must all *ascend* to prophecy. These old legs
need someone to share their work.
Young help is the perfect cure.

KREOUSA   Careful, watch your step.

TUTOR   Slow down, child.
My mind works faster than my feet.

KREOUSA   Use your stick, lean on it.   710

TUTOR   It's like me, it doesn't see too well.

KREOUSA   True, but don't give up.

TUTOR   Not willingly, but I can't use what I don't have.

(*to* CHORUS)

KREOUSA   Women! Like sisters we've shared stories
at the loom. Tell me, then, what the oracle
told my husband about children.
Give me good news, and you'll find
I don't forget those who treat me well.

CHORUS   O god!

TUTOR   A bad beginning.   720

302

CHORUS Poor woman!

  TUTOR Bad things in store, for all of us.

CHORUS What to do? Death waits for us.

KREOUSA There's fear in this song.

  CHORUS Do we speak? Keep silent? What do we do?

KREOUSA Speak. You have something for me.

  CHORUS It must be said, though I die twice for telling.
            There is for you, dear lady, no child to take
            into your arms and hold to your breast.

KREOUSA Then let me die.   730

  TUTOR Dear daughter ...

KREOUSA   Pure pain
              shrieks in me.
              It must end here.

  TUTOR Child.

KREOUSA   *Ai   Ai*
              Grief stabs
              my heart.

  TUTOR Don't cry out yet.

KREOUSA   The grief is here.   740

  TUTOR Not till we know ...

KREOUSA   What's left to know?

  TUTOR Whether your husband shares the grief,
            or if you suffer alone.

CHORUS Apollo gave *him* a son, old man —
a private joy that cuts her off.

KREOUSA Evil, and worse, worse yet
rips through me with every word.

TUTOR This "son" you mentioned, is he waiting
for a mother, or is he born already? 750

CHORUS Already born, and grown,
Apollo's gift. We saw it all.

KREOUSA What? Unspeakable!
Don't tell me that.
It scalds my ears.

TUTOR Tell me clearly now, precisely,
what the oracle said, and who the child is.

CHORUS The first one seen, the first your husband met,
leaving the shrine — he was the son, the god's gift.

KREOUSA No! And *my* child? 760
I'll be barren, bereft,
childless, alone in my house.

TUTOR What happened then? Whom did he meet?
Did he see anyone when he came out?

CHORUS Remember, my queen, the young man
sweeping the temple? He is the child.

KREOUSA If I could soar from this earth, this Greece,
through the light-steeped air
to far fields of western stars . . .
O friends, I'm torn too much by grief. 770

TUTOR His name. What name did his father give him?
Has the oracle revealed that, too?

CHORUS Ion. Because he was the first one seen.

TUTOR And the mother?

CHORUS   That I can't say.
         I do know they've gone to make a birthday offering
         in the sacred tent. Your husband took the boy, in
                                                   secret.
         He plans a sacrifice and public feast for his new son.

TUTOR We've been betrayed, both of us, by your husband.
       He has designed events to serve himself
       and force us from your father's ancient house.   780
       My love for you outsteps my old regard for him.
       The facts speak for themselves: He came to Athens
       a foreigner, full of promise; by marrying you,
       he took up your inheritance. But soon he began
       to sleep with other women, begetting children,
       and all in secret. In *secret*, because he sees
       you can't have children, and he won't share that
                                                   affliction.
       So he takes to bed some slave girl, who bears
                                                   his child,
       who he then gives over to a friend in Delphi.
       Nameless, bred in hiding, the boy grows up   790
       like a sacred beast on holy ground until, finally,
       your husband persuades you to come to Delphi
       because you're still childless. By now, the boy
                                                   is grown.
       It's not the god who lied, it's your husband,
       patient all these years while he spun his web.
       If we expose his treachery here, he'll simply
       blame the god. But if he makes it back to Athens,
       he'll contrive to bring his son to power.
       And that name! A travesty of origins—
       "Ion." The first he set his eye on!   800
       There's no "first" here, just an old conspiracy.

CHORUS I hate clever men whose talents
        disguise vicious intent.
        I'll take my friends from simple honest men,
        not from those too clever to be good.

TUTOR The worst for you is still to come,
          when a slave's man-child, a nameless no man's child,
          is made master of your house. Your husband
          had another choice, bad though it was —
          he could have said *We need a son, of a freeborn
                                        woman.*   810
          You're barren; I can save the house. If you refused,
          he could have married one of his own kind.
          Now *you* must act. Act as any woman should.
          Kill your husband. Sword, poison, deceit, anything.
          Kill the youngster, too. But do it now,
          before they murder you. Bitter enemies
          can never share the same house.
          I'll share the work, and the bloodshed.
          I'll go now where they're feasting.
          Live or die, I'll repay all the kindness   820
          you have shown me. A slave's disgrace
          lies only in his name. In virtue
          he can stand equal to a freeborn man.

CHORUS We, too, will share with you what happens,
          either death or a decent life.

KREOUSA Silent still, Kreousa?
          Stop now and say no more?
          Or flood down light
          on that dark bed?
          What holds you back? Match   830
          your husband's shame with your own?

          My husband, traitor, robs me
          of house, robs me of children,
          hope's human shape, that hope
          now gone. Why silent about
          that other marriage, silent
          about that wept-for child?

          By Zeus' starry throne, by Athena,
          mistress of our citadel who reigns

at the sacred shore of Triton's lake,   840
I will not hide my marriage,
but heal myself and tell,
as tears flood my eyes and my soul breaks,
    how men and gods betrayed me,
    disgraced me in their beds.

        From seven strings
        strung between the bull's bright horns,
        you pluck soft songs,
        O Leto's child, Apollo.
        To sunlight's jury I cry   850
        my charge against you:
            Bright God,
        you came to me, sunburst
        in your hair, in the fields
        where I was plucking
        soft yellow petals
        that fluttered to my lap
        and sang back dawn's bright gold.
            Your hand grabbed and locked
            this pale wrist, dragged me   860
            to the cave bed, while I
            shrieked *Mother*. There you worked
            Aphrodite's shameless grace.
        In misery, I bore you a son.
        With a mother's terror,
        I put him back, left him
        to die on our dark bed,
        where you yoked me to darkness.
        Ah, I wept, alone. Now the child
        is gone, a feast for vultures,   870
        my son and yours.

    You
        Lord of song
        you all the while
            sing self-praise, you
            chant the future

                    before the golden throne
                    at the earth's core.
            Into your ear
            I scream these words: 880
                    Vile coward lover,
                    you forced me to be your wife,
                    now you give my husband a son
                    and my house to house him.
                    You owe *him* nothing. Our child,
                    mine and yours, you left to die,
                    prey for birds, stripped
                    of cradle clothes his mother made.
                    Delos, where your mother
                    labored you into life,   890
                    hates you. And the laurel
                    sprung up there
                    beside the feathery, bloodroot palm—
                    the laurel hates you,
                    seed of highest Zeus.

CHORUS   The treasure hoard of evil opens.
                It would make the whole world weep.

  TUTOR   Daughter, your face fills me with pity.
                I feel I'm going mad—no sooner
                do you clear my mind of recent trouble   900
                than another wave of words shocks me,
                surging away from evils we've just known
                toward more wretched painful ones to come.
                So, now, voice your charge against Apollo.
                Who is the child? Where did you bury him?
                Go over it for me once again.

KREOUSA I feel shame, but I will speak.

  TUTOR   I know how to share your sorrow.

KREOUSA Listen. There is a cave, on the north slope
                of the acropolis, called the Long Rocks.   910

TUTOR I know it. Near Pan's shrine and altar.

KREOUSA I struggled there, it was dreadful.

TUTOR Say it. I'll grieve with you.

KREOUSA The Bright God forced himself on me. My miserable
                                                        wedding.

TUTOR I was right when I thought ...

KREOUSA You guessed?

TUTOR Your hidden illness. The sighs and groans.

KREOUSA Now I can reveal my secret.

TUTOR But how did you hide Apollo's "marriage"?

KREOUSA Can you bear to hear it? I had his child.   920

TUTOR Where? Did you labor all alone?

KREOUSA All alone, in the cave that watched him rape me.

TUTOR Where's the child? Child! You have a child!

KREOUSA He's dead, exposed to wild beasts.

TUTOR Dead? Apollo did nothing to help?

KREOUSA Nothing. The child grew up in Hades' house.

TUTOR But who exposed him? Surely not you.

KREOUSA Yes. I swaddled him, and I left him.

TUTOR Who else knew? Who went with you?

KREOUSA Misery, secrecy—they never forget what's hidden. 930

TUTOR Your own child, how could you just leave it in
                                                    the cave?

KREOUSA How? With a torrent of words and pity.

TUTOR Ah, god,
          cold-hearted what you did, but Apollo did worse.

KREOUSA You should have seen him, his tiny hands reaching
                                                    out...

TUTOR Hungry for your breast.

KREOUSA That place was his, and I denied it. How I wronged
                                                    him.

TUTOR You must have somehow hoped...

KREOUSA that Apollo would save his own son.

TUTOR Our noble house—a storm breaks! 940

KREOUSA Why hide your head and weep?

TUTOR You and your father's name are doomed.

KREOUSA For mortals, life is change; nothing remains itself.

TUTOR No more pity, daughter, not now. Put aside this loss.

KREOUSA But what must I do? Events paralyze me.

TUTOR Pay back the god who first did you wrong.

KREOUSA I'm only a woman. He's a god!

TUTOR Burn down his shrine, oracle of the twisted god!

KREOUSA I'm afraid. I suffer enough.

TUTOR Then do what's possible. Kill your husband.   950

KREOUSA But he was, once, a good man to me.

TUTOR Then kill the child who stands against you.

KREOUSA Is that possible? How? It's something I would do.

TUTOR Your servants have weapons.

KREOUSA Let's go. Where do we get at him?

TUTOR Inside the sacred tent where he celebrates with friends.

KREOUSA Too much in the open. Besides, slaves are weak.

TUTOR And you're playing the coward. How would you do
                                                      it, then?

KREOUSA I do have a plan, insidious, workable.

TUTOR I'm with you.   960

KREOUSA Then listen. You know about the war of the giants.

TUTOR Earth's children fought the gods on the great plain

KREOUSA and Earth produced the awful Gorgon

TUTOR to help her children fight against the gods.

KREOUSA And Zeus' daughter, Pallas Athena, killed the monster.

TUTOR I heard that story long ago.

KREOUSA How Athena skinned it, made it into a breastplate,

TUTOR her armor, called the aegis

KREOUSA because the eager Gorgon struck against the gods.

TUTOR What did it look like?   970

KREOUSA A breastplate linked with rings and rings of snakes.

TUTOR What has this to do with revenge?

KREOUSA You know Erichthonios?

TUTOR Your ancestor, sprung from earth.

KREOUSA When he was newborn Athena gave him . . .

TUTOR What? Say it, get it out!

KREOUSA two drops of blood from the Gorgon.

TUTOR Which have some power against men?

KREOUSA One kills, the other cures.

TUTOR But how could a baby keep . . .   980

KREOUSA In a gold bracelet, passed down father to son.

TUTOR Till Erechtheus died and passed it on to you?

KREOUSA (*revealing the bracelet*)
I still keep it on my wrist.

TUTOR A double gift from the goddess.

KREOUSA One drop seeped from the hollow veins.

TUTOR What power does it have?

KREOUSA Repels disease, nurtures life.

TUTOR And the heartblood's second drop?

KREOUSA Kills. Poison from the Gorgon snakes.

TUTOR Do you mix them or keep them separate?   990

KREOUSA Always separate. Good and evil do not mix.

TUTOR O child, dearest girl, you have all you need!

KREOUSA With this the boy dies. You will kill him.

TUTOR *You* say where and how, *I* will do it.

KREOUSA In Athens, when he comes to my house.

TUTOR It won't work. And *you* criticized *my* plans.

KREOUSA I think I see the problem.

TUTOR Even if you're not the one who kills him, you'll
                                             be blamed.

KREOUSA The old story of the wicked stepmother.

TUTOR Kill him here, now, where you can deny it all.   1000

KREOUSA Yes, and savor the bloodshed sooner.

TUTOR And you can keep your husband's secret to yourself.

KREOUSA (*giving him the bracelet*)
         You know what to do? Take from my wrist
         Athena's ancient golden handiwork and go where
                                       my husband
         makes his secret sacrifice. When they finish eating,
         and are about to pour libations for the gods,

put a drop of poison into the boy's cup.
His cup. No one else's. Keep it apart, just for him,
who wants to rule my house. Once he drinks it,
he will never come to glorious Athens.   1010
He will die here, rooted to this ground.

TUTOR   Hurry back to where you're staying
        while I manage everything here.

                              (*Exit* KREOUSA.)

Old as I am, blood still runs fast enough in me—
that much I have in common with the boy.
I'm on the side of kings, if I can hunt the enemy
and share the murder that drives the boy from
                                    our house!
When fortune favors us, the right thing is to be good.
No law or custom holds us back when we
kill enemies who would kill us if they could.   1020

                              (*Exit* TUTOR.)

CHORUS   Crossroads Queen, who guides all things
              that loom out on roads by night,
              Demeter's daughter, Queen of Returns,
                    guide through this noonday light
                         the brimming cup,
                         death's portion caught
                    from the Gorgon's slashed throat.
                         Guide our queen's plot,
                         keep foreigners out,
                         let our city be ruled   1030
                         only by the children
              of the noble house of Erechtheus!

              If the boy's death goes unfulfilled,
              the moment's lost. If her sum
              of hope and purpose fails, she dies,
                    throat snapped by a cord

                    or heart pierced.
                         Agony
          poured upon her suffering,
                    but death is change   1040
                    at last complete.
                    Never in the sun's light
                    could she bear to see
          others in her father's house.

          Hymns sung to Dionysos,
          dawn on the twentieth day,
          torchlight rivering down
                    from Athens to Eleusis.
                    There celebrants
                    dance round the spring.   1050
                    Imagine Ion there,
                    spying on the mysteries!
          The shimmering sweep of stars,
                    the dancing moon,
                    and fifty water spirits dancing
          by the everflowing river running down to sea—
                    all hymn
                    golden-crowned Persephone
                         and Demeter
                    terrible fruitful mother!   1060
                         Apollo's beggar
                         hopes to rule there
          claiming everything we've worked for as his own.

                         O Singers
                    tell how women reign
                    more pious than unjust men.
                    Change your jangling songs
               that cry *unlawful* and *unholy*
               at a woman's love, a woman's bed.
          Sing a new and grimmer tale: 1070
                    tell what men do to us.
                    The son of Zeus, oblivious,
                    childless with our queen

turns
toward some other,
shares another's bed
and finds a bastard child.

Enter MESSENGER.

MESSENGER You women, where can I find the queen,
daughter of Erechtheus?
I've run all over town looking for her.   1080

CHORUS You're one of us. Tell us what happened.

MESSENGER We're hunted, our queen most of all.
The men of Delphi say they'll stone her to death.

CHORUS What are you saying? Have they found us out,
our plot to murder the boy, everything?

MESSENGER Exactly. And you'll be punished, too.

CHORUS How did they know?

MESSENGER Apollo uncovered it. He saw right edging out wrong
and refused to be defiled.

CHORUS Tell us how he knew.   1090
Tell it all, we beg you.
Knowing will make it easier to die.

MESSENGER When our queen's husband left the temple with
his son,
thankful for the first sight of the newborn boy, he went
to make sacrifice to the birth gods, up on Parnassos,
splashing blood on the twin crags of Dionysos that
gleam by day
and flicker with torches at night. *Wait here and set up
the tent,*
the father told the son. *If the sacrifice takes too long,*

start the feast without me. He rounded up some calves
and left, while the boy went straight to work.   1100

He erected the frame—roofpoles, guylines, all that—
then dressed the tentskin over the bones. Not a tent,
                                                     really,
but a billowing, broadbacked pavilion, measured off
                                                     exactly,
"from the middle point," as the wise men say.
                                    Foursquare,
a hundred feet to a side, huge enough to house all
                                    of Delphi.
Most of all he wanted the walls cambered just right,
to hold off noon's burst of sun, and sundown's sharp
spilled radiance. Then he brought out sacred tapestries,
from the temple's secret hoard. Dazzling,
fabulous bolts of cloth that Herakles, son of Zeus,   1110
seized in his war with the Amazons then offered to
                                    Apollo.
Draped high over the roofpoles, they made a second
                                    heaven,
a celestial cover, up there, where heaven musters
                                    all its stars
in the circle of sky, while the horses of the sun,
chasing day's last light, drag the Evening Star behind.
There it shines! And night in its chariot rides forth,
dark-gowned, striding slow, the stars holding close.
And there, the Pleiades, good companions, ford the sky.
And Orion with his sword, poised midstride forever.
And the Great Bear, curling its golden tail round the
                                    polestar.   1120
And high in heaven's festive weave, the white full moon
fractions the year, carves the months with blades of light,
till the breeding Hyades, clear sign that steers the sailor,
are chased away, with all the other stars, by dawn's light.
He hauled out other stuff, strange Asian things to drape
                                    the walls.
Odd scenes, Greek ships locking hulls with the Persian
                                    fleet.

Monstrous creatures, half man, half beast. Horsemen
                                        running down deer
and spearing lions in the wild. At the tent door,
they hung an image of Kekrops, Athens' first king,
snake-king, flanked by his daughters—an offering   1130
from some Athenian. In the middle of it all
he placed a golden mixing bowl; and a herald,
very proud of himself, stood at the door
calling everybody in Delphi to the feast.
Soon the place was packed. The guests decked garlands
                                        on their heads
and ate to their hearts' content. When they had their
                                        fill,
some old man barged into the middle of things, fussy,
                                        madcap,
playing the role of wine steward. *Let me get the water
                                        bowls.*
*Wait! Let me wash your hands. Permit me to light some
                                        incense.*
Why don't I just clear away those golden wine cups?   1140
After dinner, when the music started and the flutes got
                                        going,
the large wine bowl was mixed and everyone held his
                                        cup.
Then the old slave shouts *Stop! Too small! These cups,
they are surely too small. Let me fetch bigger ones.
Take your pleasures quick, I say. Big cups, big bellies!*
When each guest has a big gold-and-silver cup,
the old man offers one to the young new master,
the brimming cup laced with poison. A gift, they say,
from our queen, that the boy might leave the light.
No one knew a thing. The boy raised his own cup,   1150
along with the rest of us, when someone—a servant, I
                                        think—
said something, a dark word, a piece of wrong speech
that the boy, raised on prophecies, took for an evil
                                        omen.
So he ordered a new bowl filled, and that first libation,

for the gods, he gave to the earth, commanding the
                                                    others
to do the same. Silence all around. A servant then
remixed pure water and the best wine in the common
                                                    bowl.
But then, a riot of doves, sacred and free to roam the
                                                    precinct,
came careening in. They swooped down where the
                                                    wine
soaked the dust, they dipped and wetted their beaks,   1160
the drops trickling down their feathered throats.
The wine didn't bother them, except for one that
                                                    alighted
at the feet of the new son. Its bonecage quivered,
it shook like a bacchant, it screeched words no prophet
                                                    could unlock,
while everyone, dumbstruck, stood and watched.
                                    The young thing rattled
and died. Its blood-red claws and brittle legs sagged.

Ion burst from his place, bare arms flashing from
                                                    his cloak,
and shouted *You wanted me to drink from that cup,*
                                                    old man,
Who's trying to kill me? He grabbed the old man by
                                                    the wrist,
searched him, found the poison, but the slave, even
                                    under torture,   1170
held out a long time before he revealed the plot,
                                    how everything
was meant to work out. The boy ran at once to
                                    call all the people,
he addressed the lords of Delphi: *By the sacred Earth,*
                                                    this child
of Erechtheus, this foreign woman, our guest, tried
                                                    to poison me.
The lords easily reached a vote: Kreousa will be stoned
                                                    to death

for plotting to kill the god's servant, for conspiring
                                         to pollute
the precinct with blood. The whole city's after her now.
                                               Childless,
already miserable, she races farther down misery's
                                       long road.
She came to Apollo yearning with desire for children.
                                     But now
she has destroyed herself, her own body, her hope
                                   for children.   1180

                                     Exit MESSENGER.

CHORUS No way out. No way to turn death
          back, fly free from it.
          All too clear. Snakeblood poison
          mixed with wine that flows
          from the grapes of Dionysos—
          shining too clear
          our own wretched lives
          like any sacrificial thing,
          and my queen stoned to death . . .

          If I could fly unharmed through falling stones   1190
             or hide within the shadow-folds of earth
          or race off in a chariot swift as wind
             or sail fast and sure to open sea . . .

          No help, no hiding,
          unless a god steals us away.
          O queen, what waits
          for you now? Will we suffer
          the evil consequence
          of the evil we have planned?

                                     Enter KREOUSA.

KREOUSA They're after me. I'll be slaughtered like a beast   1200
          for sacrifice. Condemned by the vote. Betrayed.

CHORUS We've been told the whole fateful story.

KREOUSA I got out just in time and somehow made it
through their lines. But now where do I hide?

CHORUS The altar, of course.

KREOUSA   What good is that?

CHORUS It's unholy to kill a suppliant.

KREOUSA   I am condemned by law.

CHORUS They have to lay hands on you first.

KREOUSA   They're close
behind,
and they have swords.

CHORUS   Quick, sit by the altar flame.
If they kill you there, your blood will be a curse
on all their heads. We must bear whatever comes.   1210

(KREOUSA *moves to the altar, sits, and wraps her arms
around it.*)
Enter ION, *followed by a crowd.*

ION Fireblooded dragon snake spawned
by the bull-shaped river god,
you tried to kill me, your nature
vile as those drops of Gorgon's blood.
Grab her! I'll pitch her off Parnassos,
the rocks will comb her hair while she hoops
and tumbles down. Some god smiles on me.
Before I went to Athens to become
my stepmother's victim, I measured up
your vicious hatred here, among allies.   1220
If I'd gone to that home of yours,
you would have caught me in your trap

then cast me down to Hades' house.
But nothing will save you now, no altar,
no temple of Apollo. I have no pity
for you. I pity myself, and my mother.
Though not here in the flesh,
her name is never far from me.
Look! Look at the monster,
weaving lies with other lies,   1230
who cowers at the altar,
as if that will set her free and clear.

KREOUSA I'm warning you. Don't kill me, not here.
For my sake, and for the god whose ground this is.

ION What could you and the Bright One have in common?

KREOUSA I give my body into the god's keeping.

ION You tried to poison Apollo's child.

KREOUSA No longer Apollo's. You are your father's son.

ION I've just become my father's son, I've always been
Apollo's.

KREOUSA You're not what you once were. But now, *I* am
Apollo's.   1240

ION *You* are sacrilege! Everything I did was holy.

KREOUSA You became my enemy, so I tried to kill you.

ION I didn't bring war to Athens.

KREOUSA You'd have torched the house of Erechtheus.

ION With a burning brand, I suppose?

KREOUSA You'd have lived in my house, taken it by force.

ION My father gave me the land he won.

KREOUSA What has the son of Aiolos to do with Athens?

ION He saved your city with a sword, not with words.

KREOUSA Allies don't lay claim to every city they help.   1250

ION You'd kill me for fear of what I *might* do!

KREOUSA To save myself, before you killed me first.

ION You're jealous. My father found me, and you have
                                                  no child.

KREOUSA Do you steal homes from those who have no children?

ION Do I get no share? Nothing from my father?

KREOUSA Nothing but a sword and shield. That much is yours.

ION Get away from the altar, it's holy ground.

KREOUSA Go preach to your mother, wherever she is.

ION You'll pay the price for trying to kill me.

KREOUSA Butcher me, if you want, but you will do it here.   1260

ION At Apollo's altar? Is that your pleasure?

KREOUSA To torture Apollo as he once tortured me.

ION No!
    All's terror if the gods make vile laws—
    their unconsidered acts outrage good sense!
    To let a criminal sit here at the altar.
    You should drive them off! No stained hands
    touch this holy shrine. Keep and protect

323

only those who suffer, falsely charged.
Don't give refuge equally   1270
to both the godless and the good.

(*He is about to grab* KREOUSA *when the temple doors*
open.
The PYTHIA *enters, carrying a wicker cradle.*)

PYTHIA Stop. Look at me, my son.
I stand outside the temple, leaving the sacred tripod
entrusted to me by Apollo's law.
I am the Bright One's prophetess, selected by all
the Delphians.

ION Dear mother.

PYTHIA I like that name, though it's only a name.

ION You've heard how she plotted to kill me?

PYTHIA I have heard. But being savage, you act wrongly.

ION Why not pay back killers in kind?   1280

PYTHIA Stepmothers against stepsons—always the same story.

ION And still true. *This* stepmother...

PYTHIA No more. You must leave the shrine and head for
home.

ION What are you telling me?

PYTHIA Go to Athens, under good omens, your hands clean
of blood.

ION A man is clean who kills his enemies.

PYTHIA You're wrong. But there's a story you need to hear.

ION You know I'll listen.

PYTHIA (*Holding up the wicker cradle.*)
What do you see?

ION I see an old cradle, with little garlands.   1290

PYTHIA I found you in it when you were a baby.

ION What? I can hardly believe this.

PYTHIA I kept these things in silence. Now I tell their story.

ION Why did you hide it from me for so long?

PYTHIA Apollo wanted you to serve him at the shrine.

ION And now he doesn't need me? I want more proof
than this.

PYTHIA He gave you a father, so it's time for you to leave.

ION And you saved all these things?

PYTHIA The god's words are slanted light, they spoke in me.

ION What words? Tell me!   1300

PYTHIA To save this thing I found, until the ripened time.

ION To harm or profit me?

PYTHIA Hidden inside are your swaddling clothes.

ION My mother! A clue to the story.

PYTHIA It's what the god wants now.

ION An incredible day—one new thing after another.

PYTHIA Take it. Now work to find the one who bore you.

ION How? I'll have to look everywhere—all over Asia,
                                                    Europe . . .

PYTHIA That's for you to figure out. I nursed you,
        my son, for the Bright One's sake. Without words,   1310
        he told me what to take, what to save,
        though I never learned why. No mortal knew
        I kept these things, or where I hid them.
        I give these things back to you. Goodbye
        forever. I give you a mother's embrace.
            Look for her here. Ask yourself first
        if some unmarried girl from Delphi left you;
        if not, see if it was a girl from elsewhere.
        You know now all the god and I can tell.
        He, too, has a share in this.   1320

ION O gods, not this. My heart streams back
        to where my mother made her secret marriage,
        had me, sold me, secretly, never fed me
        at her breast, but gave me up
        to a nameless life, slave to the shrine.
        The god is good, but some shadow
        of what he does weighs hard on me.
        She and I, mother and mother's son,
        lost from each other. An infant's joy,
        a mother's loving comforting arms, lost   1330
        to me, those happy times lost to us both.
            The cradle, Apollo, I offer up to you,
        that I be saved from knowing what I don't want
        to know. If my mother was in fact a slave,
        let silence cover all. "O Bright God,
        I offer to your temple all these things . . ."
        What am I *doing*? I'm fighting the god's will.
        He saved these scraps of my mother's past.
        I can't escape this. My fate lies right here.
        (*opening the basket*)
        Sacred garlands, little nest, what have you kept   1340

hidden, wrapped up for me these many years?
Look! The wrappings around the shell look new,
cleanly plaited, nothing has rotted away.
Time has left no stain. Have you
come down, untouched, all these years?

KREOUSA A sign from the heavens, beyond my wildest hopes.

ION Quiet, you.

KREOUSA I won't be quiet. Don't preach to me,
for I see the shell where once I put you.
You are my child. You were just a baby,   1350
babbling when I left you there
by the Long Rocks, near the caves of Kekrops.
I'll leave the altar, even if it means I'll die.

(*She lets go of the altar and rushes to embrace* ION.)

ION Grab her! Some god has made her crazy.
She's left the god's image. Tie her up!

KREOUSA Kill me, go ahead. Don't stop. I *will*
hold on to you, and these hidden signs of you.

(ION *backs away.*)

ION Too strange. You, too, want to stake a claim.

KREOUSA Claim what's mine. Love owns what it finds.

ION Me? Love? You tried to kill me.   1360

KREOUSA I love you, my son. What more can a mother want?

ION Stop lying. I've got you now.

KREOUSA That's what I came for.

ION All right. This cradle, is anything in it?

KREOUSA The swaddling clothes I once wrapped you in.

ION Let's hear you name them, sight unseen.

KREOUSA If I'm wrong, I'm yours to kill.

ION Speak. Your boldness chills me.

KREOUSA Once, as a child, I wove a little thing.

ION Like what? All girls weave.   1370

KREOUSA Mine was unfinished, my first try.

ION I'm no fool. What was it like?

KREOUSA Gorgons woven dead center of the cloth.

ION O Zeus! What fate hunts me down?

KREOUSA Fringed with snakes, like Athena's aegis.

ION Look!
This is it, found like perfect prophecy.

KREOUSA Soft echo of my girlhood after all these years.

ION You were lucky once. Is there anything else?

KREOUSA Snakes. A golden clasp. Athena's gift   1380
that retells the tale of Erichthonios,
a reminder the children of our race still wear.

ION What is it used for?

KREOUSA Worn around the neck of a newborn, my son.

ION Here it is. I long to know a third thing . . .

KREOUSA A tiny garland of olive leaves, from the tree
Athena first brought to our city on the rock.
I put it around your head. Still green and blooming,
isn't it? Born of that first and purest olive!

ION (*embracing* KREOUSA)
Dearest mother, I see you, I touch your cheek—
pure joy.   1390

KREOUSA O child, to this mother's eye
brighter than the sun itself
(may the Bright God forgive me)
I never dreamed I'd find you
but thought you shared the earth
and darkness with Persephone.

ION Dear mother, I was dead once, now in your arms
I'm alive again.

KREOUSA To heaven's bright unfolding,
my joy sings,
shouts high and far.   1400
Joy I never imagined—
Where does it come from?

ION I'm yours, mother. I can't imagine anything but that.

KREOUSA And yet I'm shaking with fear.

ION That holding me, you don't really *hold* me?

KREOUSA I exposed my hopes
long ago.
O priestess, what hands brought
my own son to Apollo's house?
What arms placed him in yours?   1410

329

ION The gods did it. But as things come round,
    may new happiness match our old despair.

KREOUSA   Child, I moaned and cried
        as you were born. I wept
        and pushed you out of reach.
            Now my breath
            warms your cheek,
        the most perfect pleasure gods can give.

ION Your song is one we both can sing.

KREOUSA   No more, no more childless house,   1420
          the hearth is lit,
         the land has its kings,
        the house of Erechtheus thrives,
         blinks awake from night
        and gazes toward the high bright sun.

ION Mother, he's here, too, my father. Let him
    share the pleasure that I've given you.

KREOUSA   Child,
    what are you saying? No.
    Keep my secret.   1430

ION Secret?

KREOUSA   Someone else. Your father was someone else.

ION God! You weren't married. What does that make *me?*

KREOUSA   No torchlight streamed me to my bed,
    No wedding hymns or dance
        swept me kindly
        to your birth.

ION *Ai* So I'm lowborn. But, mother, then who…

KREOUSA   By the goddess who slew the Gorgon

      ION Please talk sense!   1440

KREOUSA   And who broods over the city's crag
                    where the sacred olive grows

      ION Mother, no more lies. Talk straight.

KREOUSA   Where nightingales sing on the rocks
                    the Bright God

      ION Bright God?

KREOUSA   Took me
               to that secret bed.

      ION Apollo? The story's changing. This is wonderful.

KREOUSA   When nine months came full cycle, I labored   1450
               and bore you, Apollo's secret child.

      ION I love what I'm hearing, if it's the truth.

KREOUSA   Girlish things, my loom's
                    vague wanderings,
               they had to do a mother's work.
               I never put you to my breast,
               never washed you with these hands,
                    I left you there
                    in a desolate cave,
                    blood-feast for birds,   1460
                       a gift to death.

      ION A strange, awful thing for you to dare, mother.

KREOUSA   All tangled in my fear,
               I threw your life away,
               killed you against my will.

331

ION   I tried to kill you, too.

KREOUSA   Strange and terrible then, strange
          and terrible now.
          Stormwinds lash us, bad luck
          churns on every side,   1470
          then the winds change
          and the sea lies calm.
          Let it stay that way. The past
          blew hard against us, but now
          let's hope to run full sail before the wind.

CHORUS   Here's proof: Let no one ever think, not ever,
         that anything lies utterly past hope.

ION   All these switchbacks of luck and circumstance.
      One minute we suffer, the next we're healed.
      Is luck some goddess who brought us to the point   1480
      where you would kill me, and I'd kill you?
      My god!
      The sunlight's bright embrace today helps us
      make sense of all that's happened. I've found you,
      mother, dearest of all things to me; I'm glad
      my origins were better than I thought,
      but I still want to know the whole truth.

          (*Drawing her aside so that no one else will hear.*)

                                        I promise,
      I'll bury all of it in darkness,
      just tell me who my father really is.
      Maybe, as young girls do, you fell   1490
      into a secret love? No need to blame me
      on a god, to save me from shame
      by saying that Apollo did it
      when it was no god at all.

KREOUSA   By Warrior Athena, Victory Bringer,
          who fought with Zeus against the earthborn giants;

I swear your father was no mortal man,
but Apollo, your patron, the god of slanted light.

ION How could he give his own son to another father
and say I was Xouthos' natural child?   1500

KREOUSA Not "natural," *given*, conferred,
though sprung from the god himself,
given as one friend might give
his friend a son to provide an heir.

ION Is the god telling the truth? Or does his oracle lie?
The questions trouble me, and for good reason.

KREOUSA Listen, here's what I think. Apollo did right by you,
placing you in a well-born family. As adopted son,
you're the rightful heir. But if the god declared himself
your father, imagine what you'd have lost! So, you see,   1510
he only wanted to help. Because I hid
our marriage and because I tried to kill you,
no one would ever believe you were mine and his.
He had no choice: He gave you to another father!

ION No, that doesn't work. I want the truth spelled out.
I will go inside his house and ask point-blank.
Am I the son of mortal man
or of the God of Twisted Light?

> ION *turns to enter the temple but is stopped in his tracks
> by the arrival of* ATHENA *from above.*

Up there! Where the incense rises,
a god's face where the sun should be!   1520
Run, mother. We must not look on things divine
unless the right time has corne for us to see.

ATHENA Do not run from me. I am not your enemy.
I bring you good will, here, and in Athens,
the town that bears my name. From there I come,

sped down the road by Apollo. He thought it best
not to reveal himself to you, lest he be blamed,
in public, for all that's happened.
He sent me here to tell you this:

(*to* ION)

You are her son, born of father Apollo.   1530
He gives you to others whom he has chosen
not by blood, but to place you in a royal house.
He planned to wait until you got back to Athens
before revealing the truth of these things,
that you were their son—hers and Apollo's.
But all the god preferred to leave unsaid
has burst into the open; so Apollo had to intervene,
and save you both when you contrived
to kill each other. Now to fulfill the oracle
and bring things to a close, I have come here.   1540
So listen:

(*to* KREOUSA)

              Take this child home and make him prince
of Kekrops' land, for he's descended from Erechtheus.
And it is just that he rule my city, my earth.
And he shall be famous throughout Greece,
and four sons shall spring from one root,
whose names will become the Four Tribes
clustered around the crag which is our home:
GELEON   HOPLES   ARGADES   AICIKORES
At the fated time their sons shall settle
island cities of the Kyklades, and coastal towns   1550
to strengthen Athens, and also along the twin shores
of Asia and Europe. They will be named IONIANS,
rooted in his name, and they will be famous.
Xouthos and you together will have sons:
Doros, father of the Dorians, whose city
will be famed in song; and Achaios,
who shall rule the land of Pelops all the way
to Rhion on the coast, and his name shall be the name

borne by a great people—the proud Achaeans.
Apollo has worked it all out perfectly.   1560
First he gave you good health in your pregnancy,
so that no one would suspect the secret.
Then he told Hermes to take the child, still dressed
in the clothes you swaddled him in, and bring him here,
where the god nurtured his son and did not let him die.

Absolute silence! Breathe not a word
of how you got your child. Let Xouthos cherish
his sweet illusion. Go, but keep this good news
to yourselves. Farewell. Be happy.
After all your troubles, I bring you news: 1570
Your fate, filled with the god, is blessed.

ION Athena, daughter of almighty Zeus, I cannot
not believe what you say. But I accept, I believe,
I am the son of her and the God of Various Light.
Even before, this was not unbelievable.

KREOUSA Hear me, too. I did not praise Apollo,
but I will praise him now, for he gives me back
the child he once ignored.

(She touches the temple doors.)

These golden doors,
once hateful, leering, smile now.

(She embraces the door knocker.)

I say goodbye
and cling to the god's bright doors   1580
that close him in.

ATHENA I commend your change from blame to praise of the god.
For the gods always work in their own good time,
and, in the end, they use what power they have.

KREOUSA (*to* ION)
      My child, let's go home.

ATHENA   Go, and I will follow.

KREOUSA Our safe conduct on the road.

ATHENA   I love my city.

KREOUSA Come claim your rightful power.

ION   For me, a worthy
                                         possession.

         ATHENA, ION, KREOUSA *leave the theater, followed by*
                                  CHORUS.

CHORUS Goodbye, Apollo, Son of Leto and Zeus.
      Now we have learned to give the gods their due
      and to take heart when we're driven by disaster.   1590
      In the end, the good get what's good.
      The bad, by nature, get what's bad.

NOTES

1–163 / 1–183 The prologue consists of Hermes' speech (1–70 / 1–81) and Ion's *monody*—
a solo aria accompanied by the *aulos* (a kind of oboe) and by the actor's
dance steps and mimetic gestures (71–163 / 82–183).

3 / 2–3 *a goddess* Pleione, according to the mythographer Apollodoros, but Hermes
does not name his grandmother and the tradition seems to have been
uncertain.

6 / 5 *the world's core* A white egg-shaped stone at Delphi called the *omphalos* (navel)
marked the earth's center, the place where two eagles, set flying in
opposite directions by Zeus, finally met. For a description, see lines
209–11 / 225–26.

6 / 6 *Bright Apollo sings to men* The god known here and often by the cult name
Phoibos, Bright One, is said to sing to men because oracles in verse were
chanted or delivered to petitioners in written form by his chief priest
after consultation with the Pythia whom he inspired (cf. 83–86 / 91–93).

11 / 10–11 *raped her* Literally, "yoked in marriage by force." The violence of the union is
emphasized repeatedly in the course of the play; see Introduction, p. 257.

20 / 23 *daughters of Aglauros* King Kekrops of Athens and his wife Aglauros had three
daughters, Herse, Aglauros, and Pandrosos, to whom Athena entrusted the
baby Erichthonios for safekeeping. The story is told at lines 254 ff. / 265 ff.

31 / 36 *Apollo Who Speaks Two Ways at Once* The cult name here is Loxias (Oblique
One), which may originally have referred to "slanting" (riddling) oracles
or to the inclination of the ecliptic traversed by the sun. Apollo is
referred to by this name twenty-three times in the course of the play.

66 / 76 I'll hide Euripides gives Hermes, "the gods' lackey" (**5 / 4**), the sort of exit into hiding just out of sight associated with conniving slaves in later Greek comedy.

152–58 / 166–76 Delos . . . Alpheios . . . the Isthmus Sites of important shrines, respectively, of Apollo, Zeus (Olympia), and Poseidon (Isthmus of Corinth). Ion's shooing of the birds to other sacred precincts to avoid defilement of this one gives his devotion a comic quality; at the same time his threat to shoot the birds to prevent pollution foreshadows his attempt at the end of the play to remove by violence Kreousa's "stained hands" (**1267 / 1316**) from Apollo's altar.

164–225 / 184–236 Parodos or choral entrance song. The Chorus enters in three rows of five, led by a flute player, but soon divides into groups to dance and sing in wonder at the sacred images. The pictures the Chorus members describe do not correspond to what we know about the sculptured program of the temple of Apollo at Delphi, although there was a Gigantomachy on the rear pediment. Euripides has rather chosen a series of scenes of victories of gods over monsters—appropriate to Delphi, where Apollo conquered the Python, connected to Athenian tradition (the same subjects were embroidered on the Panathenaic *peplos*, a ceremonial gown offered to Athena every five years), and above all appropriate to the themes of the play.

166 / 186–87 Protector Apollo is here identified as Agyieus, the divine protector of roads in whose honor incense as burned on conical pillars set before the street doors of Greek houses.

170–78 / 190–200 As one of his twelve labors, Herakles slays the Lernaian Hydra, a many-headed beast in whose blood he thereafter will dip his arrows. Iolaos, Herakles' nephew and bosom companion, appears at his side.

179–82 / 201–4 Bellerophon kills the Chimaera, described by Homer as "of divine race, not human, lion in front, serpent behind, in the middle a goat, and exhaling the fearful power of blazing fire" (*Iliad* 6. 180–82).

183–203 / 205–18 Battle of gods and giants (Gigantomachy). Earth-born monsters challenged the rule of the Olympian gods and gave battle on the plain of Phlegra (**961 ff.** / 987 ff.). Athena and Zeus are the most prominent Olympian defenders; Dionysos (**200–203** / 216–18) was sometimes depicted in sculpture and vase painting as joining the fray with Silenos and satyrs.

226–433 / 237–451 First *episode*.

251–357 / 260–368 The longest passage in Greek tragedy written in strict *stichomythia* (line-for-line exchange). Usually used either for heated debate or rapid-fire interrogation, here its effect is intensified by the unrecognized conjunction of the tales elicited from each participant in turn and the unexplored convergence of their feelings.

254 / 265 *There's a story we've all heard* As the mythographer Apollodoros tells it, Hephaistos, god of the forge, pursued Athena and, when she rebuffed him, his seed fell to Earth, who bore his child but gave it to Athena. Because the virginal Athena could not claim Erichthonios as her own, she shut him in a chest guarded by serpents and entrusted him to Kekrops' daughters with the injunction that they were never to look. They disobeyed and frightened by the snakes threw themselves from the acropolis.

266 / 277 *sacrifice your sisters* Erechtheus' sacrifice was the subject of an earlier play of Euripides, the *Erechtheus*, of which only fragments survive. In that version, only one daughter was sacrificed, here all but the infant Kreousa were offered up. Erechtheus made the sacrifice at the behest of the Delphic oracle, who told him that only so could Athens win its war against Eleusis.

270 / 281 *a rift in the earth* The mythographer Apollodoros explains that after Erechtheus killed Eumolpos of Thrace, a son of Poseidon, who had come to Attica to help the Eleusinians in their war with Athens, Poseidon angrily struck the earth with his trident, causing it to open and swallow Erechtheus.

274 / 285 *His lightning blazes there* The allusion is apparently to a customary watch of three days and three nights for lightning on Mount Parnes, north of Athens. If lightning appeared, a public procession set out for Delphi in commemoration of Apollo's first journey there. (Strabo, a Greek geographer of the Augustan period, places the lookout at the shrine of Pythian Apollo, some distance from the Long Rocks, but Mount Parnes would be visible here also, and it is possible that the sighting took place here in Euripides' day.)

292 / 303 *About crops? About children?* These are subjects about which Ion could easily guess that rulers might make inquiry, but they have a specific relevance to Kreousa and Athens; the notion of autochthony confuses crops and the children born from earth and are thus thought of as a crop (literally, "fruit of the earth").

298 / 309 *They call me Apollo's servant* Ion still has no name, for no parents have yet named him.

324 / 335 *I might help arrange it* Ion offers to be Kreousa's official local host and agent (*proxenos*); all those who wished to consult the oracle required a *proxenos* to introduce them.

395 / 410 *O Leto* Kreousa prays not to Apollo, whom she holds responsible for her sorrow, but to his mother, who she hopes will understand her need.

425 / 444 *for the sake of argument* Ion incongruously appropriates the language of the law court as if to prosecute the gods for rape. Ion in his idealism may intuitively feel that the anthropomorphism of Greek religious tradition is somehow unsatisfactory, but here as elsewhere he has no alternative way to understand the actions and motives of the gods.

434–88 / 452–509 First *stasimon,* a choral song (and dance) formally arranged in a series of pairs of stanzas connected by identical meter and music. The Chorus in effect joins the prayers for a royal child that Kreousa has gone to offer, directing its appeals to Athena, patroness of Athens, and Artemis, goddess of childbirth.

436 / 456–57 *From the head of Zeus* There is irony in the emphasis on Athena's birth from the head of a single male parent, for the child who will appear as the result of the oracle for which they here pray will appear also to be motherless and to belong neither to Kreousa nor to the Athenian royal house.

442 / 457 *Blessed Victory* Here a cult title of Athena, as again at line **1495 / 1529.**

456 / 470–71 *Let the oracle be straight and clear* Again, there is irony: the Greek here speaks of pure (*katharois*) prophecies, but Apollo will lie to Xouthos and withhold the truth from Kreousa.

474 / 496 *Three spectral daughters* Kekrops' daughters (see on **20 / 23** and **254 ff. / 265 ff.**). Their story was reflected in a ritual observed in Euripides' day in which three Athenian girls who lived for a time in Athena's precinct carried a secret object in a basket down the acropolis at night by an underground passage, returning with other objects that they left in

NOTES

Athena's keeping. They were called Arrephoroi or Hersephoroi (dew-bearers). It is presumably these girls whom the Chorus imagines dancing before the shrine.

489–644 / 510–675 Second episode.

519 / 542 *earth was my mother!* Ion, casting about for acceptable origins, unwittingly aligns himself with the Athenian traditions of autochthony that, indeed, lie behind his birth, for his mother is the child of an earthborn father and his birth, like that of Erichthonios (see **256** / 268), is the happy result of a seemingly unhappy encounter.

528 / 550 *the torchlight mysteries of Dionysos* Delphi was shared with Apollo by Dionysos, who possessed it during the winter months. Among the regular Delphic observances were ritual dances of female devotees of Dionysos, called Thyades, whose celebrations featured the waving of torches on the slopes of Mount Parnarssos.

537 / 559 *son of the son of Zeus* As Xouthos' son, Ion would strictly be Zeus's great-grandson; but as Apollo's he is, indeed, son of the son of Zeus.

632 / 661 *Ion, the first I set my eye on* In Greek the pun works off the participle *ion* (equally coming and going). Xouthos was coming out (*exion*) of the temple when he saw his new son.

635 / 666 *Absolute silence* But the chorus, surprisingly, will disobey; see line **727** / 760.

645–91 / 676–724 Second *stasimon*.

680 / 717 *The wine god* Dionysos, pictured leading the rout of Thyades in celebration on the slopes of Mount Parnassos; see line **528** / 550. The Chorus assumes that Ion was conceived at such a rite.

692–1020 / 725–1047 Third episode, including a *kommos* (**753–74** / 782–803, a lyric lament in which Kreousa sings all her lines and the tutor and Chorus speak theirs in dialogue meter) and a *monody* sung and mimed by Kreousa (**826–95** / 859–922).

727 / 760 *though I die twice for telling* This refers to Xouthos' threat to kill the Chorus, who by speaking here strikingly breach tragic convention (cf. Euripides' *Hippolytos*, e.g., where the Chorus keeps a promise to remain silent and thus doom the innocent young hero). By reporting Apollo's oracle, the

341

Chorus spreads the confusion that generates the rest of the plot. It should be added the Chorus does so out of loyalty to its mistress and that the misunderstanding is not of its own making, but entirely Apollo's. (There is, of course, irony in Kreousa's response at **753–55** / 782–83, literally "unspeakable, unspeakable, unutterable the story you tell," because this is precisely the story they have been instructed never to speak.)

776 / 806 *the sacred tent* See line **1102** / 1133.

810 / 839–40 *of a freeborn woman* References in fourth-century Athenian courtroom orations to an earlier law that protected freeborn concubines who were kept for the purpose of producing free children suggest that a childless Athenian might, in fact, have imposed upon his barren wife an arrangement such as the one the tutor here suggests.

839–40 / 871–72 *who reigns / at the sacred shore on Triton's lake* One of Athena's cult epithets, *Tritogeneia* (Triton-born), was most commonly understood to refer to Lake Tritonis in Libya as her birthplace (thus, e.g., Aeschylus *Eumenides* 293).

891–93 / 919–20 *And the laurel … bloodroot palm* The laurel had strong associations with Apollo and is part of the Delphic scene in this play; the palm tree at Delos was sacred to Apollo because Leto clung to its trunk during his painful birth.

948 / 974 *twisted god!* The cult name here is Loxias; see note on line **31**.

969 / 997 *the eager Gorgon struck* Euripides constructs a punning derivation of aegis from the verb *aissein* (to strike) as a way of lending credibility to his version of its origin. In the usual story, Perseus gave the aegis to Medea after killing the Medusa.

1021–77 / 1048–1105 Third *stasimon*.

1021–23 / 1048–49 *Crossroads Queen … Queen of Returns* Persephone, the daughter of Demeter who returns to the upper world from Hades each spring, is here identified with Einodia, goddess of crossroads and patroness of sorcery. The identification serves the Chorus' purpose by bridging the murderous work of poisoning Ion and the Athenian sense of exclusivity symbolized in the Chorus by the rites of Demeter and Persephone at Eleusis, which it regards as justifying the killing of the interloper (cf. **1029–32** / 1058–60).

1045 / 1074–75 *Hymns sung to Dionysos* The Greek text mentions a "much-hymned god," presumably Dionysos in his guise as Iacchos, whom an Eleusinian ritual cry invoked.

1046 / 1076 *the twentieth day* This day of the Athenian month Boedromion was set aside for a great procession from Athens to Eleusis.

1055 / 1081–82 *fifty water spirits* These are the Nereids, sea nymphs who seem here simply to be part of a picture of all the elements celebrating the mysteries at Eleusis.

1078–1180 / 1106–1228 Fourth episode.

1102 / 1133 *Not a tent, really* We are not told explicitly whether the pavilion was regularly raised for special occasions or was simply improvised for this one, but the construction and decoration now presented in such lavish detail suggest that it may have been a fixture of Delphic celebrations. On the other hand, Euripides' elaboration of the themes of order (in the tent's perfect structure and the cosmos depicted on its ceiling) and disorder (in the violence and confusion of the life depicted on its tapestries) offers sufficient explanation for the detailed description.

1111 / 1145 *war with the Amazons* Among Herakles' labors was to bring King Eurystheus the girdle of Hippolyta, queen of the Amazons. The fabulous tapestries that Ion brings from the temple treasury are to be understood as booty won in that campaign.

1129–30 / 1163–64 *Kekrops . . . flanked by his daughters* Cf. **254 ff.** / 265 ff. Kekrops' monstrous nature as snake-man is emphasized here in accordance with the progression of images from the ordered heavens to the confusion and violence of earthly life.

1158 / 1197–98 *free to roam the precinct* The doves thus form an ironic contrast to the birds Ion threatened to shoot for polluting the precinct (**141–63** / 154–78), saving him from death and the shrine from pollution. Euripides images the flock of birds as a band of Dionysiac revelers, and in this context the dove that drinks the poisoned wine becomes a kind of substitute victim or scapegoat.

1175 / 1222–23 *stoned to death* Public execution by stoning was a punishment reserved for particularly heinous acts of treason, sacrilege, or murder of an immediate family member.

1181–99 / 1229–49 Fourth ode (in place of a *stasimon*). A short, highly emotional song that does not have the formal strophic responsion of a *stasimon*.

1200–1592 / 1250–1622 *Exodos.* This term, defined by Aristotle as the remainder of the tragedy following the final choral ode, obviously encompasses more than what we would regard as the final scene. In the *Ion*, the *exodos* includes two sudden and unexpected appearances, first of the Pythia (**1272** / 1320) and then of Athena (**1519** / 1549), and a lyric scene (**1391–1475** / 1439–1509, the emotional recognition duo in which Kreousa sings her lines and Ion speaks his in dialogue meter).

1206 / 1256 *It's unholy to kill a suppliant* Taking refuge at an altar made one the property of the god (cf. **1240** / 1289) and therefore inviolate; anyone who killed or forcibly removed a suppliant from sanctuary would be subject to the wrath of Zeus in his role as protector of the rights of suppliants.

1212 / 1261 *the bull-shaped river god* Kephisos, the embodiment of a river of Attica, is here depicted in the form of a bull, a frequent feature of the iconography of river gods but particularly appropriate to Ion's emphasis on Kreousa's bestial inheritance from her earthborn ancestors. Kephisos was the father of Kreousa's mother Praxithea.

1272 / 1320 *Stop* The Pythia's surprising intervention is quite unlike conventional entrances from the scene building, whose central door usually opens only after an announcement, as at lines 493–94. This entrance is reminiscent instead of the sudden arrival of a *deus ex machina*, which in a sense the Pythia is. (For a human character in the role of a *deus ex machina* one may compare the otherwise very different entrance of Medea at Euripides' *Medea* 1317). All the more remarkable, then, that the Pythia's intervention does not tie up all the play's loose threads and that a second "god from the machine," this time the goddess Athena, is required to put in an equally sudden appearance at line **1519** / 1549.

1373 / 1421 *Gorgons* The royal Erechtheid emblem, associated with Kreousa's attempt to murder Ion, now becomes a recognition token that unites them as mother and son.

1386–87 / 1433–34 *the tree / Athena first brought* In Athenian legend, Athena and Poseidon vied for primacy in Attica: Poseidon by striking the acropolis with his trident to make a salt spring flow there; Athena by introducing the olive tree. Athena won the contest and that first tree was said still to be flourishing.

1434 / 1473 *No torchlight* An important part of the Greek marriage ritual was a torchlight procession to lead the bride from her father's to her husband's house.

1445 / 1482 *the Bright God* The cult name here is Phoibos; see note on line **6**.

1498 / 1531 *the god of slanted light* The cult name is Loxias; see note on line **31**.

1510 / 1542–43 *imagine what you'd have lost* The world of the play here subtly shifts (once again) to contemporary Athens. The Greek literally says, "you wouldn't have had your inherited house and a father's name." Adoption law requires naming the biological father, and "son of Apollo" would not be suitable for this purpose!

1546 / 1577 *the Four Tribes* In classical times, the old Ionian tribes survived only for the purposes of certain archaic religious observances, but they no doubt retained a certain prestige based on their evident antiquity and derivation from the sons of Ion.

1554 / 1589 *Xouthos and you together will have sons* Euripides has changed the earlier traditions that made Doros the brother of Xouthos to bring both Dorians and Achaeans into Athens' orbit. His purpose in so doing has been variously interpreted. Athenian patriotism might obviously be at work in making Doros younger than Ion and the son of a mortal, but it would also seem possible that in underlining the ancestral relationship of Ionians, Dorians, and Achaeans, Euripides opposes a Panhellenic perspective to the Athenian exclusivity that dominates much of the play.

GLOSSARY

ACHAIA: The name of two different regions of Greece: one in the northern Peloponnesos, and the other, Achaia Phthiotis, in northern Greece adjacent to Thessaly.

ACHAIOS: Son of Xouthos and Kreousa; ancestor of the Achaians.

ADRASTOS: King of Argos and commander in chief of the Seven against Thebes. He alone escaped from that expedition alive. His son Aigialeus was the only one of the sons of the Seven to die when they attacked Thebes.

AGLAUROS: Wife of Kekrops.

AIGEUS: Son of Pandion and ninth legendary king of Athens. Initially childless, he went to Delphi for an oracle; while visiting Pittheus at Troizen on his way home, he fathered Theseus by Aithra, though in many accounts the real father is Poseidon.

AIGIALEUS: Son of Adrastos. He avenged the defeat of the Seven against Thebes and although the assault was successful, he was killed, causing his father to die of grief.

AIGIKORES: Son of Ion; ancestor of one of the four Ionian tribes.

AIOLOS: Son of Zeus, who made him king of the winds; father of numerous children, including Xouthos.

AITHRA: Daughter of Pittheus, wife of Aigeus, and mother of Theseus. Her role in persuading her son to recover the Argive war dead at Thebes appears to be a Euripidean invention.

AKAMAS: Son of Theseus; co-ruler of Athens with his brother Demophon.

ALKMENE: Daughter of Elektryon, king of Mykenai; mother of Herakles by Zeus.

ALPHEIOS (ALPHEUS): The largest river in the Peloponnesos, which flows past the site of the shrine of Zeus at Olympia.

AMAZONS: A legendary nation of women warriors, living near the Black Sea. One of Herakles' labors was to capture the belt of their queen, Hippolyte, who later bore Theseus a son, Hippolytos.

AMPHIARAOS: An Argive hero and seer; son of Oikles, brother-in-law of Adrastos, married to Eriphyle. Polynices bribed Eriphyle to persuade her husband to take part in the expedition against Thebes although Amphiaraos foresaw that all but Adrastos would die in that battle. When the others were killed and Amphiaraos fled from the field, Zeus threw a thunderbolt in front of him, opening a chasm into which Amphiaraos, his chariot, and his charioteer vanished. In death, Amphiaraos became a chthonian god of healing and oracles.

AMPHION: A Theban hero who, with Zethus, built the walls of Thebes by playing the lyre. His grave was near the North Gate.

APHRODITE: Goddess of erotic love, reproductive life, and beauty; variously said to be the daughter of Zeus and Dione, or to have been born of Ouranos (Sky), when his sexual organs, cut off by his son Kronos, chief god of the Titan generation, fell into the sea. See also KYPRIS.

APOLLO: Son of Zeus and Leto; twin brother of Artemis; god of prophecy whose chief oracular shrine was at Delphi; associated also with many of the civilized arts, including poetry, music, healing.

ARES: Son of Zeus and Hera; god of war and the personification of strife.

ARGADES: Son of Ion; ancestor of one of the four Ionian tribes.

ARGIVE: Adjective from Argos; sometimes used to refer generically to anyone or anything Greek.

ARGOS: A city and its surrounding area in the northeastern Peloponnesos.

ARIADNE: Daughter of Minos, king of Crete; Theseus freed her from the Minotaur when she helped him escape from the labyrinth.

ARTEMIS: Daughter of Zeus and Leto, twin sister of Apollo; maiden goddess of the hunt and the wild, chastity, and also childbirth.

ASCLEPIUS: God of healing, whose chief shrine was at Epidauros; another sanctuary was at Athens under the southern cliff of the Acropolis.

ATHENA: Virgin goddess of wisdom, handicrafts and sciences, and war; born motherless from the head of Zeus. She is often invoked as Pallas Athena or simply Pallas; her associations with Athens include the gift of the olive tree (by which she won the status of Athens' patron in a competition with Poseidon) and the raising of Erichthonios from the earth.

ATHENS: The capital city of Attika.

ATLAS: Giant god of the Titan generation, punished for his part in the revolt of the Titans by being made to support the heavens on his shoulders; father of Maia and grandfather of Hermes.

ATTIKA: The southeastern peninsula of central Greece, whose capital was Athens.

BACCHOS: See DIONYSOS.

BELLEROPHON: Hero, son of Poseidon, who rode the winged horse Pegasos and slew the Chimaera.

CAPANEUS: An Argive and one of the Seven against Thebes; he married Evadne. When scaling the walls of Thebes and boasting that not even Zeus could keep him from burning the city, he was struck by Zeus with a thunderbolt and toppled from the scaling ladder.

CHALKIS: Chief city of Euboia.

CHIMAERA: Monstrous creature that is part lion, part goat, part serpent; slain by Bellerophon.

CITHAERON: Mountain range separating Boeotia (the region around Thebes) from Attika and the plain of Eleusis.

CREON: King of Thebes; brother of Jocasta and thus Oedipus' uncle by marriage.

DELOS: Island at the center of the Cyclades; birthplace of Apollo and Artemis.

DELPHI: A town situated on the lower southern slopes of Mount Parnassos, home of the most important oracular shrine of Apollo, to which pilgrims traveled for divine advice and to receive purification for acts that had polluted them. During the winter months, Delphi was inhabited by Dionysos.

DEMETER: Goddess of grain, fertility, and renewal; daughter of Kronos, chief god of the Titan generation, and his consort, Rhea; and thus Zeus' sister. At Eleusis she was honored in the Lesser and Greater Mysteries (in the spring and autumn, respectively), festivals of death and renewal. Also at Eleusis, worshiped at the Proerosia with her daughter, Persephone.

DEMOPHON: Son of Theseus; co-ruler of Athens with Akamas, his brother.

DIKTYNNA: Cult name of the goddess Artemis, associated with her worship in Crete.

DIONYSOS: God of wine and ecstatic possession, who inhabited Delphi during the winter months and led revels on the slopes of Mount Parnassos; also known as Bacchos. He was born twice, once after Zeus' lightning killed his mother Semele, again from Zeus' thigh where he had been hidden from Hera's wrath.

DIRKE: A river in Thebes; the river's nymph.

DOROS: Son of Xouthos and Kreousa, ancestor of the Dorians.

ELEUSIS: A town near Athens, site of the mysteries of Demeter and Persephone, whose initiates received revelations about eternal life.

ELEUTHERAE: Town on the southern slope of Mount Cithaeron where
there was a pass through the mountain from the plain of Eleusis
to Boeotia. The site is also the home of Dionysos Eleuthereus
(the cult god of the Theater of Dionysos), whose cult statue (a
pillar-shaped idol of the god) was transported from here to
Athens as a prelude to the Great Dionysia.

ENKELADOS: Giant who took part in a battle against the Olympian gods.

EOS: Goddess of dawn.

EPIDAUROS: Site in the southeastern Peloponnesos of a great healing
shrine of Asclepius.

ERECTHEUS: King of Athens and father of Kreousa and of other daughters he sacrificed to save Athens.

ERICHTHONIOS: Earthborn king of Athens, grandfather of Erechtheus
and great-grandfather of Kreousa.

ERIDANOS: Mythical river (and river god), usually located in the west
and sometimes equated with the Po, into which Phaëthon was
hurled by Zeus.

EROS: God of love, usually said to be the son of Hermes and Aphrodite.

ETEOKLES: Theban king, son of Oedipus and Jocasta, brother of Polynices. See POLYNICES.

ETEOKLOS: An Argive and one of the Seven; son of Iphis, brother of
Evadne.

ETRUSCAN: Adjective from a region in northern Italy, settled by a
people of unknown origin.

EUBOIA: A large narrow island just northeast of Attica.

EURYSTHEUS   Son of Sthenelos and king of Argos and Mykenai; he
imposed on Herakles the labors for which he was famous.

EVADNE: Daughter of Iphis and sister of Eteoklos; wife of Capaneus.

FATES: Visualized as three divine sisters spinning, measuring, and cutting the threads of human lives and events.

GELEON: Son of Ion; ancestor of one of the four Ionian tribes.

GORGON: Daughter of the sea gods Phorkys and Keto, killed by Athena (elsewhere by Perseus); from her blood Athena bestowed upon Erichthonios a healing drop; from the blood of the serpents that formed her hair, a drop of poison. From the Gorgon's skin, Athena fashioned the breastplate called the aegis.

GRACES: Goddesses personifying loveliness or grace, generally three in number.

HADES: God of the underworld; brother of Zeus and Poseidon; Persephone's husband. His name also is used to refer to the Underworld itself.

HEBE: Daughter of Zeus and Hera and goddess of youth; wife of Herakles after the end of his life on earth.

HEKATE: Goddess of night and the shades; protectress of enchanters and witches; honored at crossroads with statues and offerings.

HERA: Goddess of matrimony and women's life; wife and sister of Zeus; she was the patron goddess of Argos and the inveterate enemy of Herakles (born of one of Zeus' many adulterous affairs) until after his death.

HERAKLEIDAI: The children of Herakles. In the play of this name only the absent Hyllos is named, and only one (unnamed in the text, but usually referred to as Makaria) has an individual role, but there are younger sons (appearing in the play at the altar), younger daughters (in the temple), and older sons (campaigning with Hyllos). All are presumably children of Herakles and Deianeira. Herakles had had children by his first wife, Megara, but he killed them all in his madness (the subject of Euripides' *Herakles*), and he also fathered many bastard children from various liaisons.

HERAKLES (HERACLES):   Son of Zeus and Alkmene; most famous of the Greek heroes. Indentured to Eurystheus, king of Tiryns in the Argolid, he was compelled to undertake the twelve labors most famous of the Greek heroes. He was known for countless acts of bravery, strength, compassion, and sometimes violent hotheadedness. His many exploits won him deification after death.

HERMES: Son of Zeus and Maia, factotum of the Olympian gods as well as god of commerce and travel; accompanied the souls of the dead to the underworld.

HESPERIA: The "western land," where the Hesperides dwelled.

HESPERIDES: Daughters of Night, who sang with great sweetness and guarded a tree that bore golden apples. Stealing the apples was one of Herakles' labors.

HIPPOLYTOS: Illegitimate son of Theseus by the Amazon Hippolyte.

HIPPOMEDON: An Argive prince; Adrastos' brother and one of the Seven against Thebes. His son, Polydoros, was one of the sons of the Seven.

HOPLES: Son of Ion, ancestor of one of the four Ionian tribes.

HYDRA: A monstrous and poisonous water snake with many heads, which inhabited the Lernaian swamp near Argos. It was one of Herakles' labors to kill the Hydra, which he did with the help of Iolaos.

HYLLOS: The oldest son of Herakles and Deianeira.

HYMENAIOS: God of the wedding feast.

IDA: Mountain in the center of Crete, where Zeus was born in a cave.

INACHOS: Son of Ocean; he gave his name to the River Inachos, near Argos.

IOLAOS: Nephew and companion of Herakles; son of Iphikles, who was the son of Amphitryon and Alkmene, and the twin half-brother to Herakles.

IOLE: Princess of Oikhalia, whom Herakles won as a prize in an archery contest set by her father, Eurytos. When the king refused to give her to him, Herakles took her captive after killing her father and brothers and sacking her city.

ION: A temple servant of Apollo at Delphi, who in the course of this play discovers himself to be the god's son by Kreousa; future father of the eponymous heroes of the four Ionic tribes.

IONIA: The central part of the coast of Asia Minor and its outlying islands that is said to be named for Ion and whose settlement by Greeks the Athenians claimed to have organized and led.

IPHIS: An Argive; father of Evadne and Eteoklos.

ISTHMUS: The strip of land, properly the "Isthmus of Corinth," that connects the Peloponnesos to mainland Greece.

KASTALIA: Sacred spring on Mount Parnassos near Delphi.

KEKROPS: Earthborn first king of Athens, half snake and half man, to whose daughters Athena entrusted the baby Erichthonios.

KEPHALOS: Husband of Procris, the daughter of Erectheus. Eos, the goddess of dawn, fell in love with him and abducted him for a time; later he inadvertently killed Procris in a hunting accident.

KEPHISOS: The divine embodiment of the chief river of the plain of Athens, depicted in this play as having the shape of a bull; maternal grandfather of Kreousa.

KOPREUS: Herald of Eurystheus.

KORE: See PERSEPHONE.

KORYBANTES: Female companions of the goddess Kybele, the Great Mother.

KREOUSA: Daughter of Erechtheus and Praxithea, queen of Athens; married to Xouthos; mother of Ion.

KYPRIS: A cult name of Aphrodite, because in one tradition she first came ashore on the island of Cyprus, where a great temple was built in her honor.

LETO: Daughter of the Titans, Coeus and Phoebe; loved by Zeus, to whom she bore Artemis and Apollo.

MAENAD: Frenzied female worshiper of Dionysos.

MAIA: Daughter of Atlas and mother of Hermes.

MAKARIA: Daughter of Herakles and Deianeira.

MARATHON: A town and plain about twenty-three miles northeast of Athens near the sea coast; scene of the Athenian defeat of the invading Persians in 490 B.C.

MEGARA: A city on the Isthmus of Corinth, west of Athens.

MIMAS: Giant who took part in the battle against the Olympian gods.

MINOS: Son of Europa and Zeus (disguised as a bull); king of Crete, father of Phaidra and Ariadne.

MYKENAI: A city in the Peloponnesos near Argos.

ORPHEUS: The legendary poet, sometimes associated with Dionysos; founder of a mystic cult.

PALLAS: See ATHENA.

PALLENE: A town in Attika, the site of a shrine of Pallas Athena.

PAN: Son of Hermes and a nymph; god of flocks and shepherds; reputed to be the cause of sudden inexplicable fear ("Panic").

PANDION: Son of Kekrops and king of Athens, the second of this name; father of Aigeus and grandfather of Theseus.

PANHELLENIC: A term meaning "all-Greek," used to refer to the laws, customs, and festivals common to all Greeks.

PARNASSOS: The mountain on whose southern slope Delphi is situated; haunt of the Muses.

PARTHENOPAIOS: Son of Meleager and Atalanta, from Arcadia. Because of her affection for Atalanta, Artemis gave Parthenopaios heavenly arrows and showered him with ambrosia, but these gifts did not save him from a huge stone hurled from the ramparts at Thebes.

PASIPHAË: Wife of Minos, king of Crete, and mother of Phaidra; cursed with love for a bull, she had Daedalos make her a hollow wooden cow. She climbed inside, was mounted by the bull, and gave birth to the Minotaur.

PEGASOS: Winged horse; offspring of Poseidon and the Gorgon Medusa.

PELOPONNESOS: Greece's southern peninsula. The more common English name is "Peloponnese." See also PELOPS.

PELOPS: Son of Tantalos and king of Elis in the western Peloponnesos. Through dynastic marriages his descendants extended their rule over most of Greece south of the Isthmus of Korinth; hence it was named the Peloponnesos, "Island of Pelops," after him. His dishonest conduct of the race that won him Hippodameia as his wife was cited as the original cause of the curse on his line, usually called the House of Atreus after one of his sons.

PERSEPHONE: Daughter of Zeus and Demeter; wife of Hades and queen of the underworld; worshiped at Eleusis; also known as Kore ("the maiden"). Zeus gave her in marriage to Hades, but her bereft mother found her and reclaimed her for life on earth for part of the year, thus initiating the cycle of death and rebirth for grain and other flora.

PHAËTHON: Son of Helios, the sun god and the ocean nymph Clymene. Driving his father's chariot across the sky, he lost control of the horses, Zeus hurled a thunderbolt against him to prevent universal conflagration; he fell to earth at the river Eridanos. His weeping sisters were turned into poplar trees, dripping amber.

PHAIDRA: Daughter of Minos, king of Crete; sister of Pasiphae; wife of
          Theseus.

PILLARS OF HERAKLES: The western limit of land, symbolized by the
          mountains on either side of the Strait of Gibraltar.

PIRAEUS: The port of Athens.

PITTHEUS: Son of Pelops and king of Troizen in the northeastern
          Peloponnese; father of Aithra. He was renowned for his wisdom
          and respected as a seer. He arranged for Aigeus, returning from
          Delphi, to sleep with Aithra by getting him drunk.

POLYNICES: Son of Oedipus and Jocasta; brother of Eteokles, Antigone,
          and Ismene. A Theban, he instigated the attack of the Seven
          against Thebes in hopes of reclaiming the kingship of which he
          claimed his brother had robbed him. As he was dying from
          Eteokles' hand, he mortally wounded his brother in the heart.

POSEIDON: Brother of Zeus and Hades; god of the sea and of horses,
          and as Earthshaker the cause of earthquakes and tidal waves.
          Poseidon had numerous associations with Athens. He com-
          peted with Athena to be the city's patron; he killed King
          Erechtheus to avenge the death of his son Eumolpos in battle;
          he was the divine father of Theseus, who became Athens' king.

PROEROSIA: An annual festival held at Eleusis before the fall plowing in
          honor of Demeter and Persephone; celebrated on the fifth or
          sixth day of Pyanopsion (late October).

PROMETHEUS: God of the Titan generation who brought fire and other
          benefits of civilization to humankind; Euripides has him assist
          at Athena's birth from the head of Zeus, but elsewhere Hephais-
          tos is said to have opened Zeus' skull with an ax.

RHION: A city at the western mouth of the Gulf of Corinth.

SARONIC GULF: The water separating Argolis in the Eastern Pelopon-
          nesos from Attika.

SEMELE: Mother of Dionysos; Theban princess, daughter of Thebes'
          founder Kadmos and his wife, Harmonia. She died when Zeus

made love to her, at her own misguided request, in the form of a lightning bolt, but Zeus took the child and brought him to term hidden in his own thigh.

SEVEN AGAINST THEBES: A legendary attack led by Adrastos to help Polynices regain the Theban throne from Eteokles. When all but Adrastos had been killed, Thebes refused to release the corpses for burial. The Seven include Polynices, Tydeus, Amphiaraos, Capaneus, Eteoklos, Hippomedon, and Parthenopaios.

SINIS   A monstrous and murderous robber killed by Theseus in his youth. Sinis attached his victims to a pine tree bent to the ground and catapulted them to their death.

SKIRON   An outlaw slain by Theseus in his youth. Skiron would force his victims to wash his feet, then kick them off his cliff into the sea.

SKIRONIAN ROCKS, SKIRONIC COAST: Cliffs on the coast in Megarian territory, associated with Skiron.

SONS OF THE SEVEN: Known as the Epigoni (those "born after"), who, in vengeance for their fathers' deaths, captured and plundered the city of Thebes. The oracle at Delphi promised them success if Alkmaion, son of Amphiaraos, should lead them, which he did, although reluctantly, after Aigialeus' death.

SPARTA: The major city of the southern Peloponnesos.

STHENELOS: Son of Perseus; king of Argos and Mykenai; father of Eurystheus.

THEBES: The principal city of Boeotia, the region north and west of Attika; founded according to legend by Cadmus the Phoenician, it became the site of many epic travails.

THESEUS: King of Athens; son of Aigeus (or of the sea god Poseidon) and of Aithra, daughter of Pittheus, king of Troizen; husband of Phaidra, father of Hippolytos; a contemporary and friend of Herakles.

THESSALIAN: Adjective from Thessaly, a fierce province in northern Greece.

TRACHIS: A city in Malis, a region in northern Greece to the west of Thebes.

TROIZEN: A city in the eastern Peloponnesos across the Saronic Gulf from Athens; in historical times, a dependency of Athens. Aithra, mother of Theseus, was the daughter of a king of Troizen, and Hippolytos was reared and died there. Yearly rites honoring him were conducted at Troizen in the time of Euripides.

TROPHONIOS: A prophetic spirit whose oracle was located in a cave fifteen miles from Delphi, just off the road from Athens.

TYDEUS: Son of Oineus, king of Calydon; one of the Seven against Thebes. As he was dying, Athena intended to make him immortal but had a change of heart when she saw him eating out the brain of the man who had struck him a mortal wound.

VENETO; VENICE, PLAINS OF: A region in northeastern Italy famous to the Greeks for its horses.

XOUTHOS: Son of Aiolos (and thus a grandson of Zeus); husband of Kreousa; future father of Doros and Achaios (elsewhere Xouthos is son of Hellen and brother of Aiolos and Doros); banished by his brothers from his birthplace in Achaia. Xouthos became a soldier of fortune and won the house of Kreousa and the kingship of Athens by aiding in the conquest of Euboea.

ZEUS: Sky god and most powerful deity of the Greek pantheon; brother of Poseidon, Hades, and other Olympians; married to Hera and father of innumerable gods and mortals.

FOR FURTHER READING

EURIPIDES

Desmond J. Conacher. *Euripidean Drama: Myth, Theme, and Structure*. Toronto: University of Toronto Press, 1967. Still the most useful play-by-play study of Euripides.

Helene P. Foley. *Ritual Irony: Poetry and Sacrifice in Euripides*. Ithaca, NY: Cornell University Press, 1985. Important study of the uses of ritual in Euripidean tragedy, with particular reference to female self-sacrifice (as in *Children of Herakles* and *Suppliant Women*).

Ann N. Michelini. *Euripides and the Tragic Tradition*. Madison: University of Wisconsin Press, 1987. A broadly based study of Euripides and the history of Euripidean criticism, with a chapter on *Hippolytos*.

James Morwood. *The Plays of Euripides*. London: Bristol Classical Press, 2002. Brief, personal discussions of all the surviving plays.

Judith Mossman, ed. *Euripides*. Oxford: Oxford University Press, 2003. A collection of influential critical essays, including important papers on *Hippolytos* and *Ion*.

Note: Among the volumes available or soon to appear in the Duckworth Companions to Greek and Roman Tragedy series are *Hippolytus* (Sophie Mills), *Ion* (L. Swift), and *Suppliant Women* (Ian C. Storey). These are reliable introductions that provide full and up-to-date bibliographies.

CHILDREN OF HERAKLES

Peter Burian. "Euripides' *Heraclidae*: An Interpretation." *Classical Philology* 72 (1977): 1–21. A reading that attempts to explain the significance of a dramatic structure based on reversals and surprises.

Daniel Mendelsohn. *Gender and the City in Euripides' Political Plays.* Oxford: Oxford University Press, 2002. An important comparative reading of *Children of Herakles* and *Suppliant Women*, which reassesses their value while demonstrating the centrality of gender to their political debates.

David K. Roselli. "Gender, Class and Ideology: The Social Function of Virgin Sacrifice in Euripides' *Children of Herakles.*" *Classical Antiquity* 26 (2007): 81–169. A provocative article, arguing that the sacrifice of the Maiden, involving a figure who is both aristocratic and, as a woman, marginal, can serve as a model for different groups in the audience.

ION

Christian Wolff. "The Design and Myth in Euripides' *Ion.*" *Harvard Studies in Classical Philology* 69 (1965): 169–94. A classic and still valuable literary interpretation.

Froma I. Zeitlin. "Mysteries of Identity and Designs of the Self in Euripides' *Ion*," in *Playing the Other*. Chicago: University of Chicago Press, 1996: 285–338. Originally published in *Proceedings of the Cambridge Philological Society* 35 (1989): 144–97. An illuminating examination of imagery and thematics of identity, personal and public, showing among much else the presence of Dionysos and his mysteries in this "Apollonian" drama.

HIPPOLYTOS

Charles Segal. *Euripides and the Poetics of Sorrow: Art, Gender, and Commemoration in "Alcestis," "Hippolytus," and "Hecuba."* Durham, NC: Duke University Press. Chapters 6–8 (pages 86–153) are the culmination of a series of essays, beginning with "The Tragedy of the *Hippolytus*: The Waters of Ocean and the Untouched Meadow." *Harvard Studies in Classical Studies* 70 (1965): 117–69. These constitute a splendid literary commentary to this play.

Froma I. Zeitlin. "The Power of Aphrodite: Eros and the Boundaries of Self in the *Hippolytus*." *Playing the Other*. Chicago: University of Chicago Press, 1996: 219–84. Originally published in Peter Burian, ed. *Direction in Euripidean Criticism*. Durham, NC: Duke University Press (1985): 144–97. A subtle and penetrating study of identity, gender, sexuality, and self-definition.

SUPPLIANT WOMEN

Peter Burian. "*Logos* and *Pathos*: The Politics of the *Suppliant Women*." In Peter Burian, ed. *Direction in Euripidean Criticism*. Durham, NC: Duke University Press (1985): 128–55. An analysis of the conflicting claims of reason and passion in this drama.

Daniel Mendelsohn. *Gender and the City in Euripides' Political Plays*. Oxford: Oxford University Press, 2002. An important comparative reading of *Children of Herakles* and *Suppliant Women*, which reassesses their value while demonstrating the centrality of gender to their political debates.

Wesley D. Smith. "Expressive Form in Euripides' *Suppliants*." *Harvard Studies in Classical Studies* 71 (1966): 151–70. A pioneering reevaluation of this play, still of great value.

Printed in the USA
CPSIA information can be obtained
at www.ICGtesting.com
CBHW030028270224
4672CB00001B/4